GANGLAND NEW YORK

THE PLACES AND FACES OF MOB HISTORY

ANTHONY M. DESTEFANO

Guilford, Connecticut

In memory of my nephew Daniel Edward DeStefano
November 2, 1979–July 2, 2014

An imprint of Rowman & Littlefield

Distributed by NATIONAL BOOK NETWORK

British Library Cataloguing in Publication Information Available

Library of Congress Cataloging-in-Publication Data

DeStefano, Anthony M.
Gangland New York : the places and faces of mob history / Anthony M. DeStefano.
pages cm
Includes bibliographical references and index.
ISBN 978-1-4930-0600-7 (pbk.) — ISBN 978-1-4930-1833-8 (e-book) 1. Mafia—New York (State)—History. 2. Organized crime—New York (State)—History. I. Title.
HV6452.N7D467 2015
364.10609747'1—dc23

2015013522

∞™ The paper used in this publication meets the minimum requirements of American National Standard for Information Sciences—Permanence of Paper for Printed Library Materials, ANSI/NISO Z39.48-1992.

CONTENTS

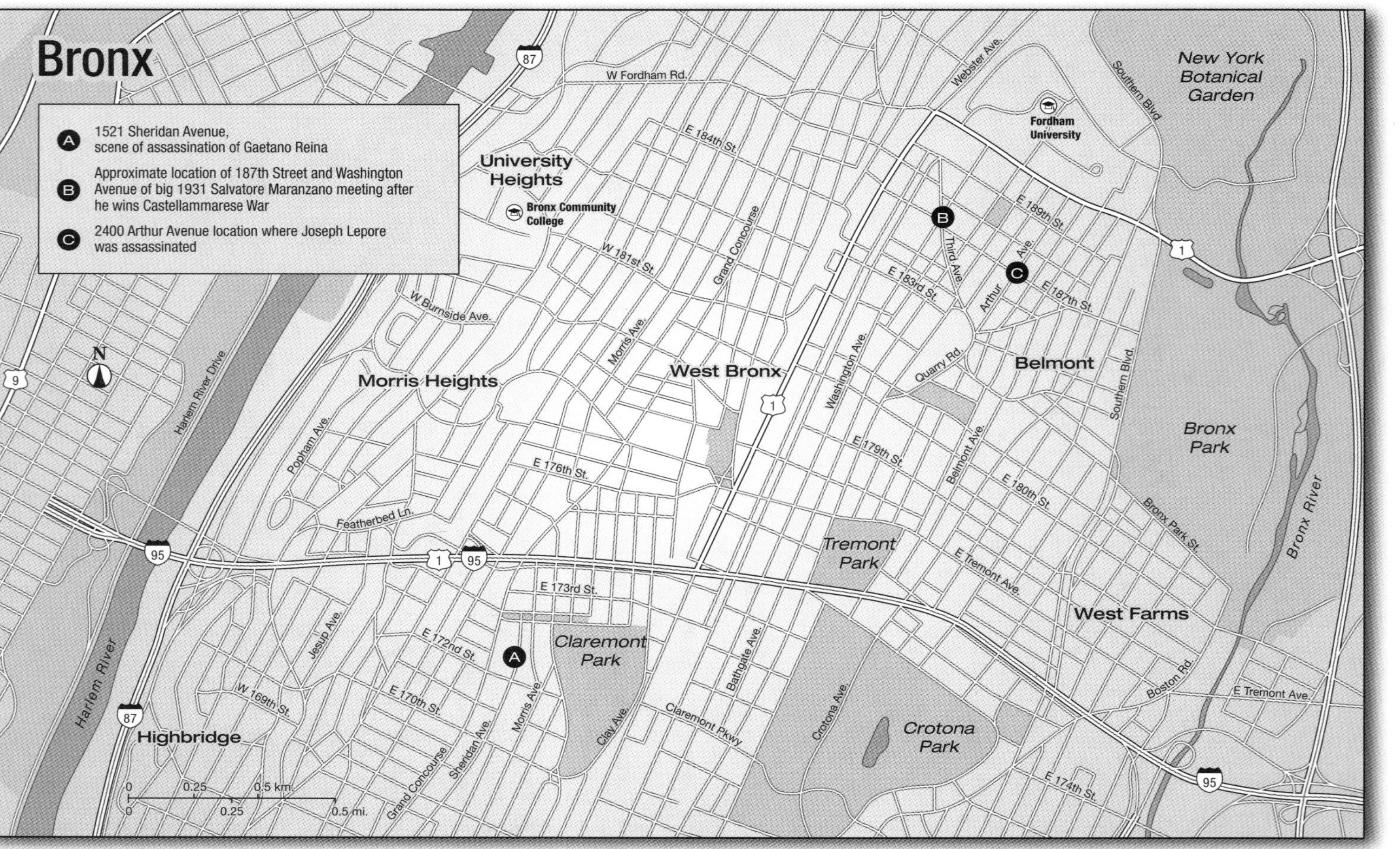
Bronx
A 1521 Sheridan Avenue, scene of assassination of Gaetano Reina
B Approximate location of 187th Street and Washington Avenue of big 1931 Salvatore Maranzano meeting after he wins Castellammarese War
C 2400 Arthur Avenue location where Joseph Lepore was assassinated
New York Botanical Garden
Fordham University
University Heights
Bronx Community College
Morris Heights
West Bronx
Belmont
Bronx Park
Tremont Park
West Farms
Claremont Park
Crotona Park
Highbridge
Harlem River
Bronx River
W Fordham Rd.
Webster Ave.
Southern Blvd
E 184th St.
E 189th St.
Third Ave.
Arthur Ave.
E 183rd St.
E 187th St.
W 181st St.
Grand Concourse
W Burnside Ave.
Morris Ave.
Quarry Rd.
Washington Ave.
Southern Blvd.
Harlem River Drive
Popham Ave.
E 176th St.
E 179th St.
Belmont Ave.
E 180th St.
Bronx Park St.
Featherbed Ln.
E Tremont Ave.
E 173rd St.
Jesup Ave.
E 172nd St.
Bathgate Ave.
Boston Rd.
W 169th St.
E 170th St.
Sheridan Ave.
Clay Ave.
Claremont Pkwy
Crotona Ave.
E 174th St.
87
9
1
95
N
0 0.25 0.5 km
0 0.25 0.5 mi.

INTRODUCTION

The American Mafia is one of our best-known secret societies.

This oxymoron stems from the fact that over the years countless investigations, informants, trials, and publicity have made the Mob and its business as familiar to us as our favorite sports teams. Stories about organized crime and its romantic notions of loyalty, blood oaths, and secret ceremonies abound. La Cosa Nostra—or *this thing of ours*, as gangsters refer to it—is really *our thing* in terms of the way the Mafia has invaded the popular culture and psyche.

Francis Ford Coppola's *The Godfather* and *The Godfather Part II* are among the top one hundred films in American history, according to the American Film Institute. Those two films and their popularity set the stage for hit television shows like *The Sopranos* and *Boardwalk Empire*. The Biography Channel has come along with its *Mobster* series, and then there is the mini franchise created by *Mob Wives*. The Mob has kept legions of writers busy—myself included—for most of our professional lives, as we track the often violent, exploitive, and, yes, sometimes exciting lives of criminals who became legends through their infamy.

But as anybody who has any awareness of organized crime knows, it is not just an Italian phenomenon. Particularly in New York City, organized crime has been a staple of life in many communities. Each immigration stream to the city helped create a series of criminal organizations that from at least the mid-nineteenth century controlled or influenced life and death. Early on, the Irish were involved, as were the Jews and the Chinese. In the early twentieth century Italian criminals earned their own reputation through the Mafia and the so-called Black Hand, a strange and terrifying kind of extortion racket which preyed on the fears and ignorance of immigrants from Italy's *Mezzogiorno*. Later came the Greek and Eastern European gangsters—notably the Albanians and Russians—who carved their own niches, and, where necessary, forged alliances with the traditional Mafia.

Let us also not forget the black and Hispanic gangsters who made money in the drug trade and other rackets, making their own accommodations and alliances with the Mafia along the way, when necessary. The long arm of the South American drug cartels has reached into the city for decades and has led to countless murders. The successors to Harlem gangsters like Leroy "Nicky" Barnes and

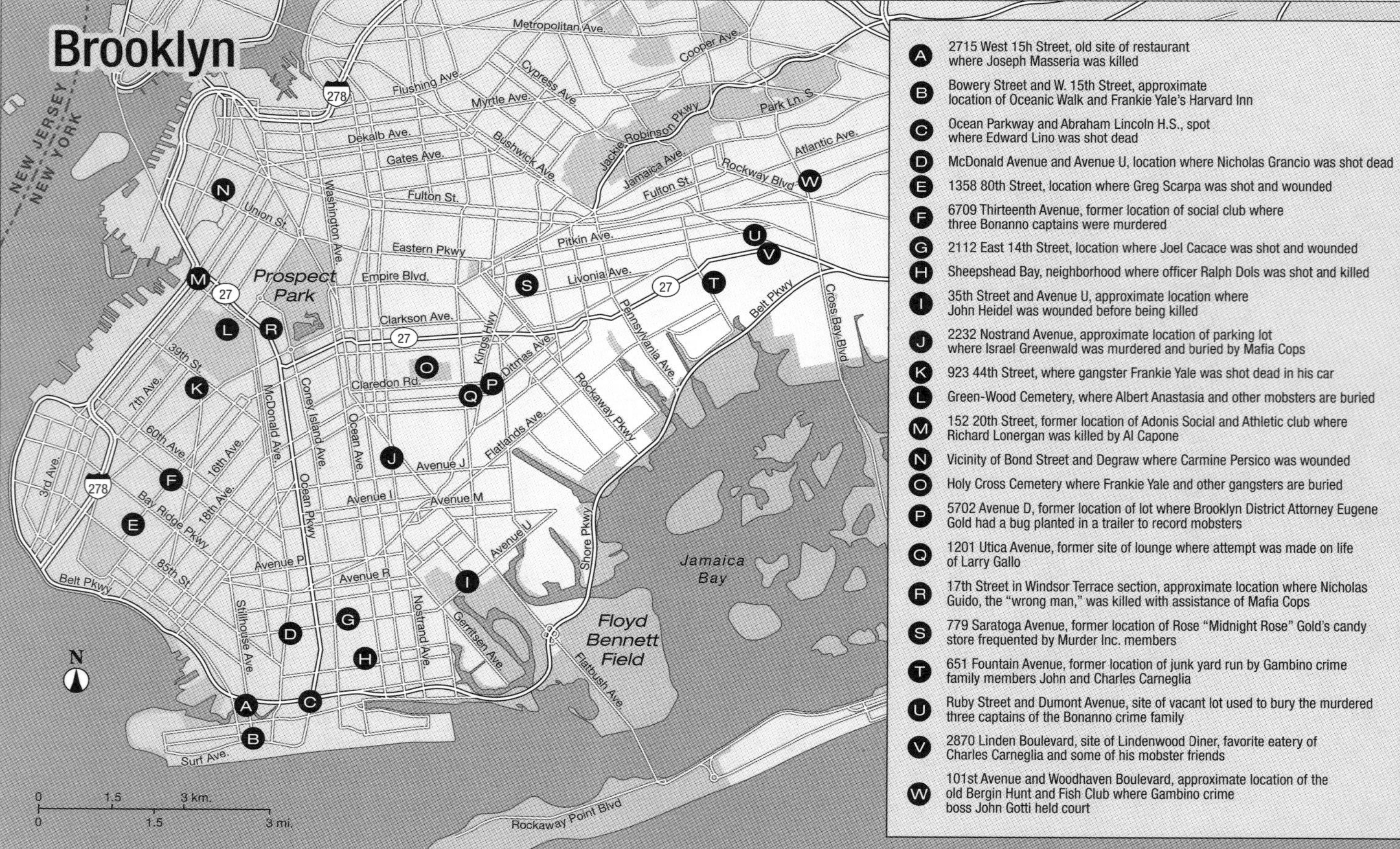
Brooklyn
NEW JERSEY
NEW YORK
A 2715 West 15h Street, old site of restaurant where Joseph Masseria was killed
B Bowery Street and W. 15th Street, approximate location of Oceanic Walk and Frankie Yale's Harvard Inn
C Ocean Parkway and Abraham Lincoln H.S., spot where Edward Lino was shot dead
D McDonald Avenue and Avenue U, location where Nicholas Grancio was shot dead
E 1358 80th Street, location where Greg Scarpa was shot and wounded
F 6709 Thirteenth Avenue, former location of social club where three Bonanno captains were murdered
G 2112 East 14th Street, location where Joel Cacace was shot and wounded
H Sheepshead Bay, neighborhood where officer Ralph Dols was shot and killed
I 35th Street and Avenue U, approximate location where John Heidel was wounded before being killed
J 2232 Nostrand Avenue, approximate location of parking lot where Israel Greenwald was murdered and buried by Mafia Cops
K 923 44th Street, where gangster Frankie Yale was shot dead in his car
L Green-Wood Cemetery, where Albert Anastasia and other mobsters are buried
M 152 20th Street, former location of Adonis Social and Athletic club where Richard Lonergan was killed by Al Capone
N Vicinity of Bond Street and Degraw where Carmine Persico was wounded
O Holy Cross Cemetery where Frankie Yale and other gangsters are buried
P 5702 Avenue D, former location of lot where Brooklyn District Attorney Eugene Gold had a bug planted in a trailer to record mobsters
Q 1201 Utica Avenue, former site of lounge where attempt was made on life of Larry Gallo
R 17th Street in Windsor Terrace section, approximate location where Nicholas Guido, the "wrong man," was killed with assistance of Mafia Cops
S 779 Saratoga Avenue, former location of Rose "Midnight Rose" Gold's candy store frequented by Murder Inc. members
T 651 Fountain Avenue, former location of junk yard run by Gambino crime family members John and Charles Carneglia
U Ruby Street and Dumont Avenue, site of vacant lot used to bury the murdered three captains of the Bonanno crime family
V 2870 Linden Boulevard, site of Lindenwood Diner, favorite eatery of Charles Carneglia and some of his mobster friends
W 101st Avenue and Woodhaven Boulevard, approximate location of the old Bergin Hunt and Fish Club where Gambino crime boss John Gotti held court
Metropolitan Ave.
Cooper Ave.
Flushing Ave.
Cypress Ave.
Myrtle Ave.
Park Ln. S.
Dekalb Ave.
Jackie Robinson Pkwy
Gates Ave.
Bushwick Ave.
Atlantic Ave.
Jamaica Ave.
Rockway Blvd
Fulton St.
Union St.
Washington Ave.
Pitkin Ave.
Eastern Pkwy
Prospect Park
Empire Blvd.
Livonia Ave.
Belt Pkwy
Cross Bay Blvd
Clarkson Ave.
Kings Hwy
39th St.
Ditmas Ave.
Pennsylvania Ave.
Claredon Rd.
7th Ave.
McDonald Ave.
Coney Island Ave.
Ocean Ave.
Rockaway Pkwy
60th Ave.
16th Ave.
Avenue J
Flatlands Ave.
3rd Ave.
Ocean Pkwy
Avenue I
Avenue M
18th Ave.
Bay Ridge Pkwy
Avenue U
Shore Pkwy
Jamaica Bay
85th St.
Avenue P
Avenue R
Belt Pkwy
Nostrand Ave.
Gerritsen Ave.
Floyd Bennett Field
Stillhouse Ave.
Flatbush Ave.
N
Surf Ave.
0 1.5 3 km.
0 1.5 3 mi.
Rockaway Point Blvd
278
27

Frank Lucas are largely twenty-something street toughs who today try to emulate the gangster life by pushing drugs in the housing projects. Decades ago, the Chinese Tongs would put up wall posters in Chinatown to warn of trouble. Now, black and Hispanic gang members foolishly brag about their exploits on Facebook or wall graffiti, all of which tips off the New York Police Department.

New York City is in a constant state of renewal. Since the early years of the twenty-first century, Manhattan's skyline has changed enormously; even the waterfront has shed its gritty and dilapidated docks, replacing them with urban recreation zones and walking paths. Where Brooklyn longshoremen used to sweat under the thumb of the Mob, young families can now rent kayaks and picnic.

However, if you know a fair amount about the crime history of the city, as I do, you can still see many of the locales that have earned a special place in criminal lore. Armed with this knowledge, anyone can easily imagine what the city was like so long ago. Embracing this history makes you aware of all the things that have come before us in this fascinating city.

Walking from my office in lower Manhattan, I often find myself heading toward Chinatown and the intersection of Worth and Baxter Streets, just outside the Daniel Patrick Moynihan Federal Courthouse. Once known as the "Five Points," for the way streets intersected, the spot was the first notorious center of crime in New York. It was popularized in Martin Scorsese's 2002 film, *Gangs of New York*. Now the area is occupied largely by Columbus Park, where on most days you will find Chinese musicians playing lyrical Asian folk tunes as men play the Chinese version of checkers, fortune-tellers ply their trade, and children play on slides or take to the artificial turf of an athletic field off Mulberry Street.

More than a century earlier, the neighborhood, known as Mulberry Bend, was home to dens of thieves and impoverished Italian immigrants who scraped by any way they could. It was a place that even in the late nineteenth century was considered so filthy and odious that the city every few days would send large trucks filled with a solution of carbolic acid, chloride of mercury, and potash to flush the gutters, streets, and houses where stale beer was sold for two cents a glass. It was around these vermin-infested hovels that photojournalist Jacob Riis took the iconic photographs of bandits hanging out at Donovan's Lane, another infamous thoroughfare of the criminal class.

Immediately to the west of Columbus Park is the courthouse complex on Centre Street, with a new house of detention. But in the nineteenth century what is now a park outside the criminal court used to be home to the Tombs, the notorious jail that was built on ground above the old Collect Pond, once a draw for the early settlers of Manhattan. The ground under the jail would inexorably sink into the saturated earth, forcing the city to abandon the site. The tens of thousands

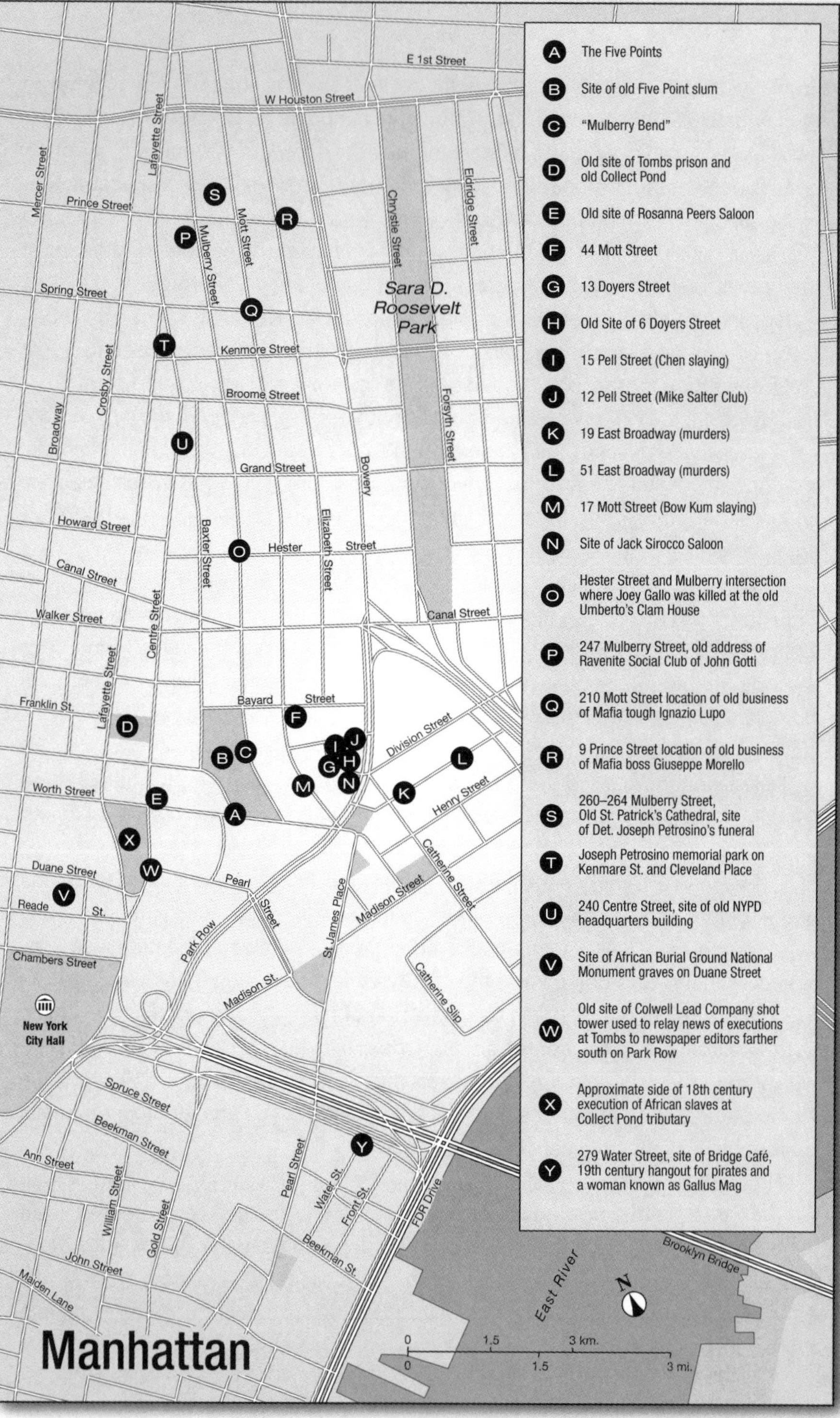

A The Five Points
B Site of old Five Point slum
C "Mulberry Bend"
D Old site of Tombs prison and old Collect Pond
E Old site of Rosanna Peers Saloon
F 44 Mott Street
G 13 Doyers Street
H Old Site of 6 Doyers Street
I 15 Pell Street (Chen slaying)
J 12 Pell Street (Mike Salter Club)
K 19 East Broadway (murders)
L 51 East Broadway (murders)
M 17 Mott Street (Bow Kum slaying)
N Site of Jack Sirocco Saloon
O Hester Street and Mulberry intersection where Joey Gallo was killed at the old Umberto's Clam House
P 247 Mulberry Street, old address of Ravenite Social Club of John Gotti
Q 210 Mott Street location of old business of Mafia tough Ignazio Lupo
R 9 Prince Street location of old business of Mafia boss Giuseppe Morello
S 260–264 Mulberry Street, Old St. Patrick's Cathedral, site of Det. Joseph Petrosino's funeral
T Joseph Petrosino memorial park on Kenmare St. and Cleveland Place
U 240 Centre Street, site of old NYPD headquarters building
V Site of African Burial Ground National Monument graves on Duane Street
W Old site of Colwell Lead Company shot tower used to relay news of executions at Tombs to newspaper editors farther south on Park Row
X Approximate side of 18th century execution of African slaves at Collect Pond tributary
Y 279 Water Street, site of Bridge Café, 19th century hangout for pirates and a woman known as Gallus Mag
E 1st Street
W Houston Street
Lafayette Street
Mercer Street
Prince Street
Mott Street
Mulberry Street
Chrystie Street
Eldridge Street
Spring Street
Sara D. Roosevelt Park
Kenmore Street
Crosby Street
Broome Street
Forsyth Street
Broadway
Grand Street
Bowery
Howard Street
Baxter Street
Elizabeth Street
Hester
Street
Canal Street
Walker Street
Centre Street
Canal Street
Franklin St.
Bayard
Street
Division Street
Worth Street
Henry Street
Catherine Street
Duane Street
Pearl
Reade
St.
Street
St James Place
Madison Street
Park Row
Chambers Street
Madison St.
Catherine Slip
New York City Hall
Spruce Street
Beekman Street
Ann Street
Pearl Street
William Street
Gold Street
Water St.
Front St.
FDR Drive
John Street
Beekman St.
Maiden Lane
Brooklyn Bridge
East River
N
Manhattan
0
1.5
3 km.
0
1.5
3 mi.

who pass by this location daily or lounge on its park benches are likely unaware that it was within the walls of the Tombs that the more notorious members of New York's original gangs—as well as other murderers—were executed by hanging from two sets of gallows.

Walking just a few short blocks north, you will come across places known for celebrated gangland murders, such as the 1972 slaying outside Umberto's Clam House of Joey "Crazy Joe" Gallo, or the 1983 shooting of Chinese gang leader Michael Chen on Pell Street. Around the corner from Pell Street is the angled Doyers Street, where the Chinatown Tong wars littered the pavement with blood and bodies during their battles of the early twentieth century. Then there is the site of the old Ravenite Social Club on Mulberry Street, where the late John J. Gotti held court and got arrested for the last time one frigid December night in 1990. Gotti's fate was sealed by secret FBI recordings made by a bug planted in an apartment three floors up from the club. Those are just a few of the sites within easy walking distance of the Five Points; walk a bit farther, and you will come across many other infamous places.

While the history and headlines of organized crime may be largely focused in Manhattan, anyone who has looked into the various mobs operating in the Big Apple knows that all the other boroughs have also earned spots on a list of important places in crime lore.

Inside the long-defunct Nuova Villa Tammaro restaurant in Coney Island one April afternoon in 1931, the feared and hated Mob boss Joseph Masseria was shot dead in a coup by his rivals while waiting for his lunch. This was one of the seismic episodes in the 1930s that set the stage for modern organized crime. On a quiet residential street in Brooklyn, the loan shark James "Jimmy Doyle" Plumeri was dumped after being strangled in 1971. Powerful Mafia captain Anthony "Little Augie Pisano" Carfano and former beauty contestant Janice Drake were shot dead in a car on a quiet Queens street in 1959. Forty years later, on a quiet Bronx street, Bonanno crime-family captain Gerlando "George from Canada" Sciascia was found with numerous bullet holes in his face and body after being killed on orders from family boss Joseph Massino, a murder which forever soured the alliance between the Canadian Mob and the Bonanno family. Another one of Massino's victims, Sonny Black Napolitano, was killed in the basement of a house on Staten Island and buried in a body bag in a wooded area near South Street.

Like Napolitano, lots of Mob-hit victims were unceremoniously disposed of without the benefits of receiving last rites, or a proper burial. Staten Island was a favorite dumping ground of killer Thomas "Tommy Karate" Pitera, because it had a lot of wooded areas and nature preserves. Then there was a vacant lot off

Ruby Street on the Queens-Brooklyn border, where in May 1981 three Bonanno crime-family captains were hastily buried after being slaughtered in a Brooklyn social club. Concrete was also a way of hiding the dead. When "Mafia Cops" Louis Eppolito and Stephen Caracappa abducted and killed diamond merchant Israel Greenwald, they forced the owner of a Brooklyn parking lot to dig a grave in a small garage, where they dropped in the body and then filled the hole with concrete.

Those who have died at the hands of La Cosa Nostra suffered terrible fates. They were shot, tortured, garroted, dismembered, dissolved in acid baths, dumped in the river, or incinerated. There was a time in the 1970s when the shoreline of Queens was littered with the torsos and limbs of errant gangsters. And of course, the mortal remains of a number of Mob victims have never been found. But taphophiles—those who are interested in all things related to cemeteries—can take heart in knowing that a number of New York City's burial grounds are graced with the burials of some infamous mafiosi who had the luxury of dying more conveniently. Very often their funerals were spectacles of the day.

St. John Cemetery in Queens is the leader, serving as the resting place for ten Mafia bosses: Carlo Gambino, Joe Colombo, John Gotti, Charles "Lucky" Luciano, Salvatore Maranzano, Joseph Profaci, Philip Rastelli, Vito Genovese, Carmine Galante, and Salvatore D'Aquila. Brooklyn's Green-Wood, the city's largest cemetery, and arguably the most historically significant, is where Joey Gallo and his brother Larry, as well as the once-feared Albert Anastasia, reside. A lesser-known Brooklyn burial ground, Holy Cross Cemetery, is where Frankie Yale was put to rest after he was shot dead in a 1928 car chase. Two of Yale's allies, the Abbatemarco brothers, are also interred there.

With so many disparate places linked to the history of the Mob, a historic guide to the places and faces of gangster life in New York City—complete with maps—seems appropriate. The result is *Gangland New York: The Places and Faces of Mob History*. Inspired by *Forgotten New York*, Kevin Walsh's delightful book about the often lost or overlooked remnants, avenues, parks, and artifacts that abound in the city, *Gangland New York* is a guide to the geography of gangster life, a traveler's companion to the Rotten Apple's landscape of crime, which doesn't have historical plaques or markers to tell us where all things criminal happened. In fact, the only signage related to the crimes of the past is a Department of Parks notice in Columbus Park by the old Five Points, which summarizes the place's former infamy.

Given the decades spanned in the pages that follow, *Gangland New York* provides a sort of archaeological tour of the city's organized-crime world, with maps to highlight the key places in this often bloody history. To aid the inquisitive reader, important addresses, street intersections, and other significant locations are highlighted in bold in the text.

The images within these pages come from a wide assortment of sources, including some old prints and etchings. Until the late nineteenth century, most newspapers, particularly those in New York, didn't rely on photographs, but instead illustrated stories with sketches, some of which have been included here. A few private sources have provided unique images. Also used are more contemporary photographs of crime scenes, evoking haunting, modern images of places that were once notorious. News and historical archives have helped to round out the source material.

In piecing together the multitude of stories, I have relied on many old newspaper accounts, public and private archives, and court records, as well as crime classics like Herbert Asbury's *The Gangs of New York*, and more contemporary books like Selwyn Raab's *Five Families*, Virgil Peterson's *The Mob*, and Jerry Capeci's great primer, *The Complete Idiot's Guide to the Mafia*. I consulted the National Archives, repository of hundreds of linear feet of records compiled by the Kefauver Committee, formally known as the Special Committee to Investigate Organized Crime in Interstate Commerce, of 1950, which riveted the national television audience with evidence about the Mafia in the United States.

A research gem I uncovered along the way was the City of New York's City Hall Library, which is a repository of a great many books about old New York, as well as documents about the police department. For years I have possessed what I believe to be one of the few original mimeographed copies of the report by the New York State Commission of Investigation to Governor Averell Harriman, on the 1957 meeting of Mafia leaders in Apalachin, New York, a treasure trove of information about some of the biggest names of La Cosa Nostra.

The result of all this research is this book, which captures some of the most important moments and personalities in Mob life in New York City, across the five boroughs and within numerous ethnic groups. These are the places where gangsters lived, worked, played, murdered, and often died. In some cases their funerals and burials became spectacles rivaling those normally reserved for heads of state.

Gangland New York is organized around each of the five boroughs and written in a chronological fashion for each area of the city. Because each chapter is driven by a time line, the entries are grouped around events that follow a sequence of years, and not necessarily because they have any special relationship. Manhattan, which since about 1850 has been the center of gangster life, has the most entries; next are Brooklyn and Queens. But each borough is represented in some fashion. This is not meant to be an exhaustive catalog of Mob history and its subjects and personalities. Plenty of murders, mostly of low-level people, aren't included. Personalities and events outside of New York City limits also don't make the cut, which is why Dutch Schultz's murder in a New Jersey restaurant isn't included in any detail. At first I tried to keep the subjects to an even one hundred, but that proved impossible with a history of organized crime in the city spanning nearly 175 years and numerous crime groups.

Another challenge was to make the subjects eclectic enough to include some of the most infamous people and events, as well as some of the more obscure and overlooked, which still played a part in the history of crime in the city. Other writers and crime buffs might have different opinions about whom and what to include, and I certainly would respect their choices. The distillation here is mine alone, based on my own expertise, historical perspective, and judgment, with a bit of serendipity thrown in as well.

I should also make a point about the many addresses and pieces of property featured in these pages: While the events depicted in *Gangland New York* happened over a long period of time, the current property owners have no connection to any of the unsavory things or crime groups involved. Of course, history will forever make a certain criminal connection to those places undeniable.

There was a time when being a gangster in New York meant enjoying celebrity status. Lucky Luciano lived in the Waldorf Astoria Hotel—until he was evicted—and Frank Costello was courted by judges and politicians. Those days are over. Anybody with a Mob pedigree is generally held at arm's length, save for the celebrity women of *Mob Wives*, who have made their somewhat attenuated ties to the Mafia a steady source of fame and income.

Although the late John Gotti was popularized by television as he tried to emulate the lifestyle of the old bosses, with his expensive suits and incessant Manhattan nightlife, in the end he was an anachronism—a showy personality who was playing the gangster role but lacked the political and social ties of those who once ruled the Mob. The public and the press may have loved the Gotti mystique, but outside of his world he had little of the clout and higher connections possessed by the likes of Costello, Luciano, and Thomas Lucchese. Make no mistake: Gotti had power in *his* world, and with one word could have someone killed. But his sphere of influence wasn't as great as what we saw in the old days of the Mob. One of the reasons is that in today's gangster world, loyalty hardly seems to matter.

"You have to understand, the world has changed," a Brooklyn detective said as he convinced Burt Kaplan, the businessman who was the Lucchese crime family's link with the infamous Mafia Cops, to cooperate with prosecutors. "The old world doesn't exist. The codes of honor are a joke. Nobody stays silent. We have guys lining up to talk to us now."

Faced with draconian sentences and aggressive prosecutors, many criminals, both young and old, simply turned into cooperating witnesses to save their skins, as Kaplan did. That's what happened to Gotti as he steadfastly remained true to his personal code even as those around him surrendered to the government juggernaut.

No matter how unappealing and marginalized real-life gangsters have become, we are still captivated by "The Life," as the Mob men call their not-so-secret society. *Gangland New York* serves as an evocative guide for those who wish to tour the neighborhoods of this historic gallery of rogues.

Anthony M. DeStefano
New York, New York

One of the oldest known photographs of the Five Points depicts the intersection of what is now Worth Street with Baxter Street. WIKIMEDIA COMMONS

CHAPTER ONE

THE RISE AND FALL OF THE FIVE POINTS (1800 TO 1895)

If ever there was a devil's cauldron for organized crime in the history of old New York City, it was a place known as the Five Points.

Adjacent to a stinking, urban swamp known both as the Collect Pond and Fresh Water Pond, the Five Points became synonymous with evil: a back alley where the poor, sailors, Irish immigrants, freed slaves, and those of a criminal mind-set coalesced around an old structure known as Coulter's Brewery. The brewery was a squalid structure that housed hundreds of men, women, and children of all ages. Wooden buildings sprouted up nearby and housed thousands more poor souls. The murderous and larcenous bent of these inhabitants earned the place the sobriquets of "murderers' alley" and "den of thieves." At the time, it was touted as the closest thing to hell on earth.

This etching of a scene in the Five Points appeared in an August 1873 edition of *Frank Leslie's Illustrated Newspaper* and depicts the squalid, dissolute life of those who lived there. PHOTO COURTESY LIBRARY OF CONGRESS

"This is the place: these narrow ways diverging to the right and left, and reeking every where with dirt and filth," was how English novelist Charles Dickens described the neighborhood in 1842 after a visit to the city.

Frontiersman Davy Crockett, no shrinking violet when it came to tough situations, once toured the area, and after seeing more drunk men and women then he had ever experienced in his travels, remarked, "I would rather rique [*sic*] myself in an Indian fight than venture among these creatures after night . . . these are worse than savages, they are too mean to swab hell's kitchen."

The neighborhood took its name from the intersection of three streets—Anthony, Cross, Orange, and the contiguity of Little Water—located roughly a quarter-mile northeast of **City Hall.** But don't look to find all of those names today. Anthony is now known as **Worth Street,** Cross is **Mosco Street,** and Orange turned into **Baxter Street.** Only Baxter and Worth intersect today. Mosco Street no longer goes to the intersection, because it is truncated by Columbus Park. Little Water Street disappeared from city maps altogether. **Mulberry Street,** although not at that precise intersection, was also considered part of the Five Points, and still exists today as a thoroughfare through Little Italy and Chinatown. Though it once surrounded a place known ironically as Paradise Square, the Five Points remained squalid and an incubator for New York's criminal life for many years.

Things were not always so bad in the Five Points. Before it turned into a large outdoor sewer, the Collect Pond (the name is said to derive from the Dutch word *kolch*, or *kalch*, meaning a small body of water) was a place for picnicking. The pond's water was used to make tea. Prior to the Dutch and English settling the area in earnest, the pond was used by local Indians, and heaps of old oyster shells on the west bank were monuments to their presence. The one macabre

This nineteenth-century engraving depicts the Collect Pond in its more bucolic state, before it became polluted and had to be filled in with landfill. *LIGHTS AND SHADOWS OF NEW YORK* BY JAMES D. MCCABE JR., 1872

element was that African slaves were said to have been executed on a spot of land known as Magazine Island, located in the midst of the water at a spot occupied today by **Pearl Street and Centre Street.** A half-block to the west is the old Negro Burial Ground, now known as the **African Burial Ground National Monument,** and signifying what is left of the place where slaves were buried in eighteenth-century Manhattan.

Fed by underground springs, the Collect was deep enough for small boats. The pond attracted a brewery, tanneries, and slaughterhouses. But all of that commerce and the large population led to pollution. By 1811, the city finally filled in the pond with earth and debris from a hill that stood approximately to the northeast. Still, despite the disappearance of the Collect, the awful living conditions in the neighborhood led to three outbreaks of cholera.

The saloons, which sprouted like mushrooms in the Five Points, attracted hordes of drunks from near and far. Charity workers visiting tenements to care for children would sometimes find all the adults in an apartment lying in a drunken stupor on the floor. Prostitution was also rampant. Some of the streets housed a brothel in almost every building. "Every house was a filthy brothel, the resort of persons of every sex, age, color and nationality," one historian wrote in 1849. The sex business also led to a particular kind of larceny in which a prostitute would

An etching published in 1872 depicts a rum shop or saloon of the kind that was prevalent in the Five Points.
LIGHT AND SHADOWS OF NEW YORK BY JAMES D. MCCABE JR., 1872

make so much noise servicing her client that the man didn't notice a wall panel open, allowing thieves to pick the pocket of his coat or pants, which had been left on a chair near the wall. This particular brothel was known as a "panel house."

Women, it turned out, did more than work in bordellos or ply drinks in the Five Points; they also nurtured some of the city's early gang culture. Rosanna Peers, who ran a grocery store noted for its rotting and barely palatable vegetables, also had a speakeasy at the intersection of what are known today as **Worth and Centre Streets.** More than a century later, newspaper columnist Walter Winchell dubbed Peers as the first owner of a speakeasy in the city. Known for its potent cheap liquor, Peers's establishment became a place where local gangsters, pick-pockets, and thieves congregated, much like the social clubs of the Mafia a century later. Eventually, the criminals coalesced into the Forty Thieves, believed to be the first organized gang in the city's history. The leader was one Edward Coleman, and children who aspired to be pickpockets (or worse) were organized into an affiliated group known, not surprisingly, as the Little Forty Thieves.

■ ■ ■

Coleman may have been more like the Dickensian character Fagan than a gang leader. It wasn't long before other criminal groups had willing recruits from the desperate residents of the Five Points and its environs, notably the Bowery area located just to the northeast. Theaters, beer halls, and concert halls took root along the **Bowery,** and for a time it drew a respectable clientele. But after a while the quality of the entertainment dropped off, and the Bowery became its own haven for gangs. Like the Five Points gangs, the Bowery mobs were sometimes made up of ethnic Irish. But ethnic solidarity—or in this case, the lack of it—didn't stop them from warring, and the fights between the Bowery Boys and the Dead Rabbits were legendary. Fighting broke out constantly in the Five Points, along the Bowery, or in an area just north of **Grand Street.**

Among the battlers for the Dead Rabbits was another gangster woman known as Hell-Cat Maggie. Stories from the time she was active, around 1840, distinguished Maggie as a ferocious fighter who had filed her teeth to points and wore claw-like nails on her hands. This made Maggie a double threat in hand-to-hand combat, as she could slash with her hands and do serious damage with her mouth.

Leaping into a street fight, Maggie was known to shriek a battle cry before she would "rush biting and clawing into the midst of opposing gangsters; even the most stout-hearted blanched and fled," said author Herbert Asbury. Maggie was an Irish immigrant of about twenty years old who fought alongside the Dead Rabbits as they did battle with the anti-Irish Bowery Boys. She would be portrayed in brutal fashion in Scorsese's 2002 movie version of Asbury's book by actress Cara Seymour. Maggie was only rivaled in reputation by another woman named Sadie Farrell, known as Sadie the Goat, who earned her moniker because her forte in street fighting was to butt her head against her opponent.

■ ■ ■

New York City was one of the largest maritime ports in the nation, and thus a target for pirates, who seemed to strike with abandon up and down the docks of Manhattan Island. One of the New York gangs that took to raiding vessels was called the Daybreak Boys, led by Nicholas Howlett and William Saul. The enterprising pair had their men strike before sunrise—hence the gang's name—reportedly raking in as much as $200,000 in booty from the vessels they targeted, a princely sum in those days.

The police of the time were unprepared to deal with this waterfront thievery and crime, readily admitting to Manhattan newspaper reporters that there was little they could do to stop the thieves. The wharves were too numerous and the opportunities for pillaging too plentiful for the police to do anything to stop the brash and ingenious pirates.

"They are like wharf rats, as much at home in the water as on shore," was how the *Brooklyn Daily Eagle* once described the pirates. "When they have committed a robbery or a murder, if too closely chased, they are prepared to jump

River pirates who plagued the waters around Manhattan often did battle with police, as depicted in this engraving. *RECOLLECTIONS OF A NEW YORK CHIEF OF POLICE* BY GEORGE WALLING, 1887

overboard, dive under a pier, and thus escape arrest or even detection, as has often been done."

The Daybreak Boys' penchant for violence is what led to the undoing of Howlett and Saul. It happened during a raid on the sloop *Thomas Watson* while it was anchored off Oliver Street on the East River (a street now cut off from the river by a housing development). When the gang shot and killed night watchman Charles Baxter with a bullet through his neck, the gunfire alerted police, who cornered the gang at the nearby Slaughterhouse Inn. After a three-hour standoff, both Howlett and Saul surrendered.

After a trial, Howlett and Saul were convicted of Baxter's murder, while a third gang member, William Johnson, cooperated with police. The sentence for Howlett and Saul was death, possibly the first instance of capital punishment meted out against a gang leader in New York City history. Their execution was slated for the Tombs, a city prison that had been built—rather unwisely—on the site of the old Collect Pond. The shifting ground under the prison would eventually lead to its demolition, but that was years in the future. The jail had a pair of gallows, and occupied the block on **Centre Street, between Leonard and Franklin Streets.**

The first Tombs prison constructed in the 1830s on Centre Street had gallows in its inner courtyard. PHOTO COURTESY LIBRARY OF CONGRESS

Howlett and Saul were executed on January 28, 1853, and the event was a spectacle. News reporters were given amazing access to the prison, with *The Times* chronicling in minute detail how they slept soundly the night before and refreshed themselves in the morning with cold water from the "Croton pipes," the new aqueduct that had been built to bring water into Manhattan. Howlett ate what was described as a "sumptuous breakfast," while a depressed Saul had no appetite. Before the noon hour of the execution, both men met briefly and shook hands with friends like William Poole and pugilist Tom Hyer, who will be mentioned in greater detail later in this chapter.

Once on the gallows it was Saul who appeared the most contrite and resigned to his fate, praying and then taking a moment to tell friends "to live in the fear of God." Howlett asked for some chewing tobacco and also prayed. "Oh God, have mercy! Oh God, protect my poor mother," exclaimed Saul as the hangman put the noose around his neck. A deputy warden who had become close to both condemned men cried as the end neared.

Both men died quickly as they dropped, although observers said Saul's arms and legs convulsed for a few moments. The crowd, which had filled the courtyard of the Tombs, dispersed and the remains were turned over to grieving friends of the dead and placed in polished mahogany coffins, which had plates engraved with their names, date of death, and ages: Howlett was nineteen years old; Saul, twenty.

■ ■ ■

Sadie "The Goat" Farrell fared better in piracy than Saul and Howlett. While head-butting gave her a reputation, Farrell needed something more substantial to make a living. Eventually, Sadie started a gang of river pirates from Charlton Street who for years plagued the Hudson River. Her crew commandeered a sloop and for months sailed north up the Hudson and raided farmhouses and stately homes, sometimes taking hostages for ransom. Eventually, the local populace got wise and took up arms, making Sadie's kind of piracy too risky. She eventually returned to her old haunts in Manhattan, making peace with her old rival, a woman known as Gallus Mag, who bit her ear off in a fight.

Gallus Mag was not a woman to trifle with. One newspaper account of 1872 reported that she had been arrested for brawling with a police officer who was investigating a bar fight in a dance house she ran at **338 Water Street.** The name *Gallus* is said to have come from the suspenders she wore, known as "galluses" back in the day. Sadie is said to have been given her ear back, which she wore in a locket around her neck for the rest of her life. After fading away, Sadie's life and exploits became fodder for twentieth-century novelists.

However, Gallus Mag, otherwise known as Mag (Margaret) Perry, persists in the city's memory through the old Hole-in-the-Wall saloon she frequented. The site of the saloon, **279 Water Street,** is now known as the Bridge Café, near the current site of the South Street Seaport. During the heyday of river piracy the saloon was a hangout for the Daybreak Gang. The popular Bridge Café, about two blocks from the East River, was damaged during Hurricane Sandy in 2012, but survived and is being refurbished, its aging clapboard siding a reminder of its vintage. It is reputed to be the oldest saloon in New York City.

■ ■ ■

Gambling, politics, and gangs worked well together in the mid-nineteenth century in Manhattan. Gambling parlors were all over the area around City Hall, and some of the establishments were top-shelf, complete with servants, food, and musicians

Bare-knuckle boxer John Morrissey went from Manhattan gang leader to the US House of Representatives in the nineteenth century. PHOTO COURTESY LIBRARY OF CONGRESS

at the ready to entertain clientele. With nicely appointed furniture and fixtures, the places resembled the best-run brothels, which weren't very far away. A man eager to make his mark and earn a good wage could look to the gambling halls for a job. Such was the case with John Morrissey, an Irishman from upstate Troy who excelled at using his fists as a bare-knuckle fighter.

The problem for Morrissey was that he decided early in his career to run up against two other street fighters who were just as good as he was: Tom Hyer and William Poole. Hyer, a heavyweight boxing champion, and Poole, butcher by trade from Christopher Street, were among the special group of gangsters who had said farewell at the gallows in January 1853 when Saul and Howlett were hanged for the murder of the watchman aboard the vessel *Thomas Watson*. Poole and Hyer were two gang leaders closely allied politically to the Know-Nothing Party, a deep-seated national movement that counted among its adherents former president Millard Fillmore, who became the party standard-bearer in the 1856 presidential race, but lost.

During the election of 1854 in New York, Poole and his gang of toughs put out the word that they were going to intimidate voters, a threat that some citizens took seriously, forcing them to form their own group to protect polling places. Morrissey joined the citizen poll watchers and amassed sufficient numbers to intimidate Poole and his toughs, who backed off from their raids on polling stations. Morrissey allied himself with Tammany Hall, the Democratic Party organization that had taken up the cause of the new Irish immigrants as a way of gaining new voters.

Know-Nothings like Poole and Hyer didn't like immigrants, particularly Catholics, Irish, and Germans who were seen as poor and living in slums like the Five Points. Morrissey, being Irish and Catholic, had two strikes against him in Poole's eyes. The Election Day standoff in 1854 didn't help matters. The men became mortal enemies.

Morrissey and Poole were such bitter foes that they couldn't stay in the same room without a fight breaking out. In fact, Morrissey attempted to shoot Poole at Stanwix Hall, **579 Broadway,** but his handgun misfired three times. Poole was getting ready to attack the befuddled Morrissey with a knife when cops arrived and placed them both under arrest, although nothing came of it.

But in the world of New York gangs, arrests weren't much of a deterrent. Morrissey and Poole had just been released from police custody when, on a February night in 1855, they both returned to Stanwix Hall, which at the time was a major entertainment complex with gambling and restaurants in lower Manhattan. To start things off, a couple of Morrissey's street-fighting friends, Jim Turner and Lew Baker, picked a fight with Poole at the bar. The situation reached a flash point when one of Baker's friends, Patrick McLaughlin, spat in Poole's face. Turner pulled a pistol but was such a bad shot that he wound up wounding himself in the arm with his first bullet. Turner managed to squeeze off another shot and succeeded in wounding Poole in the leg. Baker then weighed in and shot Poole twice—once in the stomach, and another time in the chest, near the heart. A still-feisty Poole managed to throw a knife at a fleeing Baker, but was a bit shaky and missed his mark.

William "The Butcher" Poole, from a nineteenth-century engraving. *RECOLLECTIONS OF A NEW YORK CHIEF OF POLICE* BY GEORGE WALLING, 1887

At first Poole was taken to his home on Christopher Street and expected to recover. But his condition worsened. On March 8, 1855, about two weeks after he was shot, Poole died at his home at **164 Christopher Street.** Cemetery records show that he was thirty-three years and eight months old. Legend has it that his final words from his deathbed were "Good-bye, boys, I die a true American." Poole's funeral was so large that it was described as having "almost regal pomp." He was buried at Green-Wood Cemetery (see chapter 14). Baker tried to flee the city on a brig headed for the Canary Islands, off the coast of Africa, but a nativist friend of Poole's, financier George Law, loaned his speedy yacht, the *Grapeshot*, to law enforcement officials for a transatlantic chase. The *Grapeshot* overhauled the vessel carrying the fleeing Baker, who was returned to New York. There, he was charged, along with Morrissey, Turner, and McLaughlin, in connection with Poole's death. But in three trials jurors couldn't agree on a verdict, and the case was dropped.

■ ■ ■

William Poole was part of a breed of early New York gangsters who made themselves powerful by using their muscle to help their political agendas. Similar groups, like the American Guards and True Blue Americans (who happened to be Irish), also seemed political. However, many of the other gangs existed to protect their turf and were named for their style of dress: Shirt Tails wore their shirts untucked from their pants; Plug Uglies had enormous plug hats with high crowns; the Roach Guards had blue-striped pants; the Dead Rabbits, considered by some historians to be an affiliate of the Roach Guards, wore red stripes and entered battle with a dead rabbit on a pike.

Fighting seemed to be the sport of gangs, and large-scale battles in and around the Five Points became legendary, with some volunteer firefighting companies also getting involved. The men who fought weren't just dissolute criminals. Often tradesmen after a day's work would put on their gang clothing and feel like they were a part of something much bigger than their small daily lives. Herbert Asbury in *The Gangs of New York* said some estimated these groups had over 30,000 members. Street brawls often involved up to a thousand combatants, and would leave scores bloodied.

Politics sometimes played a part in the bigger brawls. Just before the 1856 mayoral elections, the Dead Rabbits clashed with the Bowery Boys, a nativist group from the Bowery that attacked Five Points polling places. At first the Bowery group gained the upper hand, but the Dead Rabbits pulled reinforcements into the area armed with pistols, knives, and other weapons. The fighting went on for hours, and eventually the Dead Rabbits prevailed, beating back the Bowery Boys and in the process assuring victory for Mayor Fernando Wood, who was a favorite of the Irish.

But many of the street gangs, while organized in some fashion, weren't moneymaking operations. Their reasons for existing seemed more rooted in territory and the sense of self-esteem that membership provided. Other groups had a more economic imperative, and in that respect were more of the forerunners of the Mafia, which is rooted in making money. One such group was the Whyos, which grew to prominence around the Five Points in the years after the Civil War. The gang was, as Asbury described it, "as vicious a collection of thugs, murderers, and thieves as ever operated in the metropolis." It appears to have been the first Mafia-like collective of crooks and murderers. Legend had it that the Whyos acquired their name from the peculiar call uttered when they were going to a fight.

What made the Whyos different than the other gangs was the way the members organized themselves to carry out burglaries, bank robberies, and street thefts, notably pickpocketing. Operating from **Baxter Street** and the area around the **Transfiguration Church on Mott Street,** the Whyos became the preeminent gang in the 1880s and '90s. The gang had its fair share of fights, and because many of the members were armed, gunfights were constant. In one case, the Whyos got into a drunken gunfight at a saloon on the Bowery appropriately named The Morgue. It was reported that all the combatants were so inebriated they couldn't shoot straight, and nobody was hurt.

But it was cases of both reckless and deliberate shooting that ultimately led to the undoing of two men billed as the greatest leaders of the Whyos: Daniel Driscoll and Danny Lyons. One night in 1887, Driscoll and another man got into a fight after a night of drinking. As it turned out, a sixteen-year-old young woman named Elizabeth "Beezy" Garrity, described in the newspapers as "a dark-eyed, well formed girl," had developed a fascination with Driscoll, and took to hanging out with him. It was on this fateful night that Driscoll, Garrity, and some others were getting drunk in Chatham Square, and decided at 3:50 a.m. to visit a "disreputable lodging house" at 163 Hester Street. The lodging-house owner, who had fought with Driscoll in the past, tried to close the door to keep him out. But the Whyos leader drew his revolver and recklessly fired through the door, mortally wounding Garrity, who was already inside. The autopsy found she had been shot in the stomach, and noted that Garrity was a "remarkably beautiful woman." After a widely publicized trial, Driscoll was sentenced to be hanged in the Tombs.

Newspaper sketch of Elizabeth "Beezy" Garrity, who was shot to death by Whyos gang leader Danny Driscoll after a night of drinking in 1887.
EVENING WORLD, JANUARY 23, 1888

Execution days were traditionally public spectacles in New York City during this era, and on "Hanging Day," the church bells would ring when the condemned was finally swinging from the gallows at the Tombs. The newspapers, renowned for their cutthroat competitiveness in chasing a story, increased the public fervor surrounding these events. In the case of Driscoll, his hanging was something the *Evening World* newspaper covered feverishly, and in the age before smartphones, set up an elaborate Rube Goldberg–style signaling system so that the journalist could quickly get the story out on the street the moment Driscoll was dangling from the rope. A reporter in the courtyard of the Tombs would energetically wave a handkerchief the instant Driscoll's body plummeted off the gallows so that another staffer of the newspaper—stationed on the roof of a **Leonard Street**

Whyos gang leader Daniel Driscoll, who was executed in the Tombs on January 23, 1888.
EVENING WORLD, JANUARY 23, 1888

building adjacent to the Tombs—knew that the prisoner had been executed. The man on the rooftop then waved a red flag, visible to an associate at the top of the Colwell Lead Company tower, two blocks south at what is now the intersection of **Centre Street and Foley Square.**

The man at the top of the tower then faced south and waved a similar flag. At Printing House Square, where the newspaper was printed, an employee of the *Evening World* sat waiting on an office windowsill with binoculars. Once he had spotted the flag being waved at the tower, the newspaper employee alerted his colleagues, who started the presses rolling with the story that Driscoll was dead. The *Evening World* bragged that it scooped the competition by five minutes in getting the papers on the street.

Danny Lyons's demise came about eight months later in rather ignominious fashion. A street tough with a head shaped like a bullet and what was described as a "lantern jaw," Lyons had done a couple of years at Sing Sing Prison, and had only recently been freed on bail after assaulting a policeman. After taking over the leadership of the Whyos gang following Driscoll's execution, Lyons became a regular at a saloon run by Daniel Murphy at **199 Worth Street,** just due west of the Five Points, and an address no longer in existence. One August day in 1887 the twenty-eight-year-old Lyons was already three sheets to the wind from a day of drinking when he demanded that barman Walter Butler continue to serve him. Butler refused, and Lyons had a tantrum and started throwing bottles around. Murphy caught one of the bottles between the eyes and finally had enough, telling Lyons, "Come on, you have to go out."

The pugnacious Lyons reached for his pistol, but Murphy already had his own gun drawn and fired at the gang leader, striking him in the side of his head, over the right ear. Murphy promptly turned himself in to the police—a smart move, because other Whyo members who learned of the shooting wanted to take a piece out of his hide. Murphy claimed self-defense, and even gave cops the gun

Lyons had drawn. Meanwhile, Lyons was taken to the local Chambers Street Hospital, where surgeons tried in vain to prevent his death by lifting some pieces of his skull to relieve the pressure on his swollen brain.

There was no report that Murphy was ever indicted for the shooting, and business at the saloon in the days after the Lyons shooting picked up. Years later, there was some confusion about Lyons's fate, principally with Asbury's account in *The Gangs of New York*, where he claimed that the Whyos leader was executed on August 21, 1888, in the Tombs, for the murder of beloved athlete Joseph Quinn. But other news accounts note that the Daniel Lyons who was executed had no relation to the Whyos leader.

■ ■ ■

The deaths of Lyons and Driscoll didn't signal the end of the Whyos, but at the close of the nineteenth century, the geographic center of the Mob—indeed, any gang that frequented the Five Points area—was shrinking. There had been some changes over the years, as charities like the Five Points Mission, which took over the site of the Old Brewery, and the Five Points House of Industry worked to improve the situation facing residents—particularly the children. But the dilapidated and dingy houses, the narrow alleyways and filth-lined gutters, did nothing to improve the reputation of the neighborhood.

Writer James D. McCabe Jr. described the locale in *Lights and Shadows of New York Life*: "[T]he sidewalk is almost gone in many places and the street is full of holes. Some of the buildings are of brick . . . others are one- and two-story wooden shanties. All are hideously dirty." On a tour, McCabe found that every dwelling seemed to have a home distillery that produced "the vilest and most poisonous compounds" as whiskey, gin, rum, or brandy. Brothels seemed to be almost as plentiful. The city spent a small fortune regularly disinfecting the area known as **"Mulberry Bend,"** the part of Mulberry Street at the intersection with Baxter Street that was slightly angled, as it is to this day.

Something had to change, and by 1895, the city had finally approved a plan to tear down the Five Points.

In June 1895 the city began auctioning off the dilapidated buildings of the Five Points so that demolition could begin to create a park. The structures, made infamous over the years as hotbeds of gang activity, were sold for as little as $1.50. The winning bidders won the right to tear down the buildings and sell the debris for scrap. They also had the right to obtain back rent from many of the displaced tenants who were months in arrears, and spent their time scurrying around to find new lodgings.

Columbus Park after it opened in 1897, replacing the old Five Points slum and the notorious section known as Mulberry Bend, which occupied the area at the curve of the road in the upper-right-hand section of this photograph. PHOTO COURTESY LIBRARY OF CONGRESS

Demolition of the Five Points buildings on Baxter Street, Mulberry Bend, and surrounding areas began by June 8, 1895. The park to occupy the new space was designed by Calvert Vaux, who had co-designed Central Park years earlier. The approximately three-acre parkland, said to be one of New York's first urban parks, was finally opened in the summer of 1897, and was graced with curved walkways, trees, and flowers. Summer concerts gave a nod to the ethnic succession seen in the old Five Points, with a choice of music ranging from Italian operas and Irish folk tunes to standards like "My Old Kentucky Home" and "The Star-Spangled Banner."

CHAPTER TWO

THE SICILIAN AVENGERS

In the tone of its coverage, the establishment press, notably the *New York Times*, considered the Italian immigrant community as either quaint or poverty-stricken. The Italians were often portrayed as a downtrodden mass that filled the Five Points and its environs. Naturally, there was some truth behind that stereotyping. The Italians *were* poor and forced to live in crowded tenements, much as the Irish had experienced years before. The Italians were laborers, ragpickers, bootblacks, and even organ grinders with monkeys. But as Tyler Anbinder noted in his book *Five Points*, they also introduced fruit and vegetable stands to New York City neighborhoods and put their backs into much of the building and construction that came to define the skyline of the city.

Anbinder noted that an 1890 police census found that 49 percent of the Five Points residents were of Italian ethnicity, while the Irish had shrunk to just 18 percent. But Italians lived elsewhere in New York City and began having deep-seated issues that went beyond the prejudice they endured as newer immigrants. Theirs was a peculiar crime problem that would eventually overtake anything the old Five Points gangs ever did, and would contribute to the disfavor and suspicion Italians faced in later decades. It all started with what became known as the first "Mafia" murder in New York: the slaying of Antonio Flaccomio.

Pushcart peddler selling clams along Mulberry Street. The building to the right rear with the window sign "A. Cuneo Bank" housed a bank run by Italian businessman Antonio Cuneo, an early extortion victim of the Black Hand. The pharmacy on the right occupied Five Points land that is now part of Columbus Park. PHOTO COURTESY LIBRARY OF CONGRESS

While New York became the center of the five Mob families, the first appearance of the Mafia in the United States is widely considered to have been the dealings of the

Matranga and Provenzano families in New Orleans, beginning in the 1870s. Carlo and Antonio Matranga, two immigrant brothers from Sicily, parlayed their saloon and brothel earnings into a wider base of extortion and other crimes in the Italian community of that port city. They ultimately tried to target the Provenzano clan's lucrative fruit importation business, and for years the two groups were at war, a conflict that would eventually lead to the death of a police officer and the lynching of some reputed Italian Mob members.

Police in New York City were watching the situation in New Orleans and became alarmed because they feared similar outbreaks of violence among Italians in their city. "Have We Imported the Mafia along with Italian Opera?" *The Sun* newspaper asked rhetorically in a December 1888 headline for a story about an Italian extortion plot in the city. Police and Italian diplomats related stories about how Italians in New York were often the subject of such plots. It seemed as though any time Italians got together it was the making of a conspiracy.

So it seemed to police on the night of October 14, 1888, when Antonio Flaccomio, a cigar merchant, was stabbed to death outside of the Cooper Union at St. Mark's Place. Flaccomio was seen dining earlier at an Italian restaurant known as La Trinacria when he got into some loud quarreling with at least two other men with whom he had been playing a card game. Pulled away from the shouting by a friend, Flaccomio left the restaurant at **8 St. Mark's Place** and crossed to the northeast corner of the institute building. It was there that two brothers who had been with Flaccomio in the restaurant, Carlo and Vincenzo Quartararo, accosted him. Carlo Quartararo, said police, took out a knife and stabbed Flaccomio in the left chest. Back at the restaurant, the Quartararo brothers and others made a pact not to tell police about what had happened—a forerunner perhaps of the code of silence that came to be known as *Omertà*.

Antonio Flaccomio, an associate of Sicilian gangsters in Manhattan, was stabbed to death on October 14, 1888, near what is now Cooper Union in what may have been the first Mafia killing in New York City. *NATIONAL POLICE GAZETTE*, 1884

Flaccomio wasn't an angel by any means. In 1884, he was a suspect in the murder of Carmillo Farach, a tobacco dealer who was found dead on Staten Island of multiple stab wounds, including one to the left side of his chest—much the way Flaccomio died. A sword was found hear Farach's body. Although there was strong circumstantial evidence, including the fact that Farach and Flaccomio had quarreled over business and the same woman, officials didn't think prosecuting Flaccomio would be worth the cost, and let him go.

Flaccomio's murder hit the city at a time when the Mafia menace was becoming part of the public consciousness, and the newspapers lost no time in connecting the case to the Italian secret society. The killing "was ordered by the society of Sicilian avengers known as the 'Mafia,' which has secret branches in this city and New Orleans," blared the *New York Herald*, which said the crime group was a bunch of "cutthroats, counterfeiters and malefactors of all sorts." It was unclear where the newspapers were getting their information, but it appeared to be from the police. There were stories of how the inner circle of the Mafia wanted Flaccomio dead because he might have been an informant, and that they had planned his murder with treachery.

The Quartararo brothers fled the city, but while Carlo made it to Italy, his brother Vincenzo turned himself in to authorities, and after a coroner's inquest, was brought to trial for the homicide. The case was handled by Inspector Thomas Byrnes, who had a reputation as a reformer within the New York police, and who promptly fed the voracious newspapers information about the Mafia connection from his vantage point as head of the detective bureau. Vincenzo, who denied being a member of any secret society, offered the alibi that he was with his new wife of eleven days in nearby Mount Vernon around the time of the killing, and presented witnesses who were able to testify in support of his claim. It became clear during the trial that Carlo Quartararo didn't strike the fatal blow that killed Flaccomio, but could have been considered an accessory before the fact. However, there was too much doubt for the jury, which couldn't come to a unanimous decision and freed Quartararo. Upon learning of the verdict, it was said Byrnes remarked of Italians: "[T]hey can all go kill each other."

As sensational as his earlier remarks about the Mafia may have been, even Byrnes had to admit that the city wasn't being terrorized by the Italian brigands. In a November 1890 issue of the magazine *The Illustrated American*, Byrnes admitted that while members of the Mafia existed in New York City, "they have kept quiet." That was certainly true for the city compared to what had occurred in New Orleans, with the fighting and bloodshed seen among the Matranga and Provenzano clans.

But as the Italian community grew larger in Manhattan and its environs, it was only a matter of time before the Mafia would become a major criminal force. However, until the Italian Mob became a force to be reckoned with, New York City had some fearsome gangsters who inherited the roles previously held by the Whyos and the Dead Rabbits.

CHAPTER THREE

THE EASTMANS VERSUS THE FIVE POINTERS

After the death of legendary gang leaders like William Poole, Daniel Driscoll, and others, two other leaders emerged at the turn of the twentieth century to take their turn struggling for supremacy in the changing world of Mob activity. One was Paul Kelly, who led a group known as the Five Pointers, a band of criminals who took their name from the old and displaced Five Points neighborhood. The other was Monk Eastman, whose gang was named after him and known as "The Eastmans."

Eastman was a head-breaker who looked the part. Described as a short man with unruly hair, pug nose, and cauliflower ears, Eastman had a scarred face and a bull neck that added to his fearsomeness. "He always seemed to need a haircut, and he accentuated his ferocious and unusual appearance by affecting a derby hat several sizes to small," was how author Asbury described him.

Paul Kelly was actually Italian, and born Paolo Vaccarelli, while Eastman was Jewish and originally named Edward Osterman, although he would sometimes show up in court papers as "William Delaney." Kelly wasn't known as a street brawler and thug. In fact, he had the reputation of being a cultured man. But Eastman had such a reputation as a fighter that it was reported ambulance drivers at Bellevue Hospital referred to the emergency ward as the "Eastman Pavilion."

Classic mug shot of Monk Eastman, also known as Edward Osterman, the legendary leader of the Manhattan gang known as The Eastmans. PHOTO COURTESY LIBRARY OF CONGRESS

Although Kelly's Five Pointers took their name from the old criminal neighborhood in Lower Manhattan, the Mob operated all around Manhattan, particularly the Bowery. Kelly's base of operations was the New Brighton Dance Hall at **57–59 Great Jones Street,** a place that attracted a lot of upper-crust New Yorkers. The Eastmans also flourished on the Lower East Side, particularly around Allen and Rivington Streets. They included in their number a young Italian immigrant woman named Driga

Coloma, who went by the name of "Bridget." An incorrigible girl not even twenty years old, Driga cursed a blue streak to her parents, police, and judges when she was arrested in September 1903 while hiding in an Eastman gang hangout with another woman.

Driga's main role in the gang was to hide guns under her skirt and provide entertainment by dancing, or whatever else she might have done. A judge finally sent her away to a reformatory. Kelly and Eastman fell into a long Mob war of attrition that plagued the East Side and led to a big shoot-out on Rivington Street that spread to surrounding areas, and lasted from about 9:30 p.m. on September 16, 1903, until around 2:00 a.m. the next morning.

Paul Kelly, also known as Paolo Vaccarelli, the leader of the Manhattan gang known as the Five Pointers, shown in a 1905 newspaper photo.
EVENING WORLD, NOVEMBER 28, 1905

"They shot up the town in regular Wild West style," said one police detective.

The shooting actually began at a saloon on the northwest corner of **First Avenue and First Street** and spread to **Rivington and Allen Streets,** all on the Lower East Side of Manhattan. Police said some fifty men were involved, and gunshots flashed at every street corner. Bullet holes scarred numerous building facades and many windows were shattered in the fusillade. As was often the case with Eastman's crew, police were greeted only by silence when they began questioning people in the neighborhood, none of whom claimed to have seen anything.

"We have arrested them time and time again but the magistrates let them go," one frustrated police inspector said about the lack of witnesses.

Two died in the battle and others were wounded. With so many brazen shootings and beatings, political bosses had finally had enough, and demanded an end to the constant fighting. A 1903 peace conference arranged by Tammany politician Tom Foley got Kelly and Eastman to call a truce.

But Eastman, having alienated his political connections when he got arrested in a holdup, was sentenced to ten years in Sing Sing Prison in 1904. Police said that Eastman was observed shadowing the drunken son of a man who had paid

An archival photograph of Rivington Street on Manhattan's Lower East Side, where rival gangs the Eastmans and Five Pointers had a wild shoot-out on September 16–17, 1903.
PHOTO COURTESY LIBRARY OF CONGRESS

private detectives to follow the tipsy boy. Eastman was accused of trying to kill one of the private detectives during a brawl that followed. While he was being led to the courtroom from his cell in the Tombs for sentencing, Eastman heard the music of an Italian funeral band and is said to have quipped, "Thanks, gents, for this flatterin' serenade."

Kelly fared better, even if he had to thank his lucky stars at times. Although after Eastman's incarceration Kelly became the apparent master of gang bosses in Manhattan, he faced rivalry that turned deadly at the drop of a hat—his own hat, as it turned out. Early on the morning of November 23, 1905, police responded to reports of shots at Kelly's restaurant at 57–59 Great Jones Street, and, after finding the door ajar, entered and found John Harrington, one of Kelly's bodyguards, dead on the floor. Whining near his corpse was Harrington's pet cocker spaniel.

It was obvious to police that there had been a major battle at Kelly's club. Upstairs a meeting room was in disarray, with books and documents strewn around. Chairs and tables were overturned, and there appeared to be numerous bullet holes in the walls. The investigation determined that Harrington was killed in the meeting-room fight and his body brought downstairs. The battle started, police said, after four rivals of Kelly's from the rival Liberty Association came to the saloon, apparently to avenge the shooting at the club of a friend sometime earlier. The shooting sent bartenders, waitresses, patrons, and Kelly's crew scattering in all directions.

Kelly himself had fled the gunfight and was found by police at the home of his cousin James at **1228 Park Avenue** in Manhattan. The gang leader was seated in the parlor and smoking a cigar when cops entered, giving the appearance that he was ready for a night out.

"I was just starting downtown to give myself up," Kelly told the officers.

Kelly told police he had been wounded in the assault and showed them his white waistcoat, which had bullet hole in it with powder burns. Earlier, detectives had found Kelly's hat at the club with a bullet hole through the crown. Kelly had to testify at a special coroner's hearing, but was never charged.

After the killing of Harrington at the club, Kelly moved his base of operations uptown near East Harlem and became a labor leader with the Longshoremen's Union, controlling labor peace on a large section of New York's docks. Around the same time that Kelly switched careers, he also legally changed his name to "Antonio Vaccarelli," and professed a desire to live in peace with the police.

The switch didn't spare him trouble of a different sort. A dock strike Kelly fomented in 1916 caused West Coast shippers to threaten to send products by rail to the eastern United States, a move that would have increased prices for consumer goods. The strike was settled, and Kelly—or Vaccarelli, as he was also known—seemed to fade from public view. He died of natural causes in 1936.

Monk Eastman got a chance at redemption thanks to World War I. After being paroled in 1909, Eastman joined a unit of the US Army's 27th Infantry Division, eventually fighting with distinction in France during the war. Once he was demobilized, Eastman returned to New York, where in 1919 Governor Al Smith restored to him the rights of citizenship, which he had previously lost as a convicted felon. Police even offered to line him up with a legitimate job, something that didn't appeal to him.

Eastman seemed to stay away from trouble until the day after Christmas in 1920. That evening, as he started to walk up the stairs of the Blue Bird Café, **62 East Fourteenth Street,** Eastman was shot dead by an assassin who pumped four more shots into him as he lay slumped on the sidewalk. The killer, it turned out, was a federal Prohibition agent named Jeremiah Bohan, who told police that he had had an unpleasant argument with Eastman at a Brooklyn cafe some eight months earlier. It was then, said Bohan, that Eastman had pulled a revolver and threatened to shoot him. When Bohan ran into Eastman at the Blue Bird, he said an argument had started in which Eastman called him a "rat." Bohan said that Eastman, who was later found to be unarmed, reached into his right coat pocket, a furtive move the agent apparently found threatening. In response, Bohan said he shot Eastman numerous times and then fled. Eastman's killing, along with other incidents, provoked one member of Congress to say that federal Prohibition agents were out of control and in need of strong oversight.

Funeral procession to Cypress Hills Cemetery for Monk Eastman, following his death at the hands of a federal agent in December 1920.
PHOTO COURTESY LIBRARY OF CONGRESS

Back in New York, Eastman's funeral drew thousands who came to pay their respects. His body, dressed in the uniform of an army private, rested in a casket draped with an American flag. Veterans from Eastman's old unit carried the casket to a horse-drawn hearse for a funeral service at the Third Street Methodist Church. At Cypress Hills Cemetery, astride the Brooklyn-Queens border, a firing squad shot three volleys as a bugler sounded “Taps” for the old gang leader—perhaps the only gangster to ever receive that honor.

“Eastman was a thug, yet a man who seemed to have at least one redeeming quality—personal courage,” wrote columnist Henry Irving Dodge in the *New York Times*. “His career was a lurid one, involving State’s prison and winding up with a military funeral.”

Eastman’s death signaled the end of the old era of Manhattan gang leaders who ruled over hundreds of associates with a mix of loyalty, force, and bravado on the streets. Gangs in New York had evolved from cadres of street toughs in the nineteenth century, bound together mostly by camaraderie, to more economically focused bands of criminals who fought for geographic and business territories. Eastman’s old nemesis, Paul Kelly, showed that the gangsters were coming into their own as businessmen, with a seemingly legitimate facade. This would be the future path for many of the mobsters who would follow.

CHAPTER FOUR

TALES OF BLOODY ANGLE

A neighborhood in lower Manhattan considered part of the Five Points was Chinatown. Legend has it that the first Chinese immigrant set up a grocery shop in 1822 on Mott Street, which happened to be one block east of Mulberry Street. Most of the Chinese who came into the area were sailors or merchants, but enough of them settled in the area that by the mid-nineteenth century, Mott Street was the spine of a small Chinese community that slowly spread to encompass Doyers and Pell Streets.

While the Five Points neighborhood contained a heavy concentration of Irish gangs, Chinatown developed its own criminal element during the late nineteenth and early twentieth centuries. Formed hundreds of years earlier, the Tongs controlled gambling, drug dealing in the opium dens, and the importation of women for the predominantly male population of the neighborhood. Not all of the women were Asians. A substantial number of consorts and wives of Chinatown men turned out to be Caucasian, and police logs told of a number of rescue efforts to free American women who were living as virtual slaves.

The Pelham Café at 12 Pell Street was the saloon run by gangster-impresario Mike Salter, who hired a young Irving Berlin to be a singing waiter before Berlin went on to become one of America's preeminent songwriters. PHOTO COURTESY LIBRARY OF CONGRESS

The seedy reputation Chinatown acquired in the early twentieth century made it a place where the uptown crowd and the rich liked to "slum it." Private cars would come into the area late in the evening and popular nightclubs would attract the well-to-do, who became known for their slumming parties. The Pelham Café at **12 Pell Street** was run by a Jewish impresario and businessman known as "Nigger Mike" Salter, mainly because of his swarthy complexion.

Mike Salter ruled his part of Chinatown and worked with numerous gangsters, politicians, and celebrities. His Pelham Café became a popular place for the rich and famous to slum. PHOTO COURTESY PEPPER SALTER EDMISTON

His club became known for a singing waiter named Israel Baline, whose musical abilities took him further in the business to fame and fortune under the name Irving Berlin. When John Jacob Astor and his wife took a private taxi to Salter's club one evening in January 1906 for a slumming party and a few short beers, the newspapers touted the event as a night out at "Nigger Mike's." At nearby **6–8 Doyers Street,** there was the Chatham Club, which was a favorite of the white gangster element who mingled with the members of the Tongs.

The word *tong* literally meant "meeting hall" or "society," and these groups started out as fraternal benevolent associations. But it wasn't long before the Tongs were the main power in Chinatown. Asbury estimates that by the 1890s there were over two hundred gambling games along the three main streets of Chinatown, and almost as many opium dens, affiliated with the Tongs. One notable house of prostitution was located at **18 Mott Street,** although any local street or alley had its own special commercial sex establishment. Two Tongs in particular, the Hip Sing and the On Leong, were constantly vying for power and had a number of bloody conflicts over the lucrative sex and drug trade, in which local police were paid bribes to ignore the activity.

The Tong conflicts escalated with the appearance of Mock Duck, a portly man who led the Hip Sing Tong. Twice charged with murder, Duck was acquitted each time. His luck also extended to the street, where he once escaped a knife attack, no doubt with the help of a chain-mail shirt that he and other Tong fighters wore. Allied with another Chinese group known as the Four Brothers Society, Duck started a struggle for power against the On Leong Tong and its leader, Tom Lee. Sometimes the fighting was petty, and involved the On Leong members stealing the crest of its rival off the door of the Hip Sing headquarters building on Pell Street. But at other times the battles became deadly.

Lee actually preceded Duck on the Chinatown scene, and had more ability to cross over into mainstream New York politics. Many, including those in the city establishment, considered Lee the unofficial "Mayor of Chinatown," a reputation that was enhanced when he was given the position of deputy sheriff of New York County. Despite his political stature—or more likely because of it—Lee ran a substantial part of Chinatown's underground economy of gambling and opium dens, with a few brothels spicing things up. Those operations supplemented what were the legitimate businesses of Lee: restaurants and cigar stores.

For years Tom Lee was the powerful leader of the On Leong Tong in Chinatown. He often warred with his rival, Mock Duck, leader of the Hip Sing Tong. PHOTO COURTESY LIBRARY OF CONGRESS

Lee's way of doing business was reported at times to be heavy-handed. Historian Timothy Gilfoyle in his story of the underworld, *A Pickpocket's Tale*, said that armed with his sheriff's badge, Lee was able to convince Chinatown merchants to open a gambling parlor or opium den in return for a kickback of between five to ten dollars a week. Those tactics, noted Gilfoyle, made Lee unpopular among some Chinese, and led to his indictment for extortion, a charge that was later dismissed. A few attempts were made to assassinate Lee, but he survived each time, despite the fact that a bounty of over $5,000 was put on his head.

Some of the worst of the Tong war battles erupted in August 1905, during the presentation of a popular performance at the Chinese Theater at **7 Doyers Street,** a short angled street that ran between Pell and the Bowery. During the performance someone set off a string of firecrackers near the stage. The sudden noise caused a panic among the nearly four hundred patrons crowding the theater, and many tried to escape. But Hip Sing members drew pistols and started shooting at the On Leong associates who were sitting near the stage. The incident left three dead and several wounded, and police immediately suspected Mock Duck. "Get that Duck, dead or alive," said one police sergeant. Duck was found in the hallway of a Bowery building and taken back to the station house. Despite having an alibi from his lawyer, Duck was kept in jail until he was freed on bail.

Doyers Street in Chinatown, shown here around 1905, is a street with two sharp turns. It earned the name "Bloody Angle" because it was the scene of many Tong war shootings and stabbings. PHOTO COURTESY LIBRARY OF CONGRESS

Doyers Street, photographed in 2014. AUTHOR'S COLLECTION

But barely a week after the Chinese Theater incident came another murder, this one quite grisly. In retaliation for the shootings at the Chinese Theater, several On Leong members burst into the Eleventh Street laundry of Hop Lee, who was affiliated with the Hip Sing. Armed with hatchets, the assailants began hacking at Lee, cutting off his nose and slicing his face and body. They then for some strange reason began tickling his feet with feathers in what police believed was an attempt to torture Lee, who never cried out in protest. Tipped off about the attack, police arrived and rescued Hop Lee, who later died at the hospital. Five On Leong members were arrested.

The fighting at the Chinese Theater was one of a number of shootings and hatchet attacks that took place all over Chinatown, notably in crooked Doyers Street. A short street that had two sharp turns, Doyers Street earned the name "Bloody Angle" because of the casualties that mounted there during the Tong wars. Things became so bad throughout the Tong wars that the city would flood the area with policemen, who were sometimes spaced thirty feet apart on Doyers and Pell Streets, to prevent bloodshed.

But even the presence of police and a nearby station house on Elizabeth Street didn't prevent the Tong battles. The Chinese Theater became so notorious for several fatal shootings and other incidents that it was finally shut down. Ultimately, through the efforts of Judge Warren W. Foster, the Hip Sing and On Leong Tongs signed a fragile truce in 1906, which, with one interruption, lasted until 1909. By the truce terms the On Leong controlled Mott Street, and the Hip Sing got Pell Street. Doyers Street, the scene of so much bloodshed, was deemed neutral territory.

Ultimately, the death of a woman led to a resumption of the terrible hostilities.

The story of Bow Kum and her murder is one that illustrates much about Chinatown society in the early twentieth century, particularly about the stature of women at the time. Known as "Little Flower" and "Purse of Gold," Bow Kum was sold by her family as young girl in Canton province for about $150, to a man who wanted her as a servant girl, known in Chinese culture as a *mui tsai*. But the original purchaser of Bow Kum later turned around and sold her for about $3,000 ($70,000 to $80,000 in today's dollars) to another Chinese businessman in San Francisco's Chinatown. The businessman, Lau Tang, considered Bow Kum to be his wife, although he didn't treat her well. She eventually escaped and took up refuge at a Christian mission run by Donaldina Cameron. A stout woman of Scottish

Chinese girl named Bow Kum, who became the object of a dispute between two rival Tong members, which led to her death by stabbing in Chinatown on August 15, 1909. *NEW YORK HERALD*, AUGUST 16, 1909

Chinatown businessman Chin Lam, the unofficial "husband" of Bow Kum, who was murdered in a dispute over her affection between Lam and another Chinese man. *NEW YORK HERALD*, AUGUST 16, 1909

descent, Cameron was well known to police in San Francisco for helping Chinese slave girls escape from their conditions of servitude, be they prostitutes or domestic slaves.

It was through Cameron's intercession that a young, Chinese-American vegetable trucker named Chin Lam met and fell in love with Bow Kum. Though already married to a wife who lived in China, Chin Lam took Bow Kum as his wife in a Chinese ceremony, which had no legal standing in California. The couple then traveled to New York City in mid-1909 and took up residence in an apartment at **17 Mott Street.**

The couple's escape from San Francisco angered Lau Tang, who had paid $3,000 for the property rights to Bow Kum, and had suffered a terrible loss of face. He either wanted her returned to him or to be repaid the $3,000. But Chin Lam wouldn't agree to give back his bride and merely scoffed at his rival. The stage was set for some big trouble on Mott Street.

Lau Tang was a member of the Four Brothers Society, one of Chinatown's Tongs, and the group declared a state of hostility with the rival On Leong Tong, with which Chin Lam was affiliated. The declaration of war was openly noted in Chinatown through the hoisting of red flags over Tong headquarters. Brightly colored posters placed upon billboards on Chinatown streets proclaimed in Chinese script that there would be hell to pay if Bow Kum wasn't returned.

The evening of August 15, 1909, was a Saturday night, and Mott Street was filled with the sound of pianos playing in the various restaurants lining the avenue. Sometime after midnight, a suspect or suspects entered the back area of 17 Mott Street and went to the apartment where Bow Kum lived and stabbed her to death. She was found with her "oriental silks slashed in many places, and her hands clutching at the wound in her breast," according to one account. A few of her fingers were also missing.

When Chin Lam discovered his dead wife he ran from the building and yelled, "Murder, murder!" With the help of a nearby Mott Street shop owner and a policeman, Lam reentered the building through a courtyard and ran up to the second floor, where the body of Bow Kum lay on the floor of a room at the head of the stairs, in a pool of blood. Two gaslights illuminated the room. An eight-inch knife with a bone handle lay on the floor near the body. Crowds soon formed that included a number of Chinese men who lived on the premises with their Caucasian girlfriends and wives.

Police originally suspected Lam, and arrested him after they found a bloody handprint on a door and determined that it was as long as the hand of Lam (fingerprints weren't in use at the time). After further investigation, Lau Tang and his sibling Lau Shang, both members of the Four Brothers Society, were tried for the murder in January 1910, but acquitted. Nevertheless, even the court victory didn't quell the violence.

The fighting in this particular phase of the Tong wars saw a great deal of gunplay on the streets, resulting in several murders. On occasion dynamite was even used. Killings occurred not only in Manhattan but also in Philadelphia, and from the body count it seemed as though the Four Brothers got the worst of it. Tensions were high, and police found themselves constantly searching the alleys and crannies of Chinatown for suspects, often without luck.

But in one case—the assassination on Pell Street of two members of the Four Brothers—detectives were able to break the case because of the testimony of an elderly man who lived in a cubbyhole off Pell Street, and made his living selling opium and cleaning opium pipes. Opium dens were common in Chinatown, and an entire cottage industry had formed around their existence. The old man, Ching Quong Dong, was able to identify the two suspects as Low Gung and Lu Yo Fang, two members of the On Leong. The warfare only ended after the intervention of a local committee of Chinese merchants and Terence McManus, the skillful attorney for the Four Brothers, who won an acquittal for both men tried in the Bow Kum slaying.

A fragile peace was brokered in April 1910, later broken by more violence the following June. It took until early 1911 for more substantial peace to arrive in Chinatown. The cost in bloodshed was estimated to have been fifty lives. Sporadic outbreaks of violence erupted in the following years, but Chinatown was able to keep its peace until 1924, when more fighting occurred.

Later in the twentieth century, the influx of more Chinese with the liberalization of US immigration laws brought a different kind of Mob violence, a situation that existed well into the twentieth century and required more sophisticated law enforcement tactics to combat.

Luckily for Mock Duck and Tom Lee, they were able to survive the Tong wars, and both died of natural causes. Duck's story was especially poignant. He had a daughter who was part Caucasian and the offspring of a woman named Lizzie Smith, who had initially been married to another Chinese man. A child welfare agency succeeded in petitioning the courts to have the child taken from Duck. An emotionally shattered Duck then left Chinatown and went around the world, trying to gamble his way out of depression. To his good fortune, Duck won a lot of money, fortifying his stature in Chinatown. But he never did win back custody of his child. He died in 1941.

Given the assassination attempts and threats against his life over the years, Tom Lee led something of a charmed life. He had retreated to a home he owned in the Bronx when the Tong wars were at their peak. As hostilities subsided, Lee returned to the community and was considered an elder statesman, sponsoring picnics for the neighborhood. Lee died in January 1918 at the age of seventy-six, and was reputed to be one of the oldest Chinese men in Chinatown during that period.

CHAPTER FIVE

THE RISE OF THE JEWISH GANGSTER

Monk Eastman and Paul Kelly, two by-products of the Five Points criminal world, would in their own way create separate legacies. The groups they led would give rise to the next generation of mobsters who reigned in New York. It was Eastman who enabled a number of Jewish criminals to rise through the ranks. Kelly, known later in life by his true surname of Vaccarelli, did the same for some of the Italians who went on to form the basis of the legendary American Mafia.

Jewish immigrants came in droves to the Lower East Side of Manhattan in the late nineteenth and early twentieth centuries. **Hester Street, Suffolk Street, Norfolk Street,** and the surrounding areas became the destination for the influx of Eastern European Jews who had to make do with living in the crowded tenements, which in some cases were as bad as those found in the old Five Points neighborhood. Yet as bad as conditions were, even with new laws that required the barest of conveniences, like running cold water, the Jewish population made its mark. The Lower East Side became a beehive of activity with the garment sweat-shop industry. Synagogues began popping up, and a Yiddish theater flourished. There were Yiddish newspapers and eventually settlement houses, where Jews could learn what they needed to get by in the new country, coalesce, and maintain a cultural identity.

But not everybody took to life in America the same way. A significant prostitution trade developed on the East Side, one in which women were imported from Europe to work in Manhattan brothels controlled by Jewish political ward bosses. Other women worked as fences for stolen property. For some of the young Jewish men, like Max Zweifach, who had made his early mark as a bicycle thief, Monk Eastman's gang seemed an attractive career path. It was Zweifach, known by the sobriquet "Kid Twist," who eventually became the East Side's rising gangster after Eastman went away to prison in 1905.

Zweifach's tenure as a top gangster was short-lived, however. He was gunned down on May 14, 1908, in Coney Island by Louis Pioggi, also known as "Louie the

Louis "Louie the Lump" Pioggi, the Five Pointer gang member who shot and killed Jewish gangster Max Zweifach in Coney Island on May 14, 1908. *NEW YORK TRIBUNE*, 1912

Lump," a member of Paul Kelly's Five Pointers gang. The motive, according to police and gangland legend, was the fact that Zweifach and Pioggi were romantic rivals for a Canadian-born dancer named Carroll Terry.

The murder was an ambush situation in which Pioggi jumped his girlfriend Terry, Zweifach, and another man as they all walked together on Oceanic Walk, a narrow avenue no longer in existence. Zweifach was shot in the head while his friend, an Eastman gangster and Coney Island wrestler named Cyclone Louie, was hit by six bullets and also killed. Terry was knocked to the ground and wounded in the hip. Pioggi eventually pled guilty to charges of manslaughter and was given an eleven-month sentence.

After Zweifach's death, the leadership of the Eastman organization passed to Zelig Zvi Lefkowitz, who earned the moniker "Big Jack Zelig." Once just a pickpocket, Zelig developed a terrible temper, and during one November night in 1910 went into a rage at the Chatham Club at **8 Doyers Street** in Chinatown, beating up a wannabe gang tough and a couple of others in a brutal fight at the club. A month later, Zelig further burnished his reputation as a fighter at a Madison Square Garden event, where he was severely beaten by the man he had fought at the Chatham Club. He went after his assailant despite his own injuries.

For a man who had earned his stripes in the underworld as a very adept pickpocket, Zelig saw his share of gunplay. It was in June 1912 that he became involved in a hellacious fight which became known to some as "the battle of Chinatown," stretching the twelve miles from Coney Island to Chinatown in Manhattan. Initially, the cause of the battle was said to have been woman named Wanda Murphy, who had once been a hanger-on with Zelig, but who had taken up with a faction led by Italian gangster and Five Point member Jack Sirocco. However, in her biography of Zelig titled *The Starker*, Rose Keefe said that the Murphy connection to the fight was later discounted, although she did get involved in the fisticuffs that developed.

Things began just before dawn on June 3, when Zelig and his cohorts got into a fight with a waiter at a Coney Island cabaret. The evening soured by the fight,

Zelig and his group went back to Manhattan and eventually wound up at a **Chatham Square** saloon owned by Sirocco and his associate, Jack Poggi, at **12 Chatham Square.** To make a long, convoluted story short, gunfire erupted in Chinatown at **Doyers Street** and **Chatham Square,** where forty shots were fired; police moved in and made a number of arrests, including Zelig. Some reports said Zelig and three companions were able to come into Poggi's club by entering through an arcade below the old Mandarin Café at **13 Doyers Street.** The arrival of police didn't end things, as the suspects, along with Wanda Murphy, got into a brawl at the police station at **19 Elizabeth Street,** a structure which today is one of the oldest police precinct buildings in New York City.

Zelig Zvi Lefkowitz, a Jewish gangster who became known for his fighting and who terrorized parts of Chinatown. PHOTO COURTESY LIBRARY OF CONGRESS

A carload of Zelig's friend drove to the criminal court building on Centre Street, right next to the new Tombs jail, where Zelig himself had appeared for arraignment. It is there that the story got better—or worse—depending on your point of view. As he stepped outside the courthouse and was about to enter **116 Centre Street,** Zelig was shot in the neck. Clasping his wound, Zelig made his way into the building, and said when medical assistance arrived, "Doc, I guess they got me that time . . . but I don't do no squealing." Zelig's stand-up nature as a taciturn gangster helped him cultivate Tammany Hall politicians, who were able to protect him and secure his release when he was arrested.

Mandarin Café on Doyers Street, which provided access for Zelig Lefkowitz and his associates between Doyers and Chatham Square, where they got into a gun battle with rival gangsters in June 1912. PHOTO COURTESY LIBRARY OF CONGRESS

Useful political connections were a key part of the gangster life in New York, and in

Zelig's case they could have served him well had it not been for the strange series of events surrounding the murder of Herman Rosenthal.

Like many of those involved in New York's underworld in the period, Rosenthal was a gambler who started out in life as a flunky for political bosses like Tim "Big Tim" Sullivan. Although he started out on the lower rungs of the crime ladder, Rosenthal parlayed his association with Sullivan into some serious money running gambling joints. The cash made Rosenthal protective of his operations and leery of the police. As Keefe noted in her book about Zelig, Rosenthal had "an inflated sense of superiority, combined with the Sullivan connection, [which] convinced him that splitting his profits with the cops to avoid investigations and raids was beneath him."

Well, no matter what Rosenthal felt about his own sense of self-importance, the cops still hassled his clubs, raiding them periodically. He was even indicted for bribery in 1911, but beat the case in a mistrial. The last straw for Rosenthal came in April 1912 after his new club in the Tenderloin section of Manhattan—an area on the West Side running from about **Twenty-Third Street to Fifty-Seventh Street,** and encompassing the theater district—was raided and trashed by police under the command of Lieutenant Charles Becker. It was then that Rosenthal turned to Herbert Bayard Swope, a journalist at the *New York World*. (Swope would go on to become editor of the paper and win the Pulitzer Prize.)

In its time, the *World* epitomized the best—and worst—of competitive journalism. The paper was designed to shock and titillate, and did so regularly with stories about sensational murders, executions, adultery, and theft.

NYPD Lieutenant Charles Becker, a vice cop who was suspected of taking payoffs from gambler Herman Rosenthal. PHOTO COURTESY LIBRARY OF CONGRESS

When he spoke with Swope, Rosenthal alleged that cops had raided his gambling establishment a number of times. What really angered Rosenthal the most was the fact that despite a friendship he had with Becker, the officer wasn't able to protect him from police raids. Becker was part of a special squad of police who took direction from the commissioner, and even the mayor. Their main brief was to raid the underworld, cutting off gangsters from their sources of income.

The problem was that graft and corruption seemed to be endemic in the NYPD at the time, and Becker wasn't immune. Keefe reported in her book that Becker could bank $10,000 a month in numerous accounts, some under his name, others under the name of his wife and false account holders. He also reportedly paid cash for a $9,000 home in Williamsburg. It has never been definitively shown how Becker took graft and what he did in return, although there have been plenty of people who believe he was corrupt.

In any case, Becker had ties with Rosenthal that came back to haunt the officer. In July 1912, the *World* began publishing articles based on affidavits given by Rosenthal that alleged that he and Becker had a cozy friendship, one which led to the gambler borrowing $1,500 from the cop, complete with a promissory note. Along with the debt, Rosenthal alleged that Becker promised to tip him off in advance of any gambling raids, and hinted that he could squelch any case that got to the grand jury. Rosenthal said in the news story that his relationship with Becker finally soured after he had accused the captain in an argument that he had reneged on his promises of protection. Becker said he tried to "right the wrong," and went so far as to tell the Manhattan district attorney, Charles Whitman, about what Becker was doing, but was told there wasn't enough evidence for an indictment.

Swope's stories were explosive as far as the public was concerned, but the reaction from the police department was tepid. Whitman was quoted as saying that allegations of wrongdoing weren't proof of anything. Rosenthal would never be in a position to give any evidence, even if he could find it.

Manhattan gambler Herman Rosenthal, who was assassinated on July 16, 1912, at the Hotel Metropole in Manhattan after making corruption allegations against Lieutenant Becker in newspaper articles. *NEW YORK TRIBUNE*, 1912

Not long after midnight on July 16, 1912, Rosenthal walked into the Hotel Metropole, on the north side of Forty-Third Street, near the corner of Broadway. The address was **147 West Forty-Third Street,** to be exact. Rosenthal went to the Café Metropole inside the hotel and met with some gambling cronies. At about 1:30 a.m., about an hour after he had arrived at the hotel cafe, Rosenthal went outside to pick up some copies of the *World* with the latest installment of Swope's story, and returned to the cafe. A well-dressed man entered the cafe, approached Rosenthal, and said: "Can you come outside a minute, Herman?" Rosenthal complied. It was the last thing he ever did. Witnesses recalled hearing shots at around 1:57 a.m. A police officer nearby also heard the gunfire and found Rosenthal on his back, on the sidewalk, outside the hotel entrance. He was quite dead.

Although Rosenthal's murder may not have shocked many in the city, particularly among the gambling world, the reaction was different among officialdom. Prosecutor Whitman pressed police to preserve evidence and start following leads. At one point a number of cops who were in the area of the shooting weren't able to get the license-plate number right on the alleged getaway car, prompting Whitman to say that something was fishy. "It would be idle for me to say that the investigation had not been greatly hampered . . . but we will go on with it," said Whitman.

Two of the four men arrested for the murder of Herman Rosenthal; in the foreground on the left is Louis "Lefty Louis" Rosenberg, and on the right is Harry "Gyp the Blood" Horowitz. PHOTO COURTESY LIBRARY OF CONGRESS

The investigation ultimately focused on Becker after gambler Jack Rose, the prosecution's star witness, alleged in the grand jury that Becker had ordered him to kill Rosenthal because of the trouble he had been causing the police captain. Becker even reassured Rose that he wouldn't let anything happen to him. "'What do you think I am in this department? I can do as I damn well please,'" Becker said, according to Rose's grand jury testimony.

On August 20, 1912, Becker was indicted along with several other men for Rosenthal's murder. A manhunt finally tracked down two of the suspected gunmen in the Bronx, and a trial date was set for the fall. Becker was told by one journalist friend, said to be linked to Tammany Hall, that if he came clean about police corruption, prosecutor Whitman might show compassion. Whitman was seeking a mother lode of information about police corruption in Gotham, which the prosecutor said generated a cash haul of bribes amounting to $2.4 million a year paid to police. If Becker wanted to escape the electric chair, he would have to expose the system of graft rampant among the police, said Whitman. Becker didn't bite.

Zelig, the Eastman gang leader, was given a subpoena in early September to testify as a witness for the prosecution in Becker's trial. But during the evening of October 5, 1912, after getting a haircut, Zelig was shot dead on a trolley car as it passed by **Second Avenue and Fourteenth Street.** The gunman was "Boston Red" Phil Davidson, who claimed self-defense because Zelig had blackjacked him earlier in the day. Zelig had a large funeral—not as large as William Poole's, but substantial nonetheless—with about ten thousand mourners gathering outside a tenement located then at **286 Broome Street** on Manhattan's Lower East Side.

Becker's case had a tortuous legal history, but after his first conviction was reversed and a new trial ordered, Becker was convicted a second time of the conspiracy to murder Rosenthal. Four other gamblers and gangsters were convicted: "Dago Frank" Cirofici, Whitey Lewis, Harry "Gyp the Blood" Horowitz, and Louis Rosenberg. All four were executed on April 13, 1914.

Phil Davidson admitted he shot gangster Zelig Lefkowitz on October 5, 1912, but claimed he did it in self-defense. *NEW YORK TRIBUNE*, 1912

Becker was executed on July 30, 1915, in the Sing Sing Prison electric chair, the only New York City police officer to face capital punishment. The execution was an excruciating event in which it took Becker more than nine minutes to die from numerous jolts of electricity. By the date of his execution, prosecutor Whitman had gone on to be elected governor of New York State. Becker had sought clemency from Whitman, who by all rights should have recused himself from hearing Becker's plea because of the conflict of interest he had in deciding whether to spare Becker's life. Whitman turned down the plea for clemency. Becker's wife placed an engraved plaque on his wooden casket: Charles Becker, Murdered July 30, 1915, by Governor Whitman. Becker went to his death protesting his innocence, and a number of organized-crime historians believe he was framed. He was buried in Woodlawn Cemetery in the Bronx.

Charles Becker, third man from left in bowler hat, on his way to Sing Sing Prison, where he would be executed in 1915. PHOTO COURTESY LIBRARY OF CONGRESS

CHAPTER SIX

"MIO FIGLIO!"

The murder in 1888 of Antonio Flaccomio and the press hoopla about the Mafia was the first time New York City saw substantial publicity given to Italian organized-crime groups. At that point police at least had a glimmer of awareness that they were facing a new crime problem; they just didn't know much yet about who was involved.

Giuseppe Morello is credited with being the first Mafia boss of any substance in the city. In terms of physical appearances, Morello was a far cry from the dapper hoods who later became part of Mafia folkore, such as Frank Costello and John Gotti. Morello dressed like a laborer and with his thick, droopy mustache fit the stereotype of an Italian immigrant portrayed in the press. Known as "the Clutch Hand" because of a congenitally deformed right hand, Morello had emigrated from Sicily, where he had lived in the town of Corleone—yes, that Corleone, which became popularized in Mario Puzo's *The Godfather* as the inspiration for the name of his title character, Don Corleone. History is unclear as to when Morello arrived in New York, but by 1902 he was working out of a store located at **9 Prince Street,** where he sold olive oil, spaghetti, and more of what the newspapers called "Italian products."

Morello is said to have left Sicily before authorities there were able to prosecute him for a murder. He was apparently convicted in absentia for counterfeit-related offenses for which he received a prison sentence. Despite being handicapped with his withered hand, Morello earned a reputation for being a ruthless killer. His group was suspected of murdering an associate, putting his body in a sack, and tossing it off a cliff by the harbor in Bay Ridge, Brooklyn. Morello's main criminal stock-in-trade was counterfeiting, but he hired a bunch of enforcers who took care of the homicides to enforce discipline in their criminal group, and to protect it from police. One of the head-breakers was Ignazio Lupo, known as "the Wolf," who married Morello's sister and thus cemented a family loyalty between the two men.

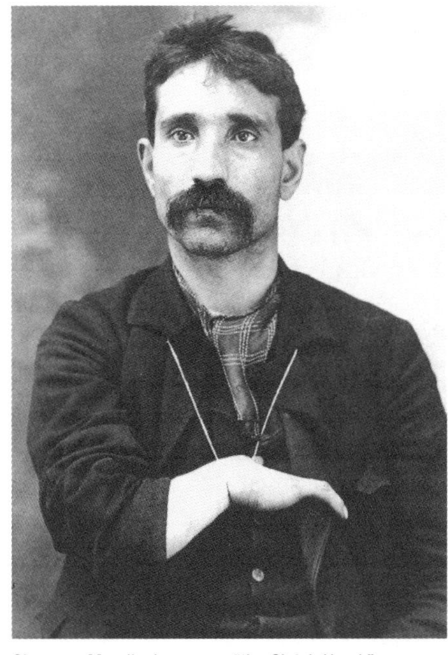

Giuseppe Morello, known as "the Clutch Hand," was one of the first Mafia-style bosses in New York City, and is shown here in an NYPD mug shot. An immigrant from Sicily, Morello ran a band of counterfeiters and killers in Little Italy. WIKIMEDIA COMMONS

The brutality practiced by Morello's gang included the peculiar method of the barrel murder. Victims were slain and their remains folded up and placed in a large wooden barrel, such as the kind used for wine, and placed in a conspicuous public place so that cops would find the body. The first recorded Mafia barrel murder in New York occurred in April 1903 when police found the corpse of Benedetto Madonia of Buffalo in a barrel in front of a building at **743 East Eleventh Street,** near Avenue D in Manhattan. Madonia's throat was cut from ear to ear and his body pocked with at least eighteen stab wounds. The doctor who performed the autopsy said that it appeared Madonia had been asleep when he was attacked, or held down while being tortured. An NYPD captain said it was one of the most remarkable cases he had seen in years. Barrels with bodies inside would pop up around the city for years to come.

As luck would have it, a group of federal Secret Service agents, as well as a New York City policeman named Joseph Petrosino, had been watching Morello and his gang in a counterfeiting investigation.

Petrosino, himself an Italian immigrant, was involved because he had been specially assigned to investigate crime in that immigrant community, and was gaining a name for himself for his proficiency in developing leads about the Mafia. The federal agents identified the man found in the barrel as a person they had seen a few days earlier as he entered a butcher shop at 16 Stanton Street, in the company of the Morello gang. Police then moved quickly, raiding Morello's apartment at **178 Chrystie Street,** where they found a trunk filled with letters written in Italian. A raid at a small pastry cafe at **226 Elizabeth Street,** another address associated with Morello, uncovered some incriminating evidence: a barrel identical to the one in which the body of Madonia had been found. There was even

The legendary NYPD detective Joseph Petrosino, on left in bowler hat, escorting Mafia hit man Tommaso Petto outside the new Tombs prison in Manhattan. PHOTO COURTESY LIBRARY OF CONGRESS

sawdust found on the floor of the cafe that appeared similar to that found in the death barrel.

Petrosino determined that Madonia was believed to have been on the verge of exposing the operations of Morello's US-based counterfeiting ring. Petrosino also learned that Madonia's brother-in-law had earlier been convicted of counterfeiting, and may have been trying to have Madonia recover a share of the profits. However, Madonia may have been more deeply involved in the counterfeiting ring than merely serving as an errand boy. One of the letters confiscated by police in the murder investigation revealed that Madonia had been sent by the Morello gang to revive a counterfeiting operation in Pittsburgh. But Madonia apparently didn't do a good job and, after complaining that Morello had unfairly criticized him, was preparing to quit and return home to Buffalo.

Morello and seven other members of his group were arrested and held for a coroner's inquiry, the standard practice back then in New York City whenever there was a suspicious death. The evidence against the Morello group was at best circumstantial, and there didn't appear to be anything linking the gang to Madonia's murder. But because the federal agents and Petrosino had developed some evidence that Morello and his band had associated with the dead man in the hours before he died, the coroner ruled that they were all accessories to the killing and had them held. When the ruling was announced, the wives of some of the gang members became hysterical, and police had to separate them from their husbands before the courtroom bailiffs took the men away.

The lack of evidence in the barrel murder case forced prosecutors over an eight-month period to dismiss charges against Morello and a number of his men. Finally, in January 1904, the court released the last defendant to be held, Tommaso "The Ox" Petto, effectively ending the prosecution. The murder of Benedetto Madonia remains officially unsolved. For Petto, so strong that it took as many as three police officers to arrest him, things didn't end well. In October 1905, Petto, living under the name "Luciano Perrini," was shot dead near Wilkes-Barre, Pennsylvania.

But Morello seemed to thrive, consolidating his power and becoming a major mafioso in the city. Among his confederates was another tough Sicilian-born gangster named Joseph Masseria. A flinty-eyed man with a gluttonous appetite for food, Masseria had ambition and cunning. His time as a man to be reckoned with in the Mafia would come later. In the meantime, Morello kept his organization focused on counterfeiting. It would lead to his undoing.

■ ■ ■

Since the barrel murder of 1903, federal officials and New York police were keeping a closer eye on the Mafia, and the related phenomenon known as the "Black Hand." Police officer Joseph Petrosino was instrumental in the formation of the NYPD Italian Squad, which focused on investigating organized crime in the Italian immigrant community in the early twentieth century. While both the Mafia and the Black Hand were seen as synonymous—they both exploited Italian immigrants—there was a difference. Whereas the Mafia existed to make money for the organization through rackets, such as counterfeiting, the Black Hand was more a state of mind in the community, causing immigrants to be fearful of anonymous criminals who used extortion as a way to squeeze money out of their victims. Mafiosi did use extortion, but more often the Black Hand struck by sending notes, unsigned except for crude drawings of daggers or guns, demanding money. At times victims who ignored those demands had their places of business dynamited.

Police officer Joseph Petrosino and others in the Italian Squad spent a good portion of their time going after Black Hand extortionists, as well as the more-traditional Sicilian gangsters. One case they solved was the attempted extortion of opera star Enrico Caruso by the Black Hand. Petrosino also focused on Italian anarchists, doing such a good job that he learned of a plot to assassinate President William McKinley in Buffalo. But Petrosino's evidence was ignored, and McKinley was assassinated on September 6, 1901.

Joseph Petrosino, key member of the NYPD Italian Squad. PHOTO COURTESY LIBRARY OF CONGRESS

Whenever there was a case involving the Mafia or the Black Hand, Petrosino was involved. He did so well at his job that in 1908, Petrosino was promoted to the rank of lieutenant, and in March 1909, he set sail for Sicily on what was described as a secret mission. However, news of Petrosino's investigative trip was widely known, and on the evening of March 12, 1909, outside a train station in Palermo, the crusading detective was shot multiple times and killed. He reportedly left his handgun back at his hotel and couldn't defend himself.

Petrosino's death sparked a virulent campaign against the Black Hand, the older Camorra group, the Mafia, and any other variant of Italian organized crime. The newspaper the *World* offered a $1,000 reward for the capture and conviction of those responsible for Petrosino's murder, and the New York City government pledged $50,000 to fund a special unit to go after Italian organized crime, which now had earned its place as a public menace.

Petrosino's body was shipped back to New York City aboard the SS *Slavonia* and arrived on April 9. Four days later, Petrosino's funeral was held at the Old St. Patrick's Cathedral at **260–264 Mulberry Street,** and the procession was watched by an estimated 200,000 people. The city proclaimed the event a holiday so that people could take off from work to watch the event. Petrosino's body was then buried at Calvary Cemetery in Queens. (In 1987, a small triangular park space, bounded by **Cleveland Place and Kenmare and Lafayette Streets,** about two blocks north of the old police headquarters building at **240 Centre Street,** was dedicated in Petrosino's honor.)

Meanwhile, back in Sicily, authorities identified five men, some with ties to New York and Giuseppe Morello, naming them as suspects in the Petrosino murder. None of them were ever brought to trial.

■ ■ ■

If Morello was breathing a little easier with Petrosino's assassination, his respite didn't last very long. Morello and his crew had long been on the radar of law enforcement for counterfeiting, and eight months after Petrosino's death, Morello and and several others were arrested on charges that they had smuggled fake $2 and $5 bills into the United States from Palermo, Sicily, in tins of olive oil, crates of olives, and cartons of spaghetti. The fake paper was also said to have been nicely printed at a farm upstate, but because they were churned out quickly, the bills were dead giveaways as counterfeit because they bore the same serial number, plate number, and series. Also arrested was Ignazio "The Wolf" Lupo, one of Morello's enforcers; although he could break legs, he had a hard time running a small grocery store at **210 Mott Street,** and had previously fled New York, leaving behind a gaggle of creditors.

After a nearly monthlong federal trial, Morello, Lupo, and six others were convicted of counterfeiting offenses and hit with stiff prison sentences in February 1910. None of the mafiosi took their medicine stoically. Lupo cried into a handkerchief as the judge gave him a total of thirty years. Morello played for sympathy, holding out his deformed right hand for the judge to see. Then Morello told the court that he had a family to take care of, and that if the judge would only suspend his sentence he would return to Italy immediately. The judge was unconvinced and hit Morello with a twenty-five-year sentence, at which point the gangster collapsed in a faint and had to be helped by federal deputies.

The long prison sentences sounded like the death knell for the Morello-Lupo gang, and officials proclaimed that Black Hand extortions and Mafia counterfeiting were now relegated to the past. But this was not going to be the case. There were plenty of Sicilian gangsters eager to assert themselves, regardless of how much Morello, through his half brother Nicolo, tried to maintain control of his organization. Morello lost his appeal, and his half brother was shot dead in Brooklyn in September 1916. The power vacuum was filled by Joseph Masseria, once one of Morello's lieutenants, but now a man who pulled together the various factions to be considered the top boss of all the Mafia groups in the city.

Known as "The Wolf," Ignazio Lupo, shown here in a 1912 newspaper photo, was a key confederate of early Italian Mob boss Giuseppe Morello, who was his brother-in-law. *NEW YORK TRIBUNE*, 1912

Masseria's main focus and his big moneymaking activity soon became bootlegging, once Prohibition became the law of the land in 1918. He seemed to concern himself less with petty extortion and the business that had become known as the Black Hand.

But average Italians in New York were still vulnerable to the extortion rackets run under the mantle of the Black Hand. The modus operandi of this group was to target Italian immigrants with an extortion demand, usually via a note that wasn't signed but had a rendering of a black hand, or *mano nera.* As revealed by the Enrico Caruso case, investigated by the late Lieutenant Joseph Petrosino, Italians from all walks of life were targeted. When necessary the extortionists would kill their victims. While the popular press painted many Italian gangsters with the label of the Black Hand, the meaning of the term actually became a subject of debate. Eventually, a number of loosely affiliated groups of criminals used the fear engendered by the Black Hand to make their own extortionate demands.

One such case was the kidnapping of five-year-old Giuseppe Verotta, one of the most notorious crimes attributed to the Black Hand in the period following World War I. Giuseppe, who was also known by the surname "Varotta," was mysteriously taken from his home at **354 East Twelfth Street** on May 24, 1921, not long after his mother had given him a penny to buy some candy. The child's father was soon sent a ransom note requesting that he pay $2,500 for the safe return of his son. Little Giuseppe's father, Salvatore, got the kidnappers to agree to accept $500, his entire life savings. But instead of paying the money, Salvatore Verotta,

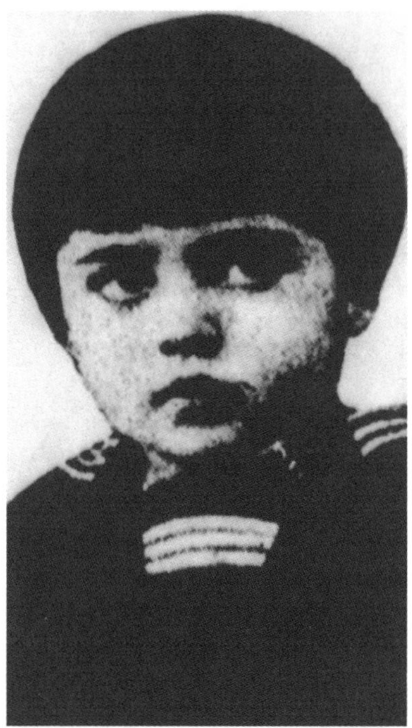

Five-year-old Giuseppe Verotta, kidnapped in May 1921 by men posing as members of the Black Hand, would later be found dead in the Hudson River north of New York City. *DAILY NEWS*, APRIL 17, 1921

working with Petrosino's Italian Squad, helped to secure the arrest of the emissary who had been passing messages to the kidnappers.

Petrosino's successor as head of the Italian Squad was Michael Fiaschetti, a cop who had the reputation of using heavy-handed tactics with suspects. He would later write a book about his career titled *You Have to Be Tough*, which indicates his approach to crime fighting. Fiaschetti was unorthodox, and not only allowed Salvatore Verotta to attend the interrogation of one of the suspects, but also permitted the father to beat the suspect in a last-ditch effort to find out what had happened to his son. But the police and Verotta were playing in dangerous territory. The kidnappers had already sent the father a crudely written note in which they threatened to not only kill Giuseppe if his family talked to the grand jury, but also to kill Fiaschetti.

Against this backdrop of threats, it really wasn't a surprise that Giuseppe's body was found two weeks after his disappearance in the Hudson River, at Piermont (near the present-day Tappan Zee Bridge). Local police in Piermont, apparently lacking mortuary facilities, buried Giuseppe's body in a makeshift grave, stripping the corpse of clothing to use for identification purposes. Traveling with a police escort to the upstate river town, Salvatore Verotta recognized the clothing—a blue sailor blouse, khaki pants, and a distinctive red garter made by his mother—as that of his son, and sat "in a stupor of grief" for hours, according to one news account. At one point the father pressed the wet clothing to his face, moaning the words "My boy, my boy" repeatedly.

Police believed Giuseppe's killing happened soon after the kidnappers' intermediary was arrested in New York by Fiaschetti's squad. Giuseppe was taken out into a boat on the Hudson River where he was garroted and his body thrown into the river. The discovery of the body resulted in a news media outcry against the

Black Hand, but did little to salve the inconsolable pain of the parents, Salvatore and Antoinette Verotta.

"*Mio figlio, mio figlio*—my son, my son!" Mr. Verotta cried out as he tried to embrace his child's casket when it was brought into the family's apartment. He then stood by the casket, talking to his son and telling him that the killers would, by the grace of God, be caught.

"May the spirit of my little boy descend upon my unborn child, that he may avenge his brother's death," said a dazed and pregnant Antoinette Verotta, referring to the child she carried within her womb.

Thousands took part in the public funeral, which filled the streets of the Union Square neighborhood where the family lived. The procession made its way to the Church of Mary, Help of Christians at **436 East Twelfth Street.** Women leaned out of tenement windows and wept. Neighbors gave the Verotta family a plate inscribed in Italian with the words "Victim of the Black Hand. We demand Justice. Let Justice be vindicated." As part of the funeral procession the child's playmates, each wearing a black armband, followed the casket through the streets.

Little Giuseppe's body was finally buried at Calvary Cemetery in Queens, also the resting place of Lieutenant Petrosino. The boy's tombstone bears an inscription proclaiming that he was kidnapped by the Black Hand, but even this symbolic act of defiance against the group drew threats. Before the modest monument was erected Salvatore Verotta received a note that promised retribution if the Black Hand was castigated on the stone. The note was turned over to police and the Verotta family ignored the warning.

Little Giuseppe Verotta's grave is located in Calvary Cemetery in the borough of Queens; his tombstone bears a barely legible, defiant inscription saying he was a victim of the Black Hand. AUTHOR'S COLLECTION

The Verotta murder was one of several blamed on the Black Hand, which had become one of the city's most odious criminal associations, as ill-defined and amorphous as it may have been. Even the *New York Times* was moved to editorialize about the child's death, commenting that "The circumstances surrounding the murder of little Giuseppe Verotta emphasize the need of bringing his kidnappers to summary justice."

Justice wasn't long in coming. Within days of the discovery of Giuseppe's body, several men were arrested for the child's murder: Salvatore Troia, Vincenzo Battaglia, Giuseppe Palestra, Santo Cusamano, Antonio Marino, John Melchionne, Joseph Ruggieri, and Robert Raffaele. Cusamano, Marino, and Raffaele were convicted and sentenced to death, although their capital punishments were changed to life in prison by Governor Alfred E. Smith.

Giuseppe's tombstone still stands at Calvary, although the passage of time has made the lettering hard to read. There is evidence that the stone once had a photograph of the child attached in a special holder, as was the common practice of the day, but that disappeared a long time ago.

■ ■ ■

Italian gangsters were the plague of their immigrant community and worked in coarse, brutal ways. At this point in history they were for the most part disorganized.

However, Jewish gangster Arnold Rothstein was the opposite of the Italian Mob. Born to a well-to-do immigrant family, his father, Abraham, a known racketeer, Arnold was known as a smart young man who had a head for mathematics and parlayed his obsession for gambling into a multimillion-dollar empire that made him rich by the time he was thirty. His main gambling salon was located on the West Side of Manhattan.

Rothstein became known as "the Fixer" and "Mr. Big," and was reputed to have been involved in the 1919 Black Sox scandal, where the World Series was fixed. An investigation found no credible evidence that Rothstein was involved, and he was later quoted as saying that while he and his friends knew about the plan, they had turned it down.

Rothstein worked quietly in the background of organized crime. Crime historians say that he was perhaps the most important racketeer of the era who convinced Italians and Irish to get organized and exploit the market potential given them by Prohibition. Rothstein offered his services as a grand *consigliere* of sorts, mediating disputes between the various Mob factions and using his high-level political connections with Tammany Hall to assert his power and put in fixes. He was also stylish, and even Charlie Luciano was quoted as giving Rothstein credit for teaching him how to dress.

Rothstein became a legendary crime figure, and thanks to writer Damon Runyon, was known as "The Brain" in popular culture, for the way he organized the flow of liquor into the the city from Europe and ran the rackets. His money was also parlayed into real estate, which he sometimes mortgaged to the hilt. Still, he stayed involved with gambling and wasn't afraid of high-stakes games, which went on for weeks.

But on November 4, 1928, Rothstein's luck and power came to an abrupt end. Two months earlier, in a bit of compulsive gambling, Rothstein had run up a debt of $320,000 ($4.4 million today) in one of a series of poker games he played. Faced with such losses, Rothstein said the games had been fixed and refused to pay. Another high roller involved, George McManus, took offense at the statement and, according to police, believed that Rothstein was the one who had fixed the game. Then, on that November day, while meeting with McManus and three other men, Rothstein was shot and seriously wounded in his room at the Park Central Hotel, at the corner of **Fifty-Sixth Street and Seventh Avenue.** Rothstein stumbled through the hotel and collapsed at the service entrance after asking the doorman to call a doctor and a taxicab. After doctors removed one bullet from his abdomen, Rothstein died on November 6. McManus had left his overcoat behind in the room and was thus a prime suspect.

Robbery was quickly ruled out as a motive, as Rothstein had over $6,000 in his pockets, although at times he carried much more. Although he had been mortally wounded, Rothstein refused on his deathbed to tell police who had gunned him down; in fact, Mob folklore has it that he told police sarcastically "me mudder did it," referring to his mother. Rothstein biographer David Pietrusza in his book said the gambler's comment to cops was more like "You know me better than that" when asked who shot him.

Although suspicion developed about several potential suspects—including the Jewish gangster, Dutch Schultz, who had his own gambling business in the Bronx—police had a rough time trying to locate the suspects, some of whom had apparently fled the city. Mayor Jimmy Walker had been pressuring his police commissioner Joseph A. Warren to show progress, and there were reports that Walker, who had his own problems, was pushing to sack Warren over City Hall's dissatisfaction with the pace of the investigation. About a month after Rothstein's murder, McManus was indicted and arrested, with Manhattan District Attorney Joab Banton saying "We have an airtight case in this Rothstein murder."

Well, as any gambler knows, there is never a sure thing, and the same holds true for an indictment. A year after he had so confidently bragged that the case against McManus was solid, Banton had to eat crow during the trial, admitting that he didn't have the witnesses or the evidence to make things stick. A judge directed a verdict of acquittal for McManus, prompting some jurors who had been hearing the evidence to remark that they would have cleared the defendant anyway.

There seemed to be something about the way big-time gamblers felt about their mothers, because as soon as McManus heard the judge toss the indictment, he turned around with tears of joy in his eyes and whispered to his brothers, "Tell Mama right away." After the jury formally pronounced him "not guilty," McManus left the courthouse to visit his mother in the Bronx.

After Rothstein's death, there was a battle over his will, which he had signed on his deathbed, apparently because of his injuries, with the notation "X." He left an estate valued as high as $25 million, which was later found to be about $2.5 million, with debts, taxes, and various claims whittling it down ultimately to $1.1 million. Rothstein's wife was left some cash, and a woman identified as girlfriend Inez Norton claimed she was to get proceeds from a $20,000 insurance policy, but lost out on her claim in court.

Eventually, the dispute over the will was settled, and Rothstein's real estate holdings in Manhattan and the Bronx were sold off at auction. Still, it remained unclear whether all of Rothstein's money could be accounted for; his criminal ventures were believed to have been split up among other gangsters. He also had an interest in a "phantom village" of 143 empty houses in Maspeth, Queens, which officials believed was part of some scam to steal from the city (see chapter 18). True to his Jewish heritage, Rothstein was buried with an Orthodox service at the Union Field Cemetery in Queens.

CHAPTER SEVEN

THE WAR OF THE BOSSES

Joseph Masseria's rise as a top mafioso was attributed to the rise of bootlegging and his own brand of luck. Over the years Masseria had dodged several assassination attempts. In one incident at the intersection of **Second Avenue and Fifth Street** in Manhattan, the stocky Masseria was able to dodge three bullets fired at point-blank range. The only thing damaged was the crown of his straw hat when one of the rounds passed right through it.

Umberto Valenti, the bootlegger believed to have arranged the failed assassination plot, wasn't so lucky; he was shot dead four days after that attempt on Masseria's life. It was suspected that Valenti was killed by a young Lower East Side hood named Charles Luciano. Masseria was questioned about the attempted hit, but the only thing he could tell police was that he had replaced the hat damaged during the attack.

Despite his twenty-five-year sentence for counterfeiting, Giuseppe Morello was let out of federal prison early after he received a pardon from President Warren Harding. With practically no power left as a Mafia boss, Morello ostensibly agreed to take a backseat to Masseria, his former underling. Morello also changed his first name to "Peter," apparently to mask his criminal past. Earlier attempts to assassinate Masseria were believed to have been instigated by Morello loyalists, so there remained an undercurrent of suspicion between the two men.

Another view of this period in Mafia history holds that one Salvatore "Toto" D'Aquila—alternately described as a cheese and olive oil importer, as well as being in real estate—had risen to power after Morello had gone to prison and become the so-called *capo dei capi*, or top dog, among Italian Mob bosses. D'Aquila had been associated with Morello, but had split off to run his own operation after old Clutch Hand was convicted. D'Aquila's rise to power was most recently discussed by author C. Alexander Hortis in his book, *The Mob and the City: The Hidden History of How the Mafia Captured New York*. Hortis cites as a key source the recollections of Nicola Gentile, a Mob associate in the 1920s.

Salvatore D'Aquila, the boss of the Mafia family which eventually became the Gambino crime family, was assassinated on a Manhattan street on October 10, 1928, while waiting for his wife to finish an appointment with her cardiologist. AUTHOR'S COLLECTION

Although he was a businessman who police said didn't seem to have a regular place of business but used his hat to keep papers, D'Aquila did have an arrest record stretching back to 1906 that included being charged as a confidence man. Whatever he did for a living, D'Aquila seemed well-off and dressed the part, wearing stylish suits, silk shirts with white collars, and expensive cravats. He lived in a nicely appointed home on Southern Boulevard in the Bronx, which he left late on October 10, 1928, to drive his wife into Manhattan to visit a cardiologist. The couple's four children also made the trip.

Leaving his wife with the doctor, D'Aquila walked outside to the corner of **Avenue A and Thirteenth Street** to check on his car. It was then that three men approached and started talking with D'Aquila for several minutes. The discussion turned into an argument, and then five shots were fired, after which D'Aquila dropped dead by his sedan. A newspaper report noted that it was lights out for D'Aquila just as the streetlights were being lit.

According to Hortis and other crime historians, the death of D'Aquila cleared the way for Masseria to become the top Mafia captain, even as he himself avoided further assassination attempts. He was viewed as *the* major boss of the Sicilian Mafia in the city at this time. Aligned with Masseria were some men who would become significant mobsters in their day: Charles "Lucky" Luciano (Lucania), Frankie Yale (Ioele), Gaetano "Tommy" Reina, and Vito Genovese.

But Masseria wasn't the only crime boss around. A number of other Italian gangsters, who traced their roots to other areas of Sicily, coalesced around other alliances. The stage was set for some inevitable major bloodshed.

■ ■ ■

What has become known as the Castellammarese War had its roots in the clannish nature of the New York Sicilian mobsters and greed. Castellammare del Golfo, a key port city in western Sicily, was the place of origin of mafiosi who were rivals of Masseria, like Salvatore Maranzano, Joseph Bonanno, Joseph Profaci, and Stefano Magaddino of Buffalo. Masseria's roots were in the nearby city of Marsala, which lay farther west. Also not to be ignored in the big picture were Chicago gangsters like Al Capone, who as a younger hood had worked out of Brooklyn, and his mentor, Johnny Torrio.

The precise beginning of the Castellammarese conflict is hard to pin down. Suspicion and deception existed for some time between one faction led by Maranzano and Masseria's group. Masseria may have struck first blood with the murder of Gaetano "Tommy" Reina, a successful ice distributor, on February 26, 1930, in the Bronx (see chapter 17). Reina's death prompted some of his supporters to shift allegiance to the increasingly powerful Maranzano. Unlike the burly and uncultured Masseria, Maranzano had an air of respectability about him. As a youth, Maranzano had expressed interest in becoming a priest, but in his native Sicily became a member of the Mafia instead. A purge by Mussolini aimed at organized crime in Italy made it inhospitable for Maranzano to remain in his homeland, so by around 1925 he had emigrated to Brooklyn, with what was said to have been a small fortune. Once in New York, Maranzano went into the business of the day for all mafiosi—bootlegging.

Maranzano was unwilling to be subservient to Masseria, and secretly began building alliances among some of his rival's supporters. Maranzano needed the element of surprise because in 1930, his group was smaller than Masseria's and had fewer resources and weapons. Maranzano was quoted as saying that Masseria wanted to "kill all of the Castellammarese," a remark aimed at preparing his friends for war.

One of the first bloody moves in the Castellammarese War was taken against the Masseria regime on August 15, 1930, when two armed men forced their way into Peter Morello's office at **352 East 116th Street** in East Harlem and shot him dead, with one bullet punching into his forehead. Morello, the old "Clutch Hand" gangster who had been a major counterfeiter in his prime, had been working what police considered "building rackets" from the offices. Another associate of Morello's, twenty-six-year-old Joseph Perrano, who was due to return to Italy the next day, was shot in the face and died. A third man, Gaspar Pollaro, was seriously wounded. Police found a car used by the gunmen but never made an arrest. The word among the mafiosi was that Maranzano's men had carried out the hit.

Maranzano's allies, those loyal to the late Gaetano Reina, struck again in September 1930. The target this time was Joseph Pinzolo, the man Masseria had appointed to take care of the criminal interests of the slain Reina. Pinzolo was one of the old-school mafiosi, a fat man with a long handlebar mustache, described by Joseph Valachi to federal investigators as a garlic-scented "grease-ball," a derogatory term for older gangsters who were quickly falling into disfavor. As Valachi would later describe in his remarks to investigators, and in his own book, he drove Pinzolo to 1487 Broadway in Manhattan where the old man had an appointment in an office suite rented by another mobster named Thomas Lucchese. It was there that Pinzolo was gunned down.

It was clear in the early days of the war that Masseria's faction was getting the worst of things. A number of the old boss's associates were getting killed all around the city. In one case, Masseria himself narrowly escaped being shot to death at an ambush in the Bronx. However, the violence was starting to disturb other Mob leaders in other parts of the country, and they told Maranzano to declare a truce, which he reluctantly did.

The peace that followed was an uneasy one. The fighting had put Masseria on the defensive, and at one point, according to Valachi's statement to the FBI, the old gangster was prepared to throw in his lot with Maranzano.

Maranzano was in a position of increasing power, and according to Valachi's later testimony to the US Congress, had about six hundred men aligned with him. Meanwhile, Masseria had only a few strong allies remaining, and the bloodshed had wreaked havoc with his rackets. Nominally, Masseria could count Luciano, Genovese, Lucchese, and Capone as his allies, but the tide had clearly shifted against "Joe the Boss," as Masseria was called.

Finally, according to one later account, during a meeting at an office on Broome Street in Lower Manhattan, Luciano, Genovese, and Frank Costello agreed that Masseria had to be killed in order to end the war. The trio secretly crossed over to Maranzano's side. According to Joseph Bonanno's biography, Luciano held a meeting with Maranzano in which it was agreed that the war would end once Luciano got rid of Masseria and took over his gang. Masseria was then lured by Luciano to a restaurant in Coney Island where he was killed on April 15, 1931 (see chapter 15). The fabled Castellammarese War was finally over.

CHAPTER EIGHT

THE RISE OF "THE COMBINATION"

After the assassination of Joseph Masseria there was little doubt that the top man in the New York Mafia was Salvatore Maranzano. Fortified by his victory over his rival, Maranzano quickly called a meeting of some of the top mobsters and associates to spell out how the world of organized crime was now going to be run. The exact date of the meeting has been lost to history, but according to the recollections of Valachi and others, it took place about a month after Masseria was killed, in a large banquet hall in the Bronx.

To further cement his position as top Mafia boss, Maranzano held a number of meetings with the heads of the Mob in Chicago and elsewhere. He then called for a large banquet stretching over nearly a week in the Bronx, in which gangsters were told to send money as tribute. Men came in and placed money on a table. Valachi recounted that $9,000 came in from Capone, with Luciano tossing in $6,000. Altogether the cash given to Maranzano amounted to over $115,000, remembered Valachi.

As organized as things seemed to be in the Mafia after Maranzano took charge, the situation was still unsettled. The problem turned out to be Maranzano himself. He appeared to have a Napoleonic complex—or in his case, a Julius Ceasar complex, because he was an admirer of the Roman leader. Maranzano also appeared to be increasingly paranoid, often telling Valachi, "We have to go to the mattress again," a phrase used to denote Mob warfare. Maranzano said that the very men he had appointed as heads or underbosses of the various families—Luciano, Mangano, Genovese—as well as Capone, had to be gotten rid of.

Maranzano contacted an Irish gangster by the name of Vincent Coll to kill Luciano and Genovese. The plan was for Luciano and Genovese to be killed after they arrived for a purported meeting at Maranzano's office at **230 Park Avenue.** But Maranzano's plot was betrayed by another Italian mobster, who tipped off the proposed victims.

Armed with the knowledge of their intended assassination, Luciano turned to a group of Jewish mobsters he had been doing business with and who were active in garment industry labor racketeering. The group included Meyer Lansky and Longy Zwillman. On September 10, 1931, at 2:00 p.m., the Lansky group had four gunmen dressed like cops go to Maranzano's ninth-floor office suite at 230 Park Avenue. The suite was actually filled with a number of people, and when the fake cops arrived, they had everyone line up against the wall.

Maranzano came out of his office to see what the commotion was all about. It was then that the gunmen, a group that included Lansky men Red Levine and Bo Weinberg, pursued Maranzano back into his office, where he was stabbed numerous times before being shot four times in the head and chest. The assassins then fled the building, running into Vincent Coll and others who were on their way up to the office to carry out the original Maranzano plan to kill Luciano and Genovese. "Beat it—the cops are on the way," Coll was told, and he fled as well.

About a dozen detectives quickly arrived at the Park Avenue office after the gunmen had fled. One of the first things disclosed in the early stages of the police investigation into the slaying was that Maranzano appeared to have been involved in a large immigrant-smuggling operation. By one account, one of the gunmen had rifled through Maranzano's desk before fleeing, pulling out a file labeled "Immigration" and placing it prominently on the desk so that detectives would find it. However, later news accounts indicated that Maranzano had been under suspicion for smuggling activity for some time. When federal agents went to look for his immigration and naturalization file, they found that it was missing.

Police took a number of people into custody for questioning about the Maranzano hit—all Italians, it seems—but made no arrests for the murder. In the meantime, Luciano quickly emerged as the top Mafia leader in New York, and set about creating an organizational structure that would help to guarantee peace, settle any disputes, and ensure that profits would continue to come in from illegal operations. Luciano, Joseph Bonanno (an old Maranzano loyalist), Gagliano, Mangano, and Profaci all agreed to serve as heads of the five individual Mafia families in New York. Luciano also established the "Commission," composed of the five New York families, as well as Chicago and Buffalo, to settle disputes and establish policies. The Commission was, as writer Selwyn Raab would later say, a sort of Supreme Court for the Mafia.

The basic five-family structure set up by Luciano became the essential core of the Mob in the city, although the names of the families would change as different leaders took over each little dynasty. With peace generally assured, the Mob went about making money.

While this made Luciano wealthy, it would also lead to many problems for him.

It was in December of 1933 that Prohibition—which had provided the Mob with so much money through bootlegging—ended with the adoption of the Twenty-first Amendment to the Constitution. The gangsters had to adapt or become extinct. Owney Madden, the head of what was the Irish Mob, decided to retire to Hot Springs, Arkansas, where he set up a nice gambling operation to serve him in his old age. Speakeasies could be converted into legitimate bars and restaurants, and because liquor was now legal, anything connected to the business also became legitimate, even if the people behind the setups were crooks. Luciano forged ahead with different business ventures, solidifying his old links to Jewish gangsters like Lansky. He also spent a lot of time getting involved in Tammany Hall politics, something the old gangsters of the earlier part of the century had done. As befit a man of his stature, Luciano moved into a suite at the Waldorf Astoria Hotel at Forty-Eighth Street and Park Avenue, registering under the name of "Charles Ross."

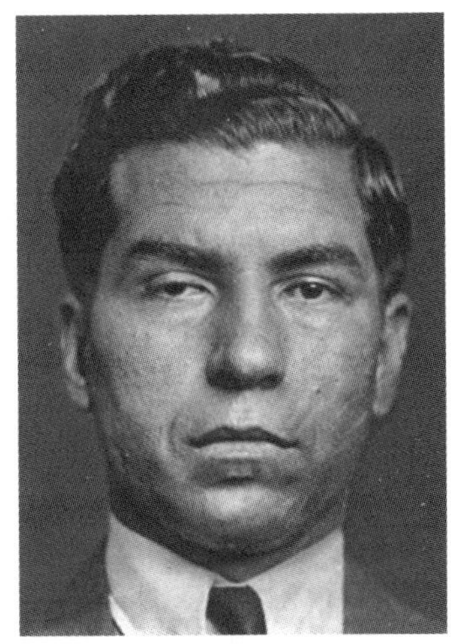

Charles "Lucky" Luciano skillfully engineered his way to the top of the New York Mafia power structure when he took part in the assassinations of bosses Joseph Masseria and Salvatore Maranzano. WIKIMEDIA COMMONS

One of the benefits of political ties for the Mob was that it helped to ensure a pliant law enforcement. It became widely known in the 1930s that the Manhattan district attorney, William Copeland Dodge, stayed away from prosecuting serious rackets and instead had his staff focus on minor crimes. This was a boon for the Mob. But in 1935, one of the grand juries regularly empaneled by Dodge became fed up with his concentration on the trivial, and demanded more serious prosecutions of racketeers. The so-called runaway grand jury became big news, and Governor Herbert Lehman picked a private attorney, Thomas Dewey, as special prosecutor. Dewey had previously served as a federal prosecutor in Manhattan for three years before going into a lucrative Wall Street legal practice.

Working out of offices at **100 Centre Street,** a court building directly opposite the location where the old Tombs jail had stood, Dewey began to look at the rackets. Eventually, after a tip from one of his woman staffers about the way prostitution cases were handled in court, Dewey started an investigation into the prostitution industry, using wiretaps to gather evidence. Through the use of the

Thomas E. Dewey made his name serving as a special prosecutor in Manhattan, successfully prosecuting Lucky Luciano for being involved in a prostitution racket. Dewey later became governor of New York State, and unsuccessfully ran for the presidency in 1944 and 1948.
PHOTO COURTESY LIBRARY OF CONGRESS

taps, Dewey's investigators tied Luciano to a citywide brothel industry, which reportedly provided the Mob—known as the "Combination"—with over $12 million in profits. Raids on brothels and subsequent arrests netted suspects, including some prostitutes, who decided to cooperate with Dewey and provide evidence that would tie Luciano into the sex rackets.

Although some legal experts and commentators would later remark that the evidence against Luciano was thin, he was nonetheless convicted in June 1936 of numerous counts of compulsory prostitution. About a month later he was sentenced to a minimum of thirty years in state prison. After his legal appeals were exhausted, Luciano stepped down as boss of his family, turning the reins over to Frank Costello. (Dutch Schultz, a tough Jewish gangster whose real name was Arthur Flegenheimer, had asked the Mafia for permission to kill Dewey because of the legal problems he had caused. But the ruling Commission of the Mob rejected Schultz's request and authorized his own assassination in October 1935, in New Jersey.)

The prostitution conviction looked like the end for Luciano, but even in prison he managed to live in style. He had special meals prepared in a kitchen set aside for that purpose by prison officials. It seemed at the least like a comfortable end for Luciano. Yet, history would prove that Luciano couldn't be written off. World War II would help him out in ways that no one could have predicted.

The war years proved quite lucrative for some in the Mob. Valachi later reported in his debriefings with the FBI that the theft and trafficking in ration tickets became a profitable sideline, particularly for Carlo Gambino, a former associate of Masseria who switched sides to Maranzano before the old boss was assassinated.

Yet there was one activity that some in the Mafia took a more patriotic interest in, particularly because it held out the prospect of some personal benefit. Faced with the threat of sabotage on the New York docks, military officials met with Joseph "Socks" Lanza, a union official who was not only politically connected to Tammany Hall, but also a member of the Luciano-Costello family. Following a meeting with US naval intelligence officials—a meeting set up with the help of the new Manhattan district attorney, Frank Hogan—Lanza agreed to help federal agents who were looking for German and Japanese saboteurs.

The issue of dock security in New York had been made critical after a fire at **Pier 88, Forty-Ninth Street and the Hudson River,** in February 1942 led to the destruction of the French passenger liner SS *Normandie*, which had been sequestered in New York City by the government because of the war in Europe, and renamed the USS *Lafayette*. An investigation ultimately determined that the fire was caused by a welding accident, but the initial fear was that the vessel was targeted for sabotage because it was being outfitted as a troop-transport ship.

Lanza controlled only a portion of the New York waterfront: the Lower East Side around the Fulton Fish Market. To assure help in protecting the rest of the New York harbor, which included the piers across the Hudson River in New Jersey, Lanza suggested that the US Navy contact the one person who could guarantee cooperation on the rest of the waterfront: Charles Luciano. What followed was one of the most intriguing episodes in the war, as the US government came to rely on Luciano for help in securing dockland in exchange for helping him get relocated to a prison closer to New York City.

Lanza recruited some fishermen to be watchful for Nazi submarines. Luciano reached out through his attorney to have Lansky have others in the underworld help get dockworkers to provide information to federal authorities about suspected saboteurs. In addition, some of Luciano's friends in the Mob helped naval intelligence agents get union books and cards so that federal agents could be placed as undercover operatives in hotels, restaurants, bars, piers, trucks, and factories.

Luciano's help also extended overseas. According to a later report done on Luciano's activities by a naval commander, the Mob contacts provided the names of "friendly Sicilian natives and even Sicilian underworld and Mafia personalities" who could be helpful in providing information for the Allied war campaign prior to the invasion of Sicily. The information provided by the Sicilians reportedly proved to be "40 percent" correct. Overall, it seems that Luciano's help proved useful to the war effort, even though it wasn't necessarily "extraordinary," as one military investigator deemed it.

As part of his deal for cooperating with the war effort, Luciano had asked for executive clemency. On January 3, 1946, with the wars in Europe and the Pacific finally over, Dewey, who was then governor of New York State, commuted Luciano's sentence to the ten years he had already served, with the condition that he go back to Italy. It was a deal Luciano took, and when the time finally came for him to be deported, he was sent to a special holding facility on Ellis Island, the old immigration station, to await transport back to Italy.

In a final bit of indulgence, two nights before Luciano left the United States for good, he was given a going-away party at the Greenwich Village Inn in

The body of Charles "Lucky" Luciano was returned to the United States in 1962 for final repose in his family mausoleum bearing the original surname "Lucania" at St. John Cemetery in Queens.
©BETTMAN/CORBIS

Sheridan Square, Greenwich Village, on February 7, 1946. Only a few close Mob friends attended, although it was reported that judges and politicians sent gifts of cash. On February 9, 1946, Luciano sailed away to Italy on the Victory ship *Laura Keene* from the Bush Terminal in Brooklyn. Aside from some newspapermen and about fifty dockworkers, there were not many people there to witness the event. The vessel also carried a cargo of flour as it made its way to its first port of call, in Genoa. Luciano lived the remainder of his days in Italy, speaking by telephone to his old mobster associates in the States. He died in 1962 of a heart attack at an airport in Naples.

CHAPTER NINE

"THIS IS FOR YOU, FRANK"

The years immediately after World War II were generally peaceful times for the Mafia in New York. The old Sicilian wars that had led to so much bloodshed were things of the past. A number of mafiosi had profited one way or another from the war, and law enforcement, either through corruption or lack of interest, had not seriously hurt the rackets. Aside from the prosecution of Luciano for prostitution, as well as some other cases of homicide, organized crime wasn't that tempting of a target.

Luciano's deportation back to Italy in 1946 allowed others to vie for control of the Mob family he left behind, although he still kept in constant contact with his old cronies. The two men who competed for power were Vito Genovese and Frank Costello, two veterans of the Castellammarese War. This jockeying for power among them continued for years. An immigrant as a boy from a town near Naples, Genovese had a reputation as a ruthless killer and drug dealer. Genovese fled the United States in 1937 when he became a suspect in the Brooklyn murder of gangster Fernando "The Shadow" Boccia three years earlier.

Vito Genovese vied for control with Frank Costello for control of the Mafia family led by Charles Luciano after he was deported to Italy in 1946. PHOTO COURTESY LIBRARY OF CONGRESS

In Italy during the war, Genovese became close to dictator Benito Mussolini, a surprising turn of events given Il Duce's long campaign to eradicate the Mafia. What apparently kept Genovese in Mussolini's good graces was the financial largesse he reportedly bestowed upon the Fascist Party. In addition, officials determined that as a further show of support for Mussolini, Genovese arranged for the assassination of prominent New York–based Italian anti-Fascist Carlo Tresca in 1943.

Tresca, publisher of the anti-Fascist newspaper *Il Martello* (The Hammer), was a well-known figure in radical politics and had a distinctive appearance, with a trimmed beard, pince-nez glasses, and flowing black cape. He was easy to spot at around 9:40 p.m. on January 11, 1943, when he came out of his office building's entrance at **2 West Fifteenth Street.** According to witnesses, a dark sedan pulled up at the curb and a gunman got out, firing three shots at close range into Tresca. Wounded, Tresca managed to walk a few steps toward his assailant before collapsing and dying at the **northwest corner of Fifth Avenue at Fifteenth Street.** He was killed despite the fact that he was under police surveillance. Mobster Carmine Galante has long been suspected of carrying out the hit.

Italian anti-Fascist newspaper publisher Carlo Tresca was gunned down in Manhattan on January 11, 1943, in a murder believed by officials to have been orchestrated by Mafia boss Vito Genovese as a favor to Italian dictator Benito Mussolini. WIKIMEDIA COMMONS

In Italy after Mussolini was deposed in 1944, Genovese managed to keep his black-market operation intact until he was targeted by US Army investigators and brazenly tried to bribe his way out of an arrest. A records check discovered the outstanding murder warrant against Genovese in New York, and he was sent back to the United States in 1945 to stand trial for the killing of Boccia. The case against Genovese seemed strong: Prosecutors had an eyewitness who could corroborate other evidence. But in the days before witnesses were protected in jails, the witness, Peter La Tempa, was found dead in a cell where he had been placed for safe keeping just before the trial was to begin. It appeared La Tempa had been given some pills to treat a chronic ailment but had actually taken poison. With no key witness, the case against Genovese fell apart.

Mafia boss Frank Costello, known as "The Prime Minister," shown here testifying before a congressional committee. PHOTO COURTESY LIBRARY OF CONGRESS

Back on the street, Genovese was in a position to battle the one man who stood in his way for control of the old Luciano family—Frank Costello. While Genovese was a cunning man, he was uneducated and lacked any kind of refinement. Costello, who resided at **115 Central Park West,** was the more-polished boss of the family, and became known as "The Prime Minister" because of his social smoothness and his ability to cultivate politicians, such as leaders of Tammany Hall, state Supreme Court justices, and other friends. He also sponsored charity events. But when the US Senate held televised hearings in 1951 on organized crime in New York, Costello became camera-shy, and would only allow his manicured hands to be shown on television as he testified.

When Genovese returned to New York, Costello realized he had a dangerous rival for leadership of the family, so he placated Genovese; thus, he was able to stay on as boss. Yet in the world of Mafia intrigue and double cross, Costello's rivalry with Genovese only intensified. On the evening of May 2, 1957, after attending a dinner party at L'Aiglon Restaurant at **13 East Fifty-Fifth Street** and visiting Monsigniore Restaurant just down the street, at **61 East Fifty-Fifth,** Costello took a cab to his apartment at **115 Central Park West,** where at about 10:55 p.m. he was confronted by a gunman in the lobby who said "This is for you, Frank," and shot him. The wound wasn't serious, but police learned that the gunman, who used a .32 caliber handgun, was a tough young aspiring boxer named Vincent Gigante. The assassination attempt was orchestrated by Genovese, who told people that Costello was actually planning to kill him. Gigante turned himself in to police and was brought to trial for the attempted murder. But Costello lived up to the Mafia code of *Omertà*—silence—and couldn't, or wouldn't, identify Gigante as the shooter. Gigante was acquitted, despite the testimony of the doorman at Costello's building, who had identified him as the gunman. Costello never retaliated; instead, he retired from active Mob leadership and died in 1973 of natural causes.

Boxer Vincent Gigante was charged with the shooting of Mafia boss Frank Costello on May 2, 1957, in Manhattan but was acquitted. PHOTO COURTESY LIBRARY OF CONGRESS

The forced retirement of Costello left Genovese as the undisputed leader of the old Luciano family, which would soon be named after Genovese. But in the Mafia, many were not satisfied to simply be named as head of the family. Genovese also feared competition from powerful Brooklyn-based mobster Albert Anastasia, the underboss to Vincent Mangano, who had disappeared in April 1951. A ruthless killer, Anastasia (whose first name in Italian was Umberto) was seen by Genovese and other Mob bosses, including Meyer Lansky, as gunning for their rackets and their lives. As it turned out, Joseph Bonanno saw the futility of another war between family bosses, and convinced both Genovese and Anastasia to sit down in 1957 for a peace dinner, where they agreed to forgo any further violence.

With the Brooklyn waterfront as his power base (his brother Anthony Anastasio was a union leader on the docks), Anastasia was a force to be reckoned with in the Mob. A tough-looking gangster, Anastasia would rather kill an opponent than talk out a problem. Intimidation was his game. Anastasia was actually convicted of murder in the 1920s and sentenced to death, but the case was dismissed on appeal. Although he never admitted it, Anastasia was suspected by his Mob cronies of orchestrating the murder of Mangano. When Mangano disappeared the Mob bosses held a meeting in Manhattan and asked Anastasia to explain the conflict he had with his old boss. After telling the other bosses that Mangano had been plotting against him, Anastasia was anointed leader of his own family and became known as "Don Umberto."

But while he struck fear in many who crossed his path, Anastasia was making enemies among the other bosses. For a start, reports circulated that Anastasia sold Mob memberships for thousands of dollars as he tried to monopolize the waterfront. Knowing Anastasia's reputation for violence, the other wary mobsters made a preemptive strike. The morning of October 25, 1957, Anastasia turned up at the barbershop in the Park Sheraton Hotel, located at the corner of **Seventh Avenue and Fifty-Fifth Street.** Anastasia would show up to get a trim and a shave about twice a month, often taking time to buy some toys at a store in the hotel lobby. "Always expensive toys, too," the store proprietor remembered.

This time Anastasia was accompanied by his nephew, Vincent Squillante, and both men took seats in the salon. Anastasia was in chair number four, while Squillante sat next to him. The barber, whose surname was Bocchino, began to cut the hair on the left side of Anastasia's head while shop owner Arthur Grasso sat at the cash register by the door. Suddenly, two armed men entered; witnesses later described them as being dark and broad of frame, with scarves over the lower part of their faces.

"Keep your mouth shut if you don't want your head blown off," one of the men said to Grasso, who stood with his mouth agape.

The gunmen approached Anastasia as the barber was working on him and fired a total of ten times, with five bullets finding their mark. One round caught Anastasia in the back, and as he stumbled out of the barber's chair, another shot hit him in the back of the head. He died in a pool of blood on the floor.

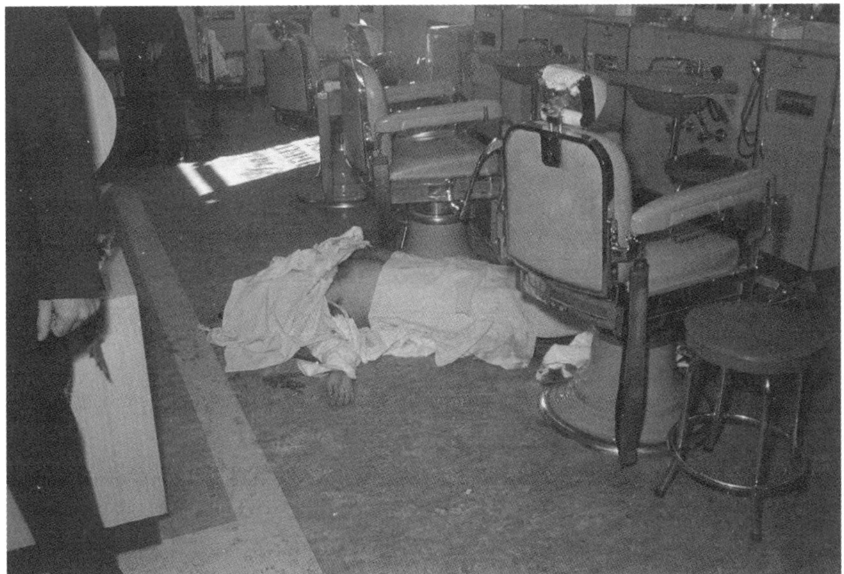

Mafia boss Albert Anastasia was gunned down as he sat in a barber’s chair getting a shave in the Park Sheraton Hotel on October 25, 1957. ©BETTMAN/CORBIS

Their job done, the killers quickly walked out of the shop, which had eleven other people besides Anastasia inside, including a manicurist, two shoeshine men, and some other customers. Police recovered one of the guns in a hotel corridor near the barbershop, while another was found in a trash can at the end of the platform of the Fifty-Seventh Street subway station, which was entered at the corner by Seventh Avenue.

The killing of Anastasia was the most sensational murder of a Mob boss since that of Maranzano in 1931, and the killers were never caught. Interestingly, Anastasia’s bodyguard Anthony Coppola was nowhere in the area at the time of the shooting, and certainly not close enough to do his job. Mob historians would later assert that Anastasia’s murder was orchestrated by Carlo Gambino and Genovese. Anastasia’s death paved the way for former ally Carlo Gambino—a little-known, hawk-nosed, and circumspect man who had entered the United States years earlier as a ship jumper—to take over the family, which came to bear his name.

As an indication of the diminished status and contempt Anastasia had garnered, his funeral was sparsely attended, aside from the usual law enforcement surveillance of the rites. There was no funeral mass, and Anastasia’s grave at

Green-Wood Cemetery in Brooklyn was not consecrated ground because the burial ground is nonsectarian. However, prior to Anastasia's interment his brother Salvatore, a priest, blessed the open grave.

Unlike other opulent Mob funerals, only Anastasia's family and a few officials from the International Longshoremen's Association attended the graveside rites, which only lasted about seven minutes. A few hundred onlookers peered through the cemetery fence along Fifth Avenue, but their line of sight was obscured by floral displays around the grave and some trees that surrounded the site. A simple flat stone marks the final resting place of the man who so many had feared. At about the same time the grave diggers in Green-Wood were shoveling the cold earth on top of Anastasia's simple metal casket, a lawyer in an appeals court in Paris claimed during oral arguments that his convicted narcotics client had had Anastasia as a customer.

The aftermath of the Anastasia murder showed just how impenetrable the Mafia had become for law enforcement. While it was true that the US Senate hearings of 1951 graphically showed the public the extent of Mob operations, particularly gambling, local police in New York City and elsewhere often found the code of silence to be a real stumbling block to any investigation. Police arrested Anastasia's bodyguard on the bogus charge of vagrancy because he didn't seem to have any visible means of support—mobsters often didn't have any if they were involved in crimes—in an effort to get him to talk, but he proved uncooperative, and a judge tossed out the charges. Meyer Lansky, the Jewish genius of crime, was questioned for about three hours, but neither he nor Frank Costello, who was interrupted in his new pastime of growing orchids at his Long Island estate to be interviewed, knew anything of value.

About a month after Anastasia died, on November 13, 1957, police near the upstate New York town of Apalachin discovered a conclave of gangsters from all over the country at the home of local resident Joseph Barbara. When the cops showed up at the meeting, touted as a barbecue, many of the mobsters scurried to get away. A number were arrested and detained for questioning. Police theorized that the purpose of the meeting was to talk about Mob gambling and narcotics operations, as well as what to do with the rackets of Anastasia.

Some participants, like Bonanno, were found trying to get away in a cornfield, while others, like Natale Evola, were stopped at a roadblock near Barbara's estate. Although police and news accounts trumpeted the meeting as a summit conference of the Mafia, officials struggled to charge the participants with anything. Even Arthur L. Reuter, chairman of the New York State Commission of Investigation, had to admit later that while the Apalachin guests "bore evil reputations," it was hard to provide proof beyond a reasonable doubt that any were "presently living as thieves and criminals." Such was the lack of hard investigative evidence about the dealings of New York City's Mafia leaders at the time.

Eventually, some of the guests were indicted on charges of conspiracy and convicted. But a federal appeals court, in a very pointed ruling in November 1960, reversed all of the convictions. The court held that the government had not proved that what had occurred at the meeting was illegal, or that the suspects had agreed to lie to investigators about what they were doing. The size of the Apalachin meeting and the publicity forced FBI director J. Edgar Hoover to finally acknowledge that the Mafia was a problem he had to deal with, but it would take decades for the agency to finally get up to speed and develop the resources to do so.

CHAPTER TEN

"BLOOD ON THE STREET"

While the FBI took baby steps in dealing with the Mob, the Mafia families in New York and elsewhere were immersed in their rackets and power struggles. Intrigue was everywhere among the organized branches of the Mafia, known as borgatas, but nowhere were things as complicated as they were with the family of Joseph Bonanno.

An immigrant from Sicily in 1924, Bonanno seemed to bridge the worlds between the Old Guard, typified by Masseri, Maranzano, and Salvatore Profaci, and the more contemporary and "liberal" bosses like Gambino, Genovese, and Thomas Lucchese. Bonanno was outwardly against drug trafficking, something for which Genovese would ultimately be indicted and imprisoned.

Mob lore has it that Lucchese and Gambino, who had a close relationship through the marriage of their daughter and son, respectively, were planning to strike against Bonanno. By now Bonanno's ally Profaci had died of natural causes, and the events that followed would require a scorecard to keep all of the players straight. Forewarned by a tip from Joseph Magliocco, the mafioso who aspired to succeed Profaci, Bonanno planned a preemptive strike against his rivals. But, as sometimes happened in the Mafia, Joseph Colombo, another aspiring gangster who had been working with Magliocco, tipped off Gambino and Lucchese about the threats against their lives. It was a classic case of Mob double-crossing, and could have cost more than a few people their lives.

Bonanno avoided getting killed, and what could have been a Mob war was avoided. But Bonanno was clearly pushing the other bosses around with arrogance and disdain. Bonanno fancied himself an intellectual and a cut above the other bosses. Fed up with his high-handed attitude, the Mafia Commission summoned Bonanno for a meeting. He refused to show up. As later recounted by New Jersey crime boss Sam "The Plumber" DeCavalcante, the other Mafia families no longer considered Bonanno a boss because of the way he had treated them.

On October 20, 1964, the day before he was to appear before a federal grand jury that was investigating his activity, Bonanno was accosted by two armed men on a Manhattan sidewalk at **Park Avenue and Thirty-Sixth Street.** One of them told Bonanno: "Come on, Joe, my boss wants you." When Bonanno's attorney, who happened to be with him, tried to intervene, one of them fired a shot at his feet. Bonanno was hustled into a car and taken away. The apparent abduction seemed like a prelude to Bonanno's execution.

There were reports that Bonanno had been spotted in Arizona, where he had a home, or in Europe. Then, some sixteen months later, on May 17, 1966, Bonanno stepped out of a car at Foley Square in Manhattan and with his attorney, Albert Kreiger, walked into the side entrance of the US District Courthouse at **40 Centre Street** to surrender to a federal judge.

Speculation about Bonanno's whereabouts in his absence would continue for decades. In his own biography, Bonanno said his abduction had been engineered by his envious cousin, Stefano Magaddino, who was a Mob boss in the Buffalo area. Maggadino even met his cousin face-to-face while he was being held at a farmhouse, Bonanno related. The truth is more likely that Bonanno had set up his own kidnapping to get away from the federal government and defuse the tense situation that had come close to open warfare on the streets of New York.

Joseph Colombo, the turncoat who had tipped off Gambino and Lucchese about Bonanno, was rewarded by the Commission in 1964 with the position of boss of the old Profaci family. Some of the old-timers viewed Colombo, who grew up in Brooklyn, as nothing more than a sycophant who fawned over Carlo Gambino. But Colombo, who had a legitimate job in real estate, developed a fluency and flair for publicity, and understood the power of the news media. To the chagrin of some mafiosi, Colombo took to the television news and talk-show circuit to denounce media depictions of Italians as gangsters. He pushed things even further by proclaiming that Italian-Americans were being persecuted by the FBI and police.

Colombo formed the Italian-American Civil Rights League, and his brash speeches against the FBI and police made him something of a champion among Italian-Americans. Donations began to pour in, and a concert at Madison Square Garden featuring Frank Sinatra pulled in $500,000. But there was a downside to all of Colombo's antics: Some mobsters feared that Colombo would goad the FBI to act. Carlo Gambino quietly sent out word that longshoremen, under the control of certain elements of the Gambino family, should not attend the 1971 Manhattan rally Colombo had planned. A few powerful mobsters resigned their positions with Colombo's group. The Mob started to edge away from Colombo, which proved to be a bad omen.

The 1971 rally of the Italian-American Civil Rights League was called Italian Unity Day, and took place on June 28 at **Columbus Circle** in Manhattan, with a heavy police and Mob presence. The towering statute of Christopher Colombus stood some eighty feet above the plaza on a pedestal that was bedecked in red, white, and green, the colors of the Italian flag.

Colombo was in his element. He was scheduled to speak at noon, and started to make his way toward the podium at around 11:45 a.m. He never got there. Suddenly, a twenty-four-year-old black man named Jerome Johnson, who had been posing as a cameraman with media credentials, fired three shots at point-blank range in Colombo's head and neck. But that didn't end things. Someone—it was never determined who—shot Johnson three times, and he fell to the pavement, dead.

Surprisingly, the Unity Day rally continued despite the shooting. The forty-eight-year-old Colombo was taken to nearby Roosevelt Hospital, where surgeons removed two bullets from his brain and neck. He never regained consciousness, remaining in a coma until his death in October 1978.

Within days of the attempt on Colombo's life, the NYPD said it had discovered evidence that the shooting of Colombo had originated with his rivals in the underworld, and that he wasn't the only intended target. Over time, it was revealed that Colombo had been viewed as incapable of running the crime family. Two factions had developed with his borgata—one led by the brash and volatile Joey Gallo, and the other by Carmine "The Snake" Persico. Detectives questioned Gallo about the Colombo shooting after it became known that he had once demanded $100,000 from Colombo to keep things peaceful in the crime family. "Put $100,000 on the table and we'll talk; otherwise, no deal," Gallo had demanded. Police pressed their investigation for months but never made any arrests.

Former NYPD chief of detectives Albert Seedman theorized that Gallo had Colombo killed in a bold bid to get back into power. "To my mind, everything about this plot, from conception to execution, bore the signature of that little guy with steel balls, Joe Gallo," Seedman said in his autobiography, *Chief!: Classic Cases from the Files of the Chief of Detectives.*

Joey Gallo didn't fade away; he went out with a bang. After his release from state prison earlier in 1972 for an extortion conviction, Gallo had wanted to break away from Colombo and start his own "Sixth Family." The group was based out of the area around President Street in Brooklyn, close to dockland. In the 1960s Gallo and his brothers had begun to challenge the leadership of the late crime-family boss Joseph Profaci in what became known as the Gallo Wars (see chapter 15). After he was released from prison, Joey Gallo became something of a media darling, talking about Sartre and Camus, whose works he had read while in prison, and hanging out in Manhattan nightclubs.

During a night of partying that began on April 7, 1972, Joey Gallo and his entourage went to the Copacabana, **10 East Sixtieth Street,** to celebrate his forty-third birthday. Along with Gallo were his new wife, Sina, her daughter Lisa, ten, his bodyguard Pete Diapoulis, and others. At the Copacabana were actor Jerry Ohrbach and his wife, Marta, who were working with Gallo on his biography. Also in the group was *New York Post* columnist Earl Wilson, who stopped by for a champagne birthday toast to the mafioso. They partied hard until about 4:00 a.m., when, hungry, the group drove down to the Chinatown area. Eventually, they went to the intersection of **Hester Street and Mulberry Street** in Little Italy, where Umberto's Clam House was still open. The seafood eatery, which had as a specialty a variety of sauces which were excellent toppings for clams, scungilli (conch), and shrimp, was owned by Matthew "Matty the Horse" Ianiello, a high-ranked member of the Genovese family.

The Gallo party was eating big helpings of seafood during the early-morning hours when a man opened the restaurant door and started shooting. Pandemonium broke out, with people screaming, tables upending, and food spilling on the floor. Gallo was killed in the fusillade. Diapoulis, the bodyguard, chased the gunman out onto Mulberry Street, but was himself shot and wounded. The killer got into a waiting car and drove away.

Gallo was buried two days later in Green-Wood Cemetery (see chapter 15). His killer or killers were never arrested. Seedman in his autobiography stated that Mob informant Joseph Luparelli described to him how Colombo family associates Carmine DiBiase and three others shot Gallo after he was spotted by chance in Little Italy. Luparelli said he drove the getaway car, noted Seedman.

New York City didn't have to wait long for there to be repercussions from Gallo's murder. But when things happened it wasn't clear what was going on, because none of the people who later lost their lives in an Italian restaurant in Manhattan had anything to do with organized crime. It all underscored how random the violence of the Mob could be.

The Neopolitan Noodle was a new restaurant at **320 East Seventy-Ninth Street,** between First and Second Avenues, that had taken over what had been a French restaurant known as Ma Pomme. The new eatery in the Yorkville section was entered by stepping down from the sidewalk and under a green-and-white awning. It had a bar near the front door and in the back were tables for lunch and dinner.

On the evening of August 11, 1972, a crowd of about twenty people was inside. Four men, accompanied by four women, were seated at the bar, and around 9:30 p.m., they got up to take a table in the back. Nearby a burly, middle-aged man placed a $10 bill on the bar to pay for his scotch and water and also got up from his seat. But the hefty man wasn't staying for dinner. Instead, without saying a word, he pulled out two long-nosed handguns and started firing at the four men.

Two of the victims were shot dead while two others were wounded. All of the men were involved in the kosher meat business, police determined. The women accompanying them were apparently unharmed. Cops at first didn't think the shooting had any connection to organized crime.

However, that quickly changed after detectives learned that four members of the Colombo crime family had been seated at the bar only minutes before the innocent businessmen took their places. The gangsters included Alphonse Persico and Jerry Langella, who were met by two other Mob associates. According to police, the mobsters were planning to discuss narcotics trafficking and what the Colombo crime family should do about it. The Mob had a mixed history when it came to drug dealing, with some crime bosses against getting involved, but others giving tacit approval for their soldiers and captains to be involved. After having drinks at the bar, the Persico group went into the back dining room to await others, thus avoiding what police later believed was an assassination attempt in retaliation for the Gallo killing.

The slaying of the innocent businessmen was an unforgiveable case of mistaken identity that shocked the city. People had become used to gangsters slaying each other, but not since a gunman had wounded an eight-year-old girl in the 1920s had innocent bystanders been hurt by Mafia gunplay.

After this shooting, Mayor John V. Lindsay ordered the police to drive gangsters out of town, and condemned the romanticization of the Mob. Lindsay told police to go after the profits of the Mafia, namely gambling, loan-sharking, and narcotics. What resulted was a case of rounding up the usual suspects. Within weeks, the FBI had conducted a raid in Brooklyn of what was the borough's "biggest gambling and shylocking (high-interest money lending) operation," issuing subpoenas to fifteen suspects for a grand jury hearing. Yet, it was clear that the city still had no cohesive plan in place to deal with the Mafia; they would have to wait for help from federal officials.

■ ■ ■

In the days after Gallo's murder there were five other murders of men linked to the Mafia in New York City, raising the fear of a Mob war. But the bigger picture was that despite the conflicts, the Mob had been prospering during the 1960s and '70s. Certain industries had become longtime moneymakers for Mafia rackets, notably the docks, the fish market, garbage collection, construction, trucking, and the garment industry. In the latter, many mafiosi—like Bonanno, Gambino, Lucchese, and others—held both legitimate interests in dress manufacturing companies as well as making illicit profits through labor racketeering, loan-sharking, and restraints of trade, particularly among garment truckers.

Emboldened by new federal racketeering laws, which gave some teeth to law enforcement, the FBI and federal prosecutors in Manhattan came up with a plan that was bold for the times. In early 1972 they focused on the garment industry, one of the city's major manufacturing industries, for two undercover operations. In one, dubbed Operation Cleveland, government informant Herman Goldfarb purchased (for $50,000 in government money) the assets of a small garment trucking company at **1441 Broadway.** The other undercover business, Operation Detroit, was a coat business known as the Whellan Coat Company, working out of **512 Seventh Avenue.** The coat company was run by Harold Whellan, scion of a garment district family, who after business reverses and squandering a family fortune saw the undercover operation as a chance to get back in business with the help of the government.

The garment industry was the type of business traditionally vulnerable to the Mob. Hard-pressed manufacturers often had to turn to Mafia loan sharks for quick cash. Trucking companies were either run by mafiosi or were part of a restrictive arrangement in which garment firms had to use certain truckers for certain locations. If manufacturers needed non-union work done, or needed to stay non-union, they often turned to connected mobsters like Thomas Lucchese for help. If some mafiosi needed to show a source of legitimate income, there was often a pliant dress company that would provide the cover of a no-show job. Seventh Avenue, the main strip for the fashion industry, became the Mob's cash register.

For two years Operation Cleveland and Operation Detroit gathered evidence on Seventh Avenue. The investigators targeted a number of loan sharks and Natale Evola, a trucker who became one of the bosses of the Bonanno family, gathering evidence against some powerful Mob captains. But those were the early years of the government's use of the new racketeering laws. The government also ran into some bad luck when one of the undercover NYPD detectives in Operation Cleveland got indicted for corruption based on his earlier years working in narcotics investigations. (He was later acquitted.)

So, the results of the investigations were mixed. There were over two dozen convictions, but the big Mafia bosses, including Evola, who died of cancer, were never touched.

CHAPTER ELEVEN

PADDY WHACKERS AND BLACK CAESARS

While the names of Mafia leaders like Gallo, Gambino, and Lucchese became household names, there were other major gangsters who would also become powerful, if not as widely known. Among them were the leaders of the Irish Mob who for decades worked out of the West Side of Manhattan in a neighborhood that became known as Hell's Kitchen. The Irish had always played a role in the major gangs in the city going back to the time when the Five Points neighborhood was the training ground for criminals. Crime historians say it was Owen "The Killer" Madden who made Hell's Kitchen a place where gangsters could thrive, and where they forged a link with the Italian Mob.

Irish gangster Owney Madden worked closely with Mafia members out of the Hell's Kitchen section of Manhattan.
WIKIMEDIA COMMONS / LIBRARY OF CONGRESS

After Madden retired to Arkansas in the 1930s, Hell's Kitchen remained a stronghold of Irish crime. For years the man considered boss of the Irish Mob was a bookmaker and gambler named Hugh Mulligan, who while little known to investigators was a major force in the underworld. Bookmakers were a dime a dozen in the city, but what made Mulligan special was his reputation as a conduit for bribes to police officers, a skill that earned him the label of "classic fixer" from law enforcement. Mulligan, a portly man with a fleshy face, would be convicted in 1971 for criminal contempt during a grand jury investigation into police corruption, linked to his gambling, loan-sharking, and other rackets. Hit with a three-year prison term, Mulligan died in July 1973 from natural causes.

Mulligan's protégé was Mickey Spillane, a handsome, dark-haired Irishman who started earning his arrest record at the age of sixteen, and was once shot by a police officer while robbing a Manhattan movie theater. Spillane married into the politically connected McManus family of the West Side, and for the rest of his life earned a reputation as a dyed-in-the-wool tough guy who, when he was indicted in 1970 for refusing to answer questions from a grand jury, took a jail sentence instead of talking.

Spillane held court at the White House Bar, **637 Tenth Avenue.** It was from this location that Spillane reportedly took a piece of the action from a number of gambling dens on Tenth Avenue. Because of his political connections through the McManus family, Spillane became something of a dispenser of jobs and advice to the Irish community.

But Spillane's gentlemanly ways weren't to last. A number of younger aspiring Irish men vied for power in Hell's Kitchen. Among them was James Coonan. In his seminal book about the Irish Mob in New York, *The Westies: Inside New York's Irish Mob*, author T. J. English traced Coonan's descent from a middle-class upbringing to a life as a hardened killer. Although his parents held stable jobs, Coonan began running with neighborhood toughs in Hell's Kitchen. The rest was history as Coonan became a fierce rival to Spillane, killing some of his trusted lieutenants.

Coonan cemented his status as a key organized-crime power on the West Side when he and his trusted lieutenant Mickey Featherstone sat down with Gambino crime-family boss Paul Castellano (Carlo Gambino had died in 1976) and agreed to do business with the Italians. Spillane had kept the Mafia at arm's length, refusing to allow the Italians to get the job for the construction of the Jacob Javits Convention Center. But Coonan agreed during his meeting with Castellano at Tommaso's Restaurant in Bay Ridge, Brooklyn, to have his crew of Irish killers serve as hired hit men for the Gambino borgata. What distinguished Coonan and his small band of Irish gangsters was the way they would dismember their victims. They weren't satisfied with just killing someone; they had to take the extra step of cutting the victim to pieces. In one case, the Westie put the head of his victim in a freezer until they could decide on a better way to dispose of it.

After the Gambino alliance, Coonan was full of himself. His recklessness extended to the way he lied to Castellano about the murder of Mafia loan shark Charles "Ruby" Stein. In the Mob, Stein was known as one of the most prolific loansharks on the street, with loans out totaling over a million dollars. As recounted by English in *The Westies*, Coonan used his 596 Club, a bar at **596 Tenth Avenue,** as an execution center. In May 1977, Stein was lured to the club where he was shot dead and dismembered, something described in detail in English's other book about Irish criminals, *Paddy Whacked: The Untold Story of The Irish American Gangster*. (The term "paddy whack" is urban slang for a beating.) Stein's body parts later washed up on a beach in Queens. Spillane was shot dead outside his home in Woodside, Queens, a few days after Stein was killed.

■ ■ ■

As strange as it might sound from a racial point of view, the Mob had been a part of life in Harlem for years. In fact, it was Irish gangster Owney "The Killer" Madden who set up one of the early nightclubs in the black community, the Cotton Club, when it was at the northeast corner of **142nd Street and Lenox Avenue.** According to author Ron Chepesiuk, the location was first known as the Douglas Casino, complete with a vaudeville theater, dance hall, and banquet room. The casino never really took off, and, according to Chepesiuk, reopened as a supper club where the person out front was former heavyweight boxer Jack Johnson. The Cotton Club opened in 1923, and Madden spared no expense, giving the club a "log cabin exterior and a 'jungle décor'," Chepesiuk writes in his book, *Gangsters of Harlem*.

"While the Cotton Club was in the heart of Harlem, a neighborhood that was becoming overwhelmingly black, it had a 'whites only' policy, although light-complexioned blacks were sometimes able to gain admission," notes Chepesiuk. However, the chorus line included some of the prettiest black women around, and the shows and music were spectacular. During Prohibition, clubs run by the Mob popped up all along **133rd Street** to cater to crowds looking for booze and excitement.

Beset by legal problems, ex-con Madden eventually had to leave New York City, and he "retired" to Hot Springs, Arkansas, in 1933. The Mob continued to assert itself in Harlem life, pushing the sale of marijuana and controlling nightclubs. As the years went by, blacks continued in the numbers racket that became the province of some memorable characters. One of them was Stephanie "Queenie" St. Clair, whose brashness and moxie became legendary. Along with her enforcer, Ellsworth "Bumpy" Johnson, St. Clair resisted the efforts of Mafia-connected gangsters like Dutch Schultz of the Bronx to squeeze her out of the business.

Eventually, the scope of the numbers business in Harlem attracted more white gangsters like Schultz, who quickly supplanted some—but not all—black operators. After Schultz was assassinated by the Mafia in 1935, other Italian gangsters came in and organized numbers operations of their own, vying with the black operators for control. St. Clair would be remembered, according to the stories that surfaced later, for sending Schultz a message as he lay mortally wounded in the hospital: "As ye sow, so shall ye reap."

But it was in narcotics that black gangsters would make their mark, ultimately breaking away from Mafia control of the heroin trade and forming their own organizations. Among the most prominent was Frank Matthews, who by the early 1970s was believed to be one of Harlem's biggest dealers of heroin and cocaine, a distinction which earned him the sobriquet "Black Caesar." It was Matthews, Chepesiuk notes, who hit upon the idea of getting all of the black and Hispanic dealers to work together to streamline the drug trade and figure out how to deal with the Mafia. However, Matthews's run as Harlem's top drug lord and leader of what became known as the "Black Mafia" quickly unraveled with his arrest in September 1972, on federal drug charges. Matthews made bail and disappeared a year later, with his whereabouts unknown to this day.

Frank Matthews became one of Harlem's biggest heroin and cocaine dealers, earning him the nickname "Black Caesar." After making bail on federal drug charges in 1972, Matthews disappeared, and his whereabouts are still unknown today. PHOTO COURTESY DRUG ENFORCEMENT ADMINISTRATION

Others were quick to fill the void left by Matthews. Among the major drug lords was Leroy "Nicky" Barnes, a strapping man who was a product of the streets of Harlem. Barnes started as a low-level drug dealer, and after a few years in prison came out and built a narcotics empire. Prison wasn't a bad thing for Barnes, as he was able to forge friendships and business alliances there with a number of mafiosi, notably Joey Gallo and Matthew Madonna. Gallo taught Barnes the value of organizing the Harlem drug trade, and Madonna, court records and news accounts stated, worked out arrangements where he supplied heroin to the Barnes organization.

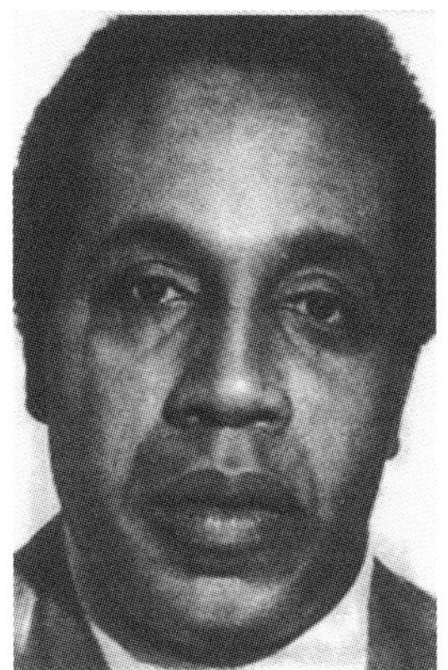

Frank Lucas was another of Harlem's preeminent heroin kingpins, and his life inspired the 2007 film *American Gangster*. PHOTO COURTESY US GOVERNMENT VIA WIKIMEDIA COMMONS

Another Harlem drug lord was Frank Lucas, whose claim to fame in the heroin racket rested with the story that he had hit upon the idea of smuggling heroin back into the United States in the coffins of dead soldiers killed in the Vietnam War. There is much doubt about whether or not Lucas ever smuggled narcotics that way, although he insisted he did. But it became clear that Lucas did engage in heroin smuggling, and over the years claimed **116th Street, between Seventh and Eighth Avenues,** as the place where the junkies could get his product. He also hooked up with Italian suppliers on nearby Pleasant Avenue. Lucas became rich, and dressed in a $50,000 chinchilla coat, flaunting his wealth. But he wound up in prison after federal and state convictions in the 1970s and '80s, later getting out early after he turned informant. Lucas's life inspired the 2007 film *American Gangster*, starring Denzel Washington. "It was worth every nickel of it," Lucas said in an interview about his past life.

Barnes also became a wealthy man from heroin and lived a flashy lifestyle. He owned so many luxury cars that he could have run a dealership, and he often bankrolled charitable events around Harlem. Barnes's organization used the Harlem River Motor Garage at **112 West 145th Street** as a place to transact many of the drug deals. Barnes, known as "Mr. Untouchable," conducted himself with a swagger and arrogance that drew the attention and considerable resources of the federal government, and he was indicted in 1977. While some saw the federal case against Barnes as problematic due to the way he insulated himself from drug deals, a jury nevertheless convicted him, and he received a life sentence without parole.

Leroy "Nicky" Barnes, who rose to the top of Harlem's heroin trade, seen in his NYPD mug shot. PHOTO COURTESY DRUG ENFORCEMENT ADMINISTRATION

But prison didn't mark the end for Barnes. Angered by reports that many of his old associates had maneuvered to take over his empire and were allegedly having sex with his wife and girlfriend, Barnes became a cooperating witness for the federal government, and helped to put many of his former associates behind bars. In August 1998 Barnes was released and placed in the witness protection program. Meanwhile, Barnes's old Mafia contact, Matthew Madonna, after serving a twenty-year sentence for drug trafficking, was freed from prison and became a captain in the Lucchese crime family.

CHAPTER TWELVE

BUGS FOR FAT TONY—BULLETS FOR DAI LO

In the 1980s the Mafia in New York City was holding on to power in a number of industries through arrangements worked out by the Commission, the governing body set up back in the 1930s by Charles Luciano. The Commission settled disputes as it had done for decades, and it did so through the powerful offices of the major crime bosses of the five New York Mafia families. With New York a major construction city, the Mob worked out a deal with major concrete producers in which bids were rigged on jobs and the crime families were assured a cut on any project over $2 million. It was a big moneymaking racket, and one of the men who enforced it was a chubby, grandfatherly man by the name of Anthony "Fat Tony" Salerno. He had risen through the ranks with Luciano, and after toiling as a bookmaker, Salerno made it to the rank of captain in what had become the Genovese crime family.

Through luck and some good defense lawyers, Salerno generally stayed out of serious trouble, until he was ultimately indicted by a federal grand jury in 1984 for his role in the concrete racket. He was convicted and given a hundred-year sentence in the famous Commission case. But until he got arrested, Salerno was viewed as the public or front boss of the Genovese crime family, a smoke screen for the likes of Philip Lombardo, who was considered the real boss.

What distinguished Salerno was his work routine. Although he had a large horse farm in upstate New York, Salerno spent a great deal of time at one of the main Mob social clubs of the time: the Palma Boys Social Club in East Harlem. Located at **416 East 115th Street,** between Pleasant Avenue and First Avenue, the Palma Boys was where Salerno could be found holding court, meeting with out-of-town gangsters or his New York Mob associates. Salerno also had a second club at **2244 First Avenue.** It was there that FBI agents approached Salerno and told him that it was unwise for the Mob to try and hurt an undercover FBI agent whose secret identity had just been revealed publicly. Salerno told the agents not to worry, that no harm would come to the agent.

On nice days, the cigar-chomping Salerno could be seen seated outside the Palma Boys, lording over the street. Why the club was named Palma Boys wasn't clear. The name could have referred to the Spanish word for *palm*, or a bay on the island of Majorca. In any case, Salerno was too comfortable in the way he used the place, too open in his activities. It was on a December night in 1983 that a secret FBI team penetrated the Palma Boys club, and while other agents operated a noisy garbage truck on the street to create noise, drilled and planted several bugs near Salerno's favorite chair. The resulting audiotapes captured not only Salerno in some incriminating conversations, but also his top captains and members of the Lucchese crime family. The tapes were used in the federal prosecution of Salerno and then Lucchese boss Anthony "Tony Ducks" Corallo in the Commission trial.

Anthony "Fat Tony" Salerno, the street boss of the Genovese crime family, with federal agents during his arrest on federal racketeering charges in March 1986. *NEWSDAY* LLC, 1986

■ ■ ■

The Mafia murders in New York got most of the attention in the 1970s because they involved some of the big names in La Cosa Nostra. But bad things were also happening in Chinatown, and very often it was all occurring under the radar. Since the liberalization of US immigration laws in 1963, migration from Chinese-speaking areas like Hong Kong and Taiwan had increased. With the new influx came families with young men who formed the basis of a new breed of organized crime—the Chinese street gangs. Chinese youth who were unable or unwilling to assimilate gravitated toward the gangs as a way of buffering themselves from the unfamiliar aspects of American society, and as a way to establish a sense of fraternity. Beginning in the mid-1970s, cities like San Francisco and New York, with their large Asian communities, saw the rather sudden appearance of gangs that began to exert criminal control over the neighborhoods.

In Manhattan's Chinatown gangs like the Ghost Shadows, Flying Dragons, White Tigers, Free Masons, and Fuk Ching carved up the turf, much like the Tongs had done in the early twentieth century. This time law enforcement officials said the Tongs took a backseat to the gangs, using them as criminal surrogates to enforce the social order in Chinatown. On **Pell Street,** the old Hip Sing Tong had an alliance with the Flying Dragons. Down on **Mott Street,** the On Leong Tong had a working relationship with the Ghost Shadows. The Fuk Ching was often unaligned, and gravitated toward the area around **East Broadway,** to the east of Chatham Square. The White Tigers emerged in the Chinese communities in Brooklyn and Queens, while the Free Masons (not connected to the larger fraternal organization with that name) worked a freelance protection racket on the eastern streets of Chinatown.

The gangs were rivals over extortion payments, which they squeezed from restaurants and other local merchants. The shakedowns became common during festivals when the gangs would ask for a certain amount of money to signify good luck. But the money never guaranteed things would be quiet on the streets of Chinatown. Gangs began to target each other, and the encounters were often deadly. Anyone who spoke out against them was targeted for retaliation, as happened in July 1977, when Man Bun Lee, a civic leader who led a local family association, was stabbed in the hallway of his restaurant on the second floor of **44 Mott Street,** in what police believe was an assassination attempt by the Ghost Shadows. Lee, who had publicly spoken out against the gang culture, survived, but others weren't so lucky. In 1979, two young members of the Chung Yeh gang were forced upstairs at **19 East Broadway** and shot dead in the back of the head. One shooting at the Pagoda Movie Theater on East Broadway led to the death of a seventeen-year-old gang member.

Then, in December 1982, close to Christmas, the gangs badly overreached with their brazen acts.

The Golden Star at **51 East Broadway** was one those Chinatown hangouts that stayed open late into the night, or even into the early-morning hours. Police knew the bar, which was entered via a flight of stairs from street level, as a gang hangout, although non-gang members would congregate there as well. Early on the morning of December 23, masked gunmen entered the club firing pistols at the patrons. Three people were killed, including a thirteen-year-old boy. Eight others were wounded. When police and paramedics arrived at the scene, the club was like a slaughterhouse.

"People were lying on chairs, people were lying on the floor bleeding from gunshot wounds, mostly to the legs and arms," said one medic. "Everybody was making noise. Friends of the victims were screaming and shouting."

Police quickly determined that the shooting was sparked by a turf fight among the gangs, a common explanation that seemed to involve many of the shootings among the Chinese. But the scope of the carnage focused more attention on the gangs, as federal and local authorities began to press investigations as a way to stem the slaughter from the wild, homicidal actions. The police acted with a major offensive against the gangs, forming a special gang task force.

But law enforcement was at a distinct disadvantage with the Asian gangs. For a start, Chinese immigrants tended to distrust the police, or were afraid of retaliation should they cooperate with law enforcement. The gangs were not large, averaging around twenty people each, about the size of the Westies on the West Side. Developing informants among the Chinese gangs was difficult, although not impossible. The Asian gangs were also diversifying by moving into heroin importation from the Far East and developing human smuggling rings so that illegal immigrants could find a way past the borders.

Though they weren't as flashy as the Mafia, Chinese gangs had their own definite structure. The bosses were known as Dai Lo, while the soldiers were known as "big brother" or "little brother," depending on their rank. Through the

Doorways for 15 Pell Street in Chinatown; the entrance on the left was where gang leader Michael Chen was shot dead in March 1983. AUTHOR'S COLLECTION

drug rackets and immigration smuggling, the gangs started to earn a great deal of money, which in turn created additional rivalries.

The one man who stood out in all of this was Michael Chen, head of the Flying Dragons.

Described as a mild-mannered, courteous young man who took care of his mother, Chen had a somewhat straitlaced image for a gang leader. He neither smoked nor drank, but he did indulge himself with nice clothing and expensive cars. Once suspected of killing two rival Ghost Shadow members in the Pagoda Theater on East Broadway, Chen was never convicted, but at one point he ordered two gang members to kill a man who had tried to dissuade young men from staying in the gang life.

Chen lived above the Hip Sing headquarters at **15 Pell Street.** On the evening of March 13, 1983, a worker entering the Hip Sing offices found Chen's body in the doorway. He had been shot five times.

Hours earlier police had found the body of another Flying Dragon member dumped on Long Island.

Chen's murder festered as a cold case for years, until May 1998 when police announced that they had traced the murder to a former associate of Chen's. The suspect and others believed that Chen's expensive lifestyle and business interests had led him to skim way too much money from the gang's illegal activities.

CHAPTER THIRTEEN

GOTTI'S GAMBLE

By the 1980s the Mafia in New York had gone through a period of transition among the Five Families. Thomas Lucchese, Joseph Profaci, and Carlo Gambino had all died of natural causes. Joseph Bonanno had retired in a fashion to Arizona, and Anthony Salerno was acting as a front man for others who were in charge of the Genovese family. Gambino was nominally considered the major boss of the New York families because of his age and the respect he commanded. When Don Carlo died in 1976, his successor was his cousin and brother-in-law, Paul Castellano. When Gambino became ill, Castellano took over as acting boss, and it was a short step to the top spot in 1976 after his cousin died. Castellano fancied himself a businessman, who read the financial newspapers and built a poultry business, investing in meat packing and other businesses.

But Castellano didn't get where he was by being smooth. He had a deadly criminal side, and as boss not only got involved in the big Mafia rackets, but also got a cut of some of the proceeds of a murderous stolen-car ring, which used the services of captain Roy DeMeo as a hardened killer. It was also Castellano who made a pact with the Westies to use the Irish Mob as contract killers. His businesses, both legitimate and criminal, made Castellano a very wealthy man. It also made him greedy for more, something that earned Castellano the deep-seated resentment and hatred of many within his own crime family.

By 1983, the resentment against Castellano was reaching the flash point. Gambino captains and soldiers openly complained about the way Castellano bad-mouthed members of his own crime family, and they resented his increasingly greedy ways. Castellano also faced the added pressure of an indictment in the car-theft ring, and the fact that some of his captains were separately charged for heroin trafficking, something he ostensibly had a strict rule against. The crew charged with drug dealing was under the leadership of a relatively obscure captain known as John Gotti from Howard Beach, Queens, who Castellano knew was aligned with the ailing family underboss, Aniello Dellacroce. The politics of

Famous photograph submitted as evidence in a Manhattan federal racketeering trial showing (standing on far left) Paul Castellano, singer Frank Sinatra (third from left), and then-Gambino crime-family boss Carlo Gambino (standing third from right). FEDERAL BUREAU OF INVESTIGATION

the Gambino family were getting very byzantine at that point. Gotti and his crew believed that it was only a matter of time before Castellano discovered how damaging government surveillance tapes were to the crime family. Fearing a deadly response from Castellano, Gotti and his cohorts decided to strike first.

The plan that ultimately emerged was for a select group of assassins chosen by Gotti to ambush Castellano in Manhattan. It was a bold and audacious plan, and not without risks, because some of the older bosses in the other crime families supported Castellano, notably the Genovese family. If word of Gotti's plan leaked out, it could mean his own death. But some of the younger members of the other families could care less if Castellano was killed; they were also fed up with his greed and imperious manner.

On the evening of December 16, 1985, the trap was set. Castellano was scheduled to meet at 5:00 p.m. with some of his captains at the high-priced Sparks Steak House at **210 East Forty-Sixth Street** in Manhattan. He was being driven that afternoon by his loyal captain, Thomas Bilotti, and before proceeding to the restaurant both men stopped by the offices of Castellano's defense attorney, James LaRossa. Meanwhile, at an athletic field near the East River, Gotti met with the men involved in the plot one final time. Included were Sammy Gravano, John Carneglia, Joseph Watts, Anthony Rampino, and Sal Scala. All of them were armed, and it was Angelo Ruggiero who gave to each of the assigned shooters the set disguise—Muscovite-style fur hats and long, beige-colored raincoats. Walkie-talkies were also handed out. Then the group, which numbered between ten to twelve men, went uptown in different vehicles.

What happened next has been recounted in federal court testimony and a number of published accounts. Carneglia was waiting with another shooter by the front door of the restaurant. Rampino was stationed opposite the restaurant on Forty-Sixth Street, as backup. Ruggiero was a short distance away from Sparks Steak House. Watching the scene in a Town Car parked near the crosswalk at **Forty-Sixth Street and Third Avenue,** just to the west of the intersection, were Gotti and Gravano.

Close to 5:00 p.m., Castellano pulled up in a Lincoln Town Car being driven by Bilotti at the very intersection where Gotti was parked, although the crime boss didn't notice him. As Castellano's car then proceeded to Sparks, Gravano radioed an alert to the gunmen. Castellano's car pulled up to the front of the restaurant and he stepped out. The two gunmen by the door suddenly approached Castellano and started firing. Five shots hit him in the head, and he crumbled to the pavement, his head near the open car door, his mouth agape and his eyes wide open. He was clutching a pair of leather gloves in his right hand.

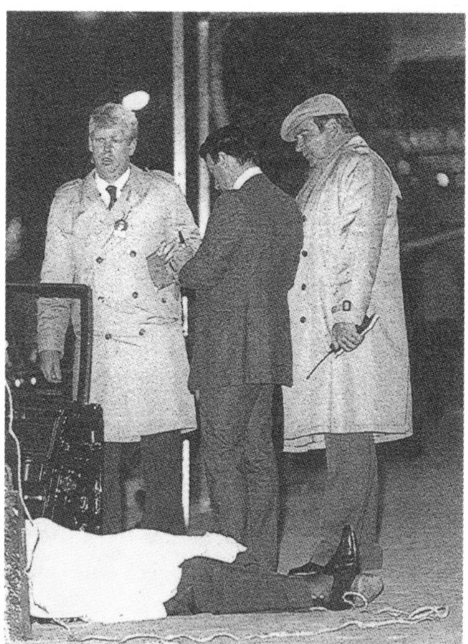
The body of Gambino boss Paul Castellano lies under a sheet at the curb outside Sparks Steak House in Manhattan after he was gunned down on December 16, 1985, by a hit team put together by John Gotti. *NEWSDAY* LLC, 1985

Bilotti had exited the driver's-side door and was apparently going around to the other side to escort Castellano when he saw the shooting and hunched down. With the death scene unfolding in front of him, Bilotti likely didn't notice the gunman who approached him and finished him off with shots to the head.

Pandemonium broke out on Forty-Sixth Street, but Gotti and his crew remained cool and followed their plan. Gotti and Gravano drove east across Forty-Sixth Street to Second Avenue, slowing down enough for Gravano to glance at Bilotti's body and remark "He's gone." At Second Avenue, Gotti turned right into the safety and anonymity of Midtown traffic. The gunmen all dispersed to hook up with their cars and drove away undetected. Back at Sparks a waiter told the men Castellano was supposed to be meeting that he would not be joining them for dinner. They all hurried away out a back exit.

The assassinations of Castellano and Bilotti were two of the most sensational Mob hits since Albert Anastasia was gunned down in the barbershop in 1957. Initially, family captains met at Caesar's East restaurant, **Fifty-Eighth Street and Third Avenue,** to discuss what happened, and were told by consigliere Joe N. Gallo that an investigation by the family was under way. Gravano would later tell the FBI that he and his cousin Edward Lino were owners of the place. A couple of weeks later, according to Gravano, all the captains met in a large recreation room in lower Manhattan to officially elect Gotti the boss.

Gotti's coup, while unopposed within the Gambino family, generated treachery. In April 1986 a bomb meant for Gotti exploded and killed his then-underboss Frank DeCicco (see chapter 16). His rule as boss made Gotti a household name and catapulted him to the status of an iconic criminal. But his celebrity became his Achilles' heel, putting Gotti directly in the sights of federal prosecutors. Gotti's tenure as boss would herald a period of instability in the Mob, a time marked by relentless prosecutions, which would hurt the Gambino family and other borgatas.

Gotti's reign started with a baptism of blood with the Castellano and Bilotti slayings, and continued with a litter of bodies all around the city. Much of the killing was done at the behest or with the assistance of Sammy Gravano, Gotti's new ally. Known by the sobriquet "The Bull," Gravano was a handsome but menacing man, a product of the streets of Brooklyn. After his induction by Castellano into the crime family, Gravano started making money for the Mob by running extortion rackets in the construction industry. He also carried out murders at Castellano's behest. After aligning with Gotti, Gravano continued as a killer, and helped to engineer the murder of Gambino captain Robert DiBernardo in June 1986, among others. Gravano would later say that Gotti knew or approved of ten of the killings.

One hit Gravano didn't actually take part in was that of Louis DiBono, his old partner in the drywall construction business. DiBono was one of those obese gangsters whose weight earned him the nickname "Jelly Belly." A man shaped like a bowling pin, DiBono was not an insignificant player in the Mob, and in 1990 had suggested to Gotti that the Mob boss get involved in drywall to take advantage of renovations being done at the World Trade Center. That suggestion of business partnership should have put DiBono in good stead with Gotti, but it didn't. The problem was that DiBono had a habit of missing appointments with his crime boss. When Gotti insisted on meeting, DiBono didn't show. Finally, Gotti had had enough, and ordered DiBono killed.

Later Brooklyn federal court testimony alleged that Gotti eventually approached his son, John Jr., to take care of DiBono. Junior Gotti continues to deny any role in the plot to slay DiBono, or any other victim; likewise, Gotti himself has never been charged with carrying out any attack on DiBono. But the testimony of witnesses in the 2009 racketeering trial of Gambino captain Charles Carneglia alleged that the younger Gotti farmed out the hit to Carneglia.

An eccentric man known for his erratic drinking and drug use, Carneglia was the younger brother of John Carneglia, a Gambino captain who was sent to prison for a federal heroin conviction. DiBono was found around October 3, 1990, dead in the front seat of his car in the underground parking garage under **Tower One of the World Trade Center.** (Three years later the garage was the site of the explosion that killed six and injured many in the first World Trade Center terrorist attack.) DiBono had been shot seven times, with four bullets entering his head. Government witness Kevin McMahon testified that it was Charles Carneglia who had performed the execution.

By the time Louis DiBono kept his appointment with the undertakers, John Gotti was himself living on borrowed time as a free man. His flashy, in-your-face

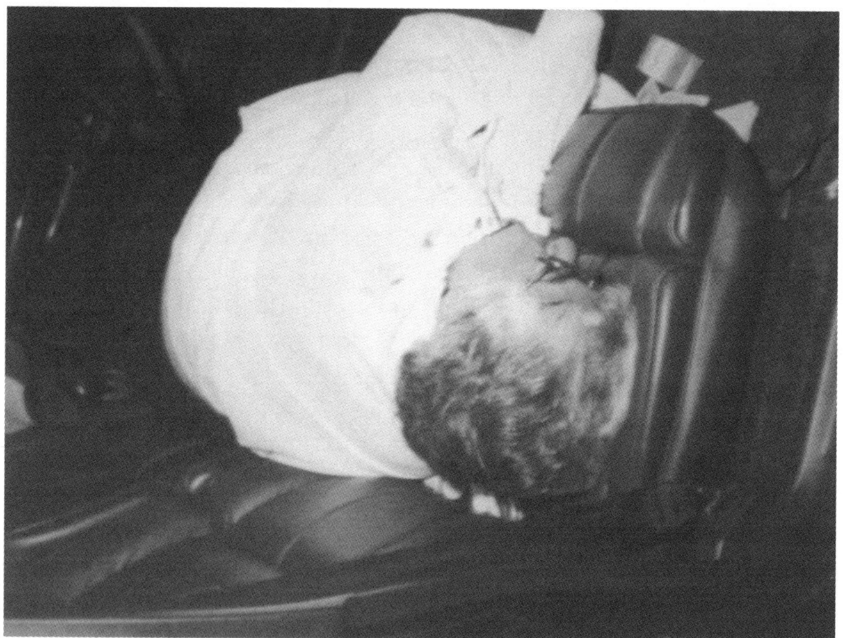

Crime-scene photo of the murder of Gambino crime-family captain Louis DiBono, slain in the underground parking lot of the World Trade Center in Manhattan in October 1990. PHOTO COURTESY US ATTORNEY'S OFFICE, EASTERN DISTRICT

Gambino crime boss John Gotti exits the Ravenite Social Club with Sammy Gravano (in turtleneck), followed by Frank LoCascio, to greet the public following Gotti's acquittal on state charges in February 1990. *NEWSDAY* LLC, 1990

style and media celebrity had energized the FBI. Working out of a nondescript office in Queens, a special FBI squad led by special agent Bruce Mouw had been patiently building a case against Gotti and his criminal hierarchy for years. It was within days of the Castellano hit in December 1985 that the FBI got strong indications that Gotti was the new boss.

The crime family, mainly the branch led by the late Aniello Dellacroce, had long used as a social club a place called the Ravenite at **247 Mulberry Street** in Little Italy. For years the Ravenite was nothing more than a storefront with large glass windows in the front and espresso machines and tables inside, typical for a Mob joint.

Social clubs like the Ravenite were a staple of Mob life, providing a place where gangsters could congregate and conduct business. By the time Gotti had taken over the Gambino family, the Ravenite had changed its appearance. Gone were the big windows in the front, replaced by a brick facade. This was done to thwart FBI and NYPD surveillance, which for years had included photographs of those who were coming and going. The bricked-up front of the Ravenite would have thwarted police use of parabolic listening devices, which were sometimes used from the law enforcement observation posts down the street. But by the

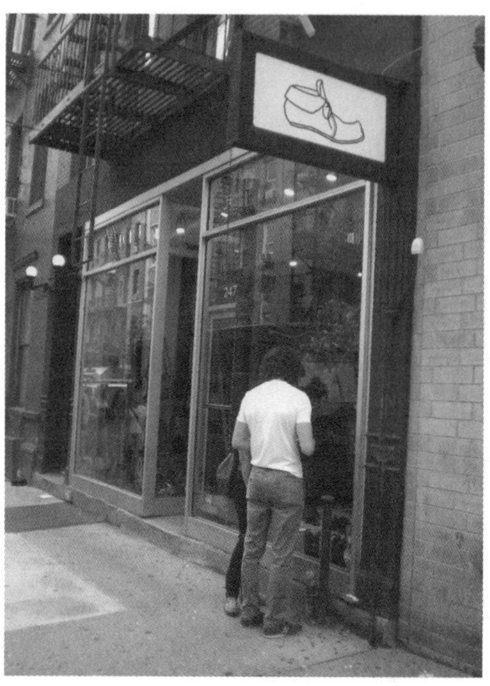

The old Ravenite club of John J. Gotti turned into a trendy shoe store on Mulberry Street. AUTHOR'S COLLECTION

time the FBI was focused on Gotti, the agents had come up with some ingenious ways to find out just what was on the crime boss's mind.

Gotti had required all his captains and major soldiers to stop by once a week at the Ravenite to pay their respects to him, check in, or even get chewed out. This practice made it easy for the FBI and NYPD to photograph lots of crime figures. Gotti's insistence that people show up allowed the FBI to identify people they had not seen before. But to build criminal cases, investigators needed recordings of the actual conversations between participants. For that the FBI technical teams penetrated the ground-floor Ravenite and planted electronic bugs. But as writer Selwyn Raab noted in *Five Families*, the bugs in the club picked up very little of value aside from gossipy tidbits.

Mouw and his team soon realized that Gotti and his captains didn't use the Ravenite for their private conversations, but instead left the club through a rear door and then went up to an apartment above the ground floor at 247 Mulberry, rented by an elderly Italian widow. It was late in 1989 that FBI teams penetrated the building with court authorization and while the widow was away planted a bug in her apartment. The surveillance device in the apartment proved to be a gold mine for agents, and captured Gotti in numerous incriminating conversations.

The results of the FBI surveillance were predictable. The night of December 11, 1990, was bone-chillingly cold. Gotti pulled up to the Ravenite with his entourage just before 7:00 p.m. and went inside. Mulberry Street had been quiet until that point. From an FBI observation post down the street an agent radioed "Number One is in," the signal that Gotti had arrived. Agents quickly descended on 247 Mulberry Street and arrested Gotti, his underboss Sammy Gravano, and consigliere Frank LoCascio. It was a peaceful arrest, and with it John Gotti's run as Gambino boss was essentially over.

As for the Ravenite, the space has become a trendy shoe boutique, emblematic of the social and demographic changes the neighborhood is going through in the twenty-first century.

■ ■ ■

Across town, on the western edge of Greenwich Village, was another Mob social club. Although law enforcement was aware of it, the club was not as high profile as the Ravenite. Known grandly as the "Triangle Civic Improvement Association," the storefront at **208 Sullivan Street** was near Bleecker Street, and not far from the apartment of Vincent Gigante's family. Gigante had earned a name for himself when as a young thug he was fingered as the shooter in the assassination attempt on Frank Costello back in 1957. Gigante beat that rap, but the next year was convicted with his mentor Vito Genovese in a heroin case, getting a seven-year prison term. His actions earned Gigante a place in the Genovese crime family, and he rose through the ranks to the position of boss in the 1980s, after Anthony Salerno was convicted in the Commission trial in 1986.

Gigante was born and bred in the Greenwich Village area and never really strayed much from his roots. The Triangle Civic club likely took its name from an intersection of streets nearby. It was described as a dingy, cramped place. It had the ubiquitous espresso machine, but not much else in terms of furnishings aside from basic tables and chairs. Gigante used the club as his hangout where he could play pinochle. The Genovese family hangers-on were aware of the FBI surveillance, and took to obscuring the windows with opaque screening. Those who got a glance inside noticed that there were warning signs, such as "The Enemy Is Listening," as a reminder about the potential for FBI bugs.

Eventually, Gigante played the role of a Mob boss battling senility as he took to shuffling the neighborhood streets in a bathrobe and slippers, mumbling to himself, escorted by his son or other associates. Unshaven and with the look of a derelict, Gigante earned the nickname of "The Odd Father," but in the end, his attempt to give the impression that he was suffering from dementia didn't fool everyone. The Genovese family was one of the major illegal earning machines of the Mafia, and Gigante was firmly in control. He was spotted through surveillance doing things that belied the notion that he was a doddering old fool, such as when he walked briskly across streets to avoid traffic, or was seen in animated conversation. In 1997, Gigante was convicted of running the rackets of the Genovese family and conspiring in the 1980s to murder John Gotti.

In 2003, Gigante was already serving a federal prison sentence when he admitted in court that he had indeed been faking his mental illness to avoid prosecution. In the end, the ruse simply got him into more trouble. Gigante died in 2005 in a federal prison medical facility and was cremated at Green-Wood Cemetery in Brooklyn.

With Gigante gone, the Triangle Civic club disappeared. The space at 208 Sullivan became a popular coffee bar and retail business.

■ ■ ■

One well-known restaurant that remained a favorite for the Mafia during this era is Rao's. Located at **455 East 114th Street** in East Harlem, the place isn't in a neighborhood known for its famous restaurants. It opened in 1896 after Charles Rao bought a small saloon at the spot from a brewery; he turned it into a restaurant where the largely Italian immigrant community could come for some good southern Italian cuisine. For locals, the place was part of the famiglia, with its signature sauce and affable staff. In 1977, Rao's got a boost into the stratosphere of restaurants when food critic Mimi Sheraton gave it a great review in the *New York Times*.

Rao's Restaurant on East 114th Street in Manhattan, a place that has been a favorite night spot for a number of New York mafiosi for decades. AUTHOR'S COLLECTION

What also added to Rao's appeal was the fact that its small space only allowed for ten tables and a bar. Reservations were hard to come by, and were booked like condominium time-shares, years in advance.

The author ate there once in 1992 with two colleagues, and remembers having ample and well-prepared dishes of chicken, Italian sausage, and pasta. Zagat has labeled Rao's cuisine "terrific," and noted its "central-casting" clientele, an apparent reference to the attraction the place holds for the gangster crowd—both the real wiseguys and those just posturing. The exclusivity of Rao's is what makes it a draw for the Mob, and John Gotti especially liked the place, as did members of the Bonanno crime family.

Things could get a bit tense because of the place's panache. In 2004, a bunch of brazen Albanian gangsters led by Alex Rudaj showed up one night and demanded they be given a table once reserved for Gotti, who by that time had been dead for two years. Table rights were reportedly then passed to Greg DePalma. The restaurant at first refused to relent, but finally gave the threatening group of Albanians the table, at least for a while.

Those who couldn't get a table were always free to drink at the bar, which also tended to be crowded. At times, there would be singing, such as on the night of December 22, 2003, when actress and chanteuse Renata Strober got up at the invitation of Rao's manager Frank Pellegrino to entertain the gathering. Strober, who had been eating dinner with a film producer, began singing "Don't Rain on My Parade," a song made popular by Barbra Streisand in the film *Funny Girl*.

But at the bar, reputed Lucchese crime-family soldier Albert Circelli wasn't just raining on Strober's parade, but also heaping insults at her vocal ability. "Ah, shut up! Get her off—she sucks," Circelli said. Nearby, Mob associate Louis "Louie Lump Lump" Barone gestured with his finger to his mouth and told Circelli to quiet down. Circelli wouldn't have it. According to court papers, Circelli then told Barone, "I'll open up your hole," and other not-at-all kind remarks.

Enraged by Circelli's verbal abuse Barone pulled out a .38 caliber Smith & Wesson and fired two shots. One hit Circelli, who died at the scene, and the other wounded a court officer who happened to be standing nearby. Barone was arrested outside Rao's and in 2004 pled guilty to manslaughter. He was sentenced to fifteen years in state prison, where he died.

Strober later started showing up at the more sedate and gentlemanly Friars Club. "I just figured old Jews with no guns is probably a better place for me," she later told a reporter.

CHAPTER FOURTEEN

THE DEAD WHO KNEW BROOKLYN

When William "Billy the Butcher" Poole died in 1855 of wounds suffered in a shooting at Stanwix Hall in Manhattan, his funeral became a spectacle of the day. For his burial, Poole's family and friends chose Green-Wood Cemetery in Brooklyn, a place that was fast becoming the cemetery of note for the city. Created in 1838, Green-Wood was styled as a rural cemetery on the most elevated point in Brooklyn, overlooking New York harbor to the west. The cemetery was established after it became clear that there was no longer grave space in Manhattan churchyards, and that the growing city would very quickly need a larger place to accommodate its deceased. With its gently sloping hills, attractive scenery, and glacial terrain, Green-Wood became a place for family outings, as well as funerals. Its main entrance is through a graceful arch at **Twenty-Fifth Street and Fifth Avenue.**

Poole's funeral procession began at his home in Manhattan and would travel some six miles to Green-Wood. His coffin was placed on an open hearse pulled by four white horses, which had been parked on Hudson Street. Poole's corpse was clothed in a dark suit, and a political badge from the Organization of United Americans was stretched across his chest. At the head of the coffin was a large gilt eagle that had been covered with black crepe. The hearse was also decked out in black velvet on each side, bearing Poole's last words—"I die a true American"—in silver letters.

The procession from Poole's old neighborhood, Christopher Street, through lower Manhattan to the ferry to Brooklyn, was said to have been witnessed by over a hundred thousand onlookers. The newspapers reported that liquor stores and cigar shops stayed open along the route. In the procession were city aldermen, politicians, gang members, noted criminals, firefighters, and members of various political clubs. Delegations came from Philadelphia and Baltimore. In an attempt to keep things peaceful, funeral organizers barred any group from displaying banners or slogans that might provoke those who had been Poole's enemies and political opponents. The marchers walked south to the South Ferry

The grave of William "Billy the Butcher" Poole at historic Green-Wood Cemetery in Brooklyn. Poole was a nineteenth-century gang leader and rabid nativist who hated foreigners. He died from a gunshot wound in 1855. AUTHOR'S COLLECTION

in Lower Manhattan, where the hearse was placed on a vessel for the short voyage to Atlantic Street in Brooklyn, which at that point in time was a separate city.

The crowds in Brooklyn were said to have been as large as those which accompanied Poole in Manhattan. Ferries from the Williamsburg section transported thousands more so they could be close to the cortege as it made its way to Green-Wood, under the watchful eyes of scores of police officers. It took about five hours for the procession to make its way from Poole's home on Christopher Street in Manhattan to the cemetery. Poole's body was placed in a receiving tomb, and four months later, on July 9, 1855, eventually placed in a grave just off the cemetery road known as Landscape Avenue.

For the longest time Poole's grave had no headstone, perhaps because his family and friends were worried about the notoriety. But in February 2003, at a time when Martin Scorcese's film *Gangs of New York* was playing in theaters, Green-Wood unveiled a three-foot-high headstone at Poole's grave. In the film, Poole was characterized as William "The Butcher" Cutting, a role played by actor Daniel Day-Lewis. Engraved into the stone were the dates Poole was wounded at Stanwix Hall, and when he died. There are also those famous last words attributed to the venerable tough guy: "Good-bye, boys, I die a true American." Cemetery president Richard Moylan did the unveiling, noting to the small crowd that Poole, who was immortalized as one of New York's early gangsters, was being commemorated as a historical figure.

■ ■ ■

Frankie Yale's livelihood as a Brooklyn gangster in the 1920s was that of a bootlegger, the career of choice for any criminal with aspirations for greatness. Yale was born in southern Italy with the name Francesco Ioele, a surname which over time turned into "Uale" and "Yale." Once in the United States, Yale gravitated toward a life of crime, and as a teenager was mentored by Johnny Torrio and brought into the Five Points Gang.

Although he was good with his fists and could elicit fear in his world, Yale also became adept at some of the early Mafia business rackets. In the days before electric refrigerators, homeowners and businesses relied on icemen to bring them blocks of ice. It was backbreaking work, and competition could be tough. Yale went into the ice business in Brooklyn and essentially got all of the companies organized into a cartel, which kept prices artificially high. Through strong-arm methods, Yale got many ice sellers to use his company as a source of supply, ensuring an additional flow of income. Yale used the same heavy-handed tactics in the laundry business, where he kept the union out of companies. He also developed a brand of cigars known as "Frankie Yales," which he forced stores to sell.

As a hedge against the relatively short longevity of his associates, Yale opened up a funeral home at **6604 Fourteenth Avenue** in the Dyker Heights section of Brooklyn, just across the street from where he lived with his family, a location that would unwittingly prove to be convenient later on. Eventually, Yale opened up a bar and dance hall in Coney Island that was given the grand name of the "Harvard Inn." The establishment, which no longer exists, was located on Seaside Walk, a popular thoroughfare not far from the Atlantic Ocean.

It was at this dance hall that another young Italian immigrant named Alphonse Capone, eager to make his way in the criminal world, took a job as a bouncer and bartender. Capone's reference for the position was Johnny Torrio, mentor to a lot of young toughs.

Capone biographer Laurence Bergreen describes the young gangster's time at the Harvard Inn: "He made himself a popular figure . . . they liked Al, the jolly way he served up the foamy beer at the bar and occasionally took a turn on the dance floor himself. It was not exalted work, but the job kept him busy and on display."

Not everyone at the bar took a shine to Capone, however. After he made a rude remark about the derriere of a patron's sister, Capone got into a fight and was slashed with a knife on the left side of his face, an injury which healed but left him with a disfiguring scar and the moniker "Scarface."

Capone would eventually go to Chicago, where he rose to prominence as a Mob boss in his own right, eventually eclipsing Yale. But back in Brooklyn, Yale and Capone remained allies, and with Prohibition in full swing, they had worked out a deal in which Yale was able to import whiskey and scotch, transporting it by truck to Capone's speakeasies in Chicago. Yale also was closely tied to a number of the up-and-coming mobsters of the day, notably Joe Adonis and Albert

A newspaper graphic showing some of the big Mob figures of the late 1920s and early '30s in New York City, including Frankie Yale, Ciro Terranova, Joseph Masseria, Al Capone, Anthony Carfano, and Richard Lonergan.
ASSOCIATED PRESS

Anastasia. Also a man to be reckoned with was Anthony Carfano, who was known by the strange nickname of "Little Augie Pisano."

As powerful as Yale was in Brooklyn, he made a lot of enemies on the way up. He even raised Capone's suspicion that he had been stealing some of the whiskey destined for Chicago. So, as tough as he was, Yale was the object of a number of assassination attempts. The first known effort came in early 1921, when gunmen fired at him as he was about to enter a nightclub in Lower Manhattan. Yale's bodyguard was killed, and Yale sustained a serious chest wound that kept him in the hospital for months.

Two years later, Yale attended a christening at a local Brooklyn church and decided to walk back to the family home, sending his wife and children ahead with his chauffeur, Frank Forte. Gunmen followed the vehicle, and as Yale's family and the chauffeur exited, they shot at Forte, apparently mistaking him for his boss.

The assassination attempts didn't slow Yale down, and in one memorable confrontation, he forced some of his Irish opponents to back off from a fight in a way that led to some long-term benefits for the Italian Mob. On the evening of Christmas Day, 1925, Yale, Capone, and a group of their Italian friends were gathered for drinks at the Adonis Social and Athletic Club at **152 Twentieth Street** in Brooklyn. A rival bunch of Irishmen known as the White Hand, led by Richard "Peg Leg" Lonergan—so named because he had a wooden leg—came to the club, demanded drinks, and began insulting the Italians with ethnic slurs like "dago" and "wop."

The result was predictable: The lights went out at the Adonis and shooting started in the darkness. In the end, three of Lonergan's men were dead, and the leader was found cowering under a piano. Capone finished off Lonergan with a shot to the head, and his wooden leg, according to Bergreen, was taken as a trophy.

The killing of Lonergan had the effect of breaking the Irish power on the docks of Brooklyn and set up the Italians as the new force on the waterfront. This would eventually become a power base for the likes of Albert Anastasia and his kin. In the meantime, Yale's position as a top Mob boss in Brooklyn was solidified by the way Lonergan and his group were so decisively dispatched.

But as is often the case in the Mafia, Yale's luck ran out—although it took a bit of trickery to make that happen. Although Capone and Yale had forged a tight relationship, the bootlegging business caused things to fray. Capone learned that Yale was hijacking booze meant for Chicago. For Capone, Yale's duplicity meant that he was effectively stealing from him. On Sunday morning, July 1, 1928, Yale was driving alone in Brooklyn in his new Lincoln, a large car with running boards, the automotive style of the day. The vehicle was bulletproof, and it is likely that Yale felt secure driving without any bodyguards.

Frankie Yale lies beside his automobile on Forty-Fourth Street in Brooklyn after he was gunned down following a car chase on July 1, 1928. ASSOCIATED PRESS

According to later police accounts, Yale noticed another vehicle to his rear with four male passengers that looked suspicious. Yale started to take evasive action and turned quickly onto Forty-Fourth Street in the Fort Hamilton Parkway section. Both cars were speeding, and then suddenly, someone in the pursuing vehicle fired a shotgun at Yale and killed him. Yale's car continued to move down the street and finally came to a stop in the front yard of **923 Forty-Fourth Street,** where a bar mitzvah party was going on. The crash took out some shrubbery and small trees in the front section of the yard. The assailants fired a burst from a submachine gun into the vehicle and then sped away. When the cops arrived at the bloody scene, they asked Yale, "Who did it?," but he was already dead.

Yale's funeral took place four days later and was one of the Mob extravaganzas of the day. The silver-colored casket was valued at $15,000. Some estimates put the crowd of mourners that lined the route at up to one hundred thousand, although that seems high even for a Mob boss. There were 35 flower cars and 250 limousines to carry the wiseguys, friends, and family members. At **Holy Cross Cemetery**—a small pocket burial ground run by the Archdiocese of Brooklyn, in Flatbush—things got even more dramatic, as two women showed up at the grave claiming to be Yale's wife. One wife was named Mary, and newspaper reports said that Yale was also married to a slim, attractive brunette named Luceida Gullioti, of Manhattan. Ultimately, it was Yale's wife Mary, the one whom he lived with and

The funeral of Frankie Yale had a cortege that drew the attention of thousands of onlookers who lined the route to Holy Cross Cemetery in Brooklyn. ASSOCIATED PRESS

had two children, who was given his personal effects at the police station. The items were a testament to Yale's wealth and style: a belt buckle with seventy-five diamonds, $2,000 in cash, and a diamond ring.

Yale's grave is in an out-of-the-way section of Holy Cross. The stone is engraved with his original Italian name, "Ioele." The curious might easily overlook the gravesite, because a low-growing tree has enveloped the headstone, creating a protective canopy of leaves in the spring and summer.

■ ■ ■

Yale's rackets and bootlegging operation were taken over by Anthony Carfano, another well-known gangster, and Michael Abbatemarco. Carfano would live a long time and graduate into the ranks of the modern Mafia to hobnob with the likes of Vito Genovese, Lucky Luciano, and Frank Costello. But Abbatemarco would barely outlive his old boss, Yale.

A handsome Italian man cut from the same cloth as Yale, Abbatemarco was known in the German-American Brooklyn neighborhood he grew up in as "Michael der Schatz," which translated to Michael "Sweetheart." As a gangster he took to flashy clothing and jewelry, spending money like it wouldn't last. He was in many ways like Yale, including in the way he died.

The end came for Abbatemarco while he was driving alone in his Nash coupe on a Brooklyn street before sunrise on October 6, 1928. A witness said a man came up from the backseat of the coupe and fired at Abbatemarco several times, killing him. The vehicle was stopped by the curb on **Eighty-Third Street, between Twenty-Fourth and Stillwell Avenues.** The first police officer on the scene looked inside and thought the driver was sleeping at the wheel, until he noticed the blood running down Abbatemarco's face.

So, three months after Abbatemarco had been at Yale's funeral, giving him a final send-off, he was back again at Holy Cross Cemetery, this time in his own $6,000 silver-bronzed casket. While the crowd wasn't as large as it was for Yale, the floral displays were just as ostentatious. Anthony Carfano sent a tower of roses topped by a fluttering dove, and Al Capone provided what was described as an "equally ornate piece."

Because he was a US Army veteran, Abbatemarco's service featured a military firing squad from nearby Fort Hamilton, which sent up an appropriate volley. But the real noise came from the women in Abbatemarco's life. His grieving wife cried, "Don't leave me, Mike. . . . You are all I have, and I love you." She fainted, as did Abbatemarco's mother and his two sisters. Since Abbatemarco's son had died three years earlier at the age of four in an auto accident, the grave diggers had exhumed the child's casket and then placed it on top of his father's before filling in the grave. Finally, a bugler blew "Taps."

■ ■ ■

Physical deformities weren't obstacles to the criminal aspirations of New York mobsters. There was Giuseppe Morello, whose congenitally deformed right hand he prominently displayed in mug shots. Another racketeer with a similar infirmity was Giuseppe Piraino, who because of his paralyzed right fingers was known as "The Clutching Hand." The moniker also was appropriate given Piraino's habits with money on the street: He didn't like to part with any of it. Like most mobsters at the time, Piraino was a bootlegger who had a soda bottling plant. Police said it was used as a place where Piraino could cut his grain alcohol and dilute the liquor. Piraino had visions of expanding his territory beyond what others in the Mob would allow, so, on March 27, 1930, Piraino and his competitors were called to attend a Brooklyn conference—a "sit-down," in modern parlance—about his straying into the territory of others. The talk wasn't productive, apparently, and Piraino left without agreeing to anything, including parting with some cash.

As Piraino walked toward **151 Sackett Street,** he looked jaunty, with a $2,000 diamond stickpin in his tie and a smaller diamond on his ring finger. As he reached the doorway he was shot, with three rounds hitting him in the heart in such a tight pattern that it was later said the holes could have been covered by a half-dollar—although Piraino probably would have preferred a silver dollar for the analogy. Piraino dropped into the gutter, and although there were dozens of people on Sackett Street, nobody saw anyone fire the shots. The lack of witnesses—or at least, those who would say anything—didn't prevent detectives from arresting a dockworker named Joseph Florino, who had once been imprisoned in Sing Sing. He was awaiting execution for the murder of Piraino before a retrial cleared him.

Funeral pomp had become expected among Brooklyn gangsters, and Piraino's family paid the price, with a $7,000 casket of metal and a cortege of seventy cars and floral tributes. His burial was at Green-Wood Cemetery, although today there is no listing for Piraino's interment, suggesting that he may have been placed in the grave of another family member. Piraino's widow claimed his death was an "accident," and tried to collect double indemnity under his $5,000 life insurance policy, which would have given her $10,000. The insurance company said Piraino wasn't an accident victim and stood firm. The case was settled for $8,000, enough to pay for his casket and then some.

As it turned out, Piraino's widow needed all the money she could get for funeral arrangements. On October 6, 1930, about seven months after Piraino was slain, his son Carmine was gunned down as he walked past **1857 Eighty-Fifth Street** in the Bath Beach section. Two gunmen had come out of a driveway and walked up behind Carmine, shooting him in the back of the head and in his chest. The assailants briskly walked into another driveway and disappeared. Police noted that Carmine died on a street within the area of Frankie Yale's bootlegging distribution ring. There was never an arrest made for the murder.

■ ■ ■

While the Italian mobsters were the major force in Brooklyn crime during the 1930s, the Jews were a potent force in their own right. Throughout a good part of the 1920s and into the '40s, a cadre of Jewish gangsters known as the "Brownsville Troop" would put many notches on their belts. Their Italian Mob counterparts who used them as hit men, notably Albert Anastasia, also recognized the convenience of their location. Historians may disagree as to how many died at the hands of this Brooklyn clique, but estimates run from scores to hundreds. The activities of the Brownsville Troop and the related Murder Incorporated (the Jewish-Italian combination) are incorporated throughout this book. They are mentioned here for the fact that they used a peculiar candy store at **779 Saratoga Avenue,** under the elevated railway in Brownsville, as a base and safe haven.

Although the shop was housed in a nondescript storefront on the first floor of the building, it occupied a special place in New York criminal history. Upstairs was the Hollywood Royal Chinese restaurant, which specialized in chow mein. Rose Gold, the Jewish mother of a hoodlum known as Sam "The Dapper" Siegal, ostensibly ran the establishment. The store's awning advertised "candy, soda, and cigars." Gold earned the nickname of "Midnight Rose" because her business stayed open throughout the night, at least for a special breed of men who hung out at the corner of Livonia and Saratoga and populated the ranks of the Brownsville Troop and Murder Inc.

Gold was said to be illiterate and didn't stay in the store all the time, but the men from the corner knew that they could enter the premises at night and do their business. In one case the candy counter was where a set of keys for a stolen auto were hidden. The car was later used in the murder of George Rudnick, a gang associate who was suspected of being an informant. When Rudnick's body was found by cops, there was a card in his pocket, allegedly signed by an assistant prosecutor, which thanked him for his help. The card was planted so that news of it would leak out and be a warning to other potential informants about what could happen to them.

Gold was more than just a kindly woman who accommodated her son's friends with a wink and a nod as they planned their mayhem. She sometimes posted bail when the Murder Inc. members got arrested. In testimony during the Rudnick murder trial, one of the prosecution witnesses, the infamous Jewish gangster Abe Reles, testified that Gold was a partner in his loan-sharking operation. A report prepared for New York governor Herbert Lehman by special prosecutor John Harlan Amen in 1941 noted that Gold handled about $400,000 in loans as part of their shylocking operation.

CHAPTER FIFTEEN

THE LAST LUNCH

Joseph Masseria, the man considered the top Mob boss in New York City in 1931, had been lucky. He had escaped a number of attempts on his life, and like a wily cat had anticipated trouble before he walked into it. But in April of that year Masseria was being challenged in ways that he had never experienced. His rival, Salvatore Maranzano, had pressed him relentlessly, picking off his allies and putting stress on his rackets. The Mob was changing, and old leaders like Masseria, who ruled by brute force and suppressed the younger gangsters eager to make money, were becoming an anachronism.

There was a glimmer of hope that the bloody conflicts could cease, and to that end Masseria met on April 15, 1931, and talked about a possible strike against their opponents with his aide, Lucky Luciano. As Luciano would reveal years later, Masseria was considering a preemptive strike against Maranzano. Around noon, Luciano suggested he and Masseria journey to Coney Island for lunch at the Nuova Villa Tammora, a restaurant owned by their friend, Gerardo Scarpato. The establishment was located at **2715 West Fifteenth Street,** and was popular, often filling up around lunchtime, although on April 15 the crowd was sparse. A total of four people were at Masseria's table and Anna Tammora, the mother-in-law of Scarpato, went out to buy some fish the diners had ordered.

Lunch for Masseria and Luciano lasted until about 3:30 p.m., and by then most of the other customers had left. Both men settled down to a game of cards, and after one hand Luciano excused himself to go to the restroom. As soon as Luciano had left the room, two or three men with firearms entered the Nuova Villa Tammora and started shooting at Masseria. Nearly two dozen shots were fired at Masseria, and five found their mark, killing him. The assailants left, got into a waiting car driven by another man, and sped away. With the shooting over, Luciano returned from the lavatory and called police. How could anyone want to harm Joe, an emotional Luciano wondered aloud after the cops arrived.

A contemporary photograph of the location where in April 1931 Mob boss Joseph Masseria was shot dead. The original building for the Nuova Villa Tammora has been replaced by a modern warehouse on West Fifteenth Street in the Coney Island section of Brooklyn. AUTHOR'S COLLECTION

Luciano put up a good act, because he was actually the one who had double-crossed Masseria, secretly going over to the Maranzano side. When the police arrived they found Masseria sprawled on the floor. A later news photograph showed Masseria on the floor with a playing card in his hand, although that might have been staged. The gunmen were later alleged to have been Joseph Stracci and Frank Livorsi, with Ciro Terranova outside driving the getaway car. No one was ever arrested for the hit, which was one of the biggest events in the history of organized crime, setting up the immediate transition to the modern Mafia and the rule of the Commission. The old restaurant location has been replaced by a nondescript brick building housing a smoked-fish purveyor. In a way, Masseria's legend now sleeps with the fishes.

The family mausoleum for slain Mob boss Joseph Masseria and kin, in Calvary Cemetery. AUTHOR'S COLLECTION

Murder Incorporated killer Abe Reles, who had decided to cooperate with police, but fell to his death from a room at the Half Moon Hotel in Coney Island, where police were keeping him. PHOTO COURTESY LIBRARY OF CONGRESS

Among all the different kinds of deaths—and there were many—which befell a gangster in the heyday of the Jewish-Italian combination known as Murder Inc., that of Abe Reles will always rank as the most bizarre and inexplicable.

Reles, a short and stocky man with curly black hair, had earned a reputation for being a vicious thug. He was among the group of Jewish racketeers who hung out around "Midnight Rose" Gold's infamous all-night candy store on Saratoga Avenue in Williamsburg and shared a lucrative loan-sharking business with her. He earned the nickname "Kid Twist," so the story goes, after another Jewish criminal named Max "Kid Twist" Zweifach, who years earlier had terrorized immigrant shop owners on the Lower East Side of Manhattan. Reles had a temper that was easily provoked, and he was once imprisoned for three years after he beat and stabbed a black car washer who didn't move fast enough.

Jewish gangster Louis "Lepke" Buchalter, after his surrender in 1939 to the FBI. He would later be convicted on charges he was among a group of men involved in the murder of George Rudnick, as well as other crimes. Buchalter was executed in 1944. PHOTO COURTESY LIBRARY OF CONGRESS

When he had to, Reles would kill for Murder Inc., or for himself. He admitted to playing a role in eleven murders, either through the use of a knife, ice pick, strangulation, or shooting. Such a body count ensured that when Reles was arrested in 1940, he would be a prime candidate for the electric chair. To save his life, Reles decided to become a government witness, and proceeded to give evidence in numerous trials, which led to the conviction and execution of Louis "Lepke" Buchalter and a number of other members and associates of Murder Inc., including Harry Maione and Frank Abbandando, who were guilty of killing George Rudnick.

Reles, while carrying a lot of baggage with such a nasty criminal record, was an effective witness, and prosecutors planned to use him to net their next big catch: Mafia member Albert Anastasia, who was accused of killing a Brooklyn dockworker. In preparation for Anastasia's trial, Reles was being sequestered under police guard at the Half Moon Hotel on the Coney Island boardwalk at **West Twenty-Ninth Street.** But at some time in the early-morning hours of November 12, 1941, for reasons no one will ever really know, a fully dressed Reles tied together two bedsheets and proceeded out the window of his room on the sixth floor. The radio he listened to at all hours was still playing in his room.

The gravestone of Louis "Lepke" Buchalter, the last major gangster to be executed in New York State, with the inscription showing his date of death. AUTHOR'S COLLECTION

Bedsheet ropes may work in comedy scenes, but in the case of Reles, there was no such luck. Reles lowered himself to the fifth floor where he tried to pry open a window screen of an empty room. It was then that the sheets came loose. Police later determined that Reles had desperately tried to kick open the window as he started to slide. Instead, he fell more than forty feet to the second-story roof ledge of the hotel kitchen, where he landed flat on his back, which broke, and killed him. Police learned of the fall after hotel staff discovered the fluttering sheets and Reles's body. He had on an overcoat, which contained a cloth cap in the pocket.

Reles's death was deemed an accident, but that didn't stop conspiracy theorists from coming up with all kinds of explanations for how he came to fall. Some thought he might have been pushed out of the window by the cops who were guarding him; it was said they disliked him because of everything from his arrogance to his poor personal hygiene. Others thought the long reach of the Mafia was involved. A police inquiry cleared the officers who were guarding Reles of any wrongdoing. The one man who greatly benefited from the demise of Reles was Albert Anastasia, whose murder trial was canceled after the prosecution lost its main witness.

Not long after Reles died, the Half Moon was turned into a military hospital during World War II. It later did duty as a maternity hospital, and in the 1970s became a senior citizens' home. The structure, one of the highest buildings in Coney Island, was finally demolished in 1995, and the site now contains an apartment complex.

■ ■ ■

In a signature scene from the film *The Godfather*, Mob enforcer Luca Brasi gets his comeuppance in a bar when he is stabbed and garroted. In real life, bars were often the setting for Mob bloodshed. Take the case of Frank "Frankie Shots" Abbatemarco. A relative of Michael Abbatemarco, who was murdered in October 1928, Frankie Shots became a policy operator for Joseph Profaci, one of the original leaders of the Mafia's Five Families after the murder of Salvatore Maranzano in 1931. "Policy" refers to an illegal poor-man's lottery scheme at the time in which bettors would choose three numbers and place a bet that they would be the ones picked in some random sequence, sometimes selected from a newspaper listing. Clients were often grandmothers and neighborhood merchants. There was no question Frankie Shots was a policy man, because he had been arrested for the activity in 1952, and it's said that his operation took in about $2.5 million a year—nice change at the time, which accounting for inflation would be $22 million now.

Like any good Mob associate, Frankie Shots had been kicking some of the policy money upstairs to Profaci. But like some Mafia bosses, Profaci became greedy and demanding. Frankie Shots then stopped making tribute payments to the boss, going into arrears that ran into the tens of thousands.

It was in a dimly lit Brooklyn bar that Frankie Shots made his final payment on the debt the night of November 4, 1959. As he left Cardiello's Bar and Grill at **256 Fourth Avenue,** Frankie Shots was wounded by gunfire, one round of which shattered the bar's door. Frankie Shots staggered back into Cardiello's and fell to the floor as two gunmen followed him and finished him off with six more shots. The gunmen wore bandanas to conceal their faces and fled in a black sedan driven by another man. None of the bar patrons could see enough of the assailants to be helpful. Police used the "Casablanca" strategy—rounding up the usual suspects among known gamblers—but made no arrest for the murder.

Rumors in the underworld said that Profaci had instigated the hit. Fed up with Profaci's high-handed tactics, the Gallo brothers—Larry, Albert, and Joey—had started a direct challenge against the elderly crime boss. What became known as the Gallo Wars consumed Brooklyn, as the brothers sought to get a bigger cut of the illegal profits from Profaci, and even went so far as to kidnap some of the crime boss's lieutenants, including his underboss Joseph Magliocco and captain John Scimone. Profaci agreed to a negotiated settlement with the Gallos to get his men freed, but later reneged on the deal.

Although bold, the Gallo brothers seemed to be under a lot of pressure from the established Profaci crowd, and were marked for death. Letting his guard down, the thirty-three-year-old Larry Gallo was lured by Scimone to the Sahara Lounge at **1201 Utica Avenue,** Brooklyn, on August 20, 1961. Seeing that

Scimone was one of those kidnapped by the Gallo brothers, Larry Gallo should have been wary about going with him to the bar. Mobsters usually don't let bygones be bygones.

Mafia boss Joseph Profaci, who became embroiled in a war with the upstart Gallo brothers of Brooklyn. PHOTO COURTESY LIBRARY OF CONGRESS

As Gallo was sitting down in a booth, two men came over from an adjacent booth and started to choke him with a piece of manila cord. Gallo would quite possibly have been a goner had not a New York City police officer entered the bar and interrupted the garroting. Gallo's two assailants, one of whom was later identified as Carmine Persico, fled the bar; one of them fired a shot into the face of the officer's partner, who was outside. Police tried to get Gallo to identify the men who were strangling him, but he remained silent when they brought a suspect to him for identification. He walked around for weeks with a rope burn on his neck, which he hid with a scarf.

The attempt on Larry Gallo's life only served to exacerbate the conflict between Profaci and the Gallo clan. Things went poorly for the Gallos, as their allies were either killed or defected to Profaci. The Gallo brothers tried to make a brave stand by "going to the mattress," living in an apartment on President Street and armed with all sorts of firearms. The crew even made an effort to blow up Persico in his car with a bomb, but the device malfunctioned, and Persico only received a concussion. Persico was also shot at on **Bond Street,** on the block between Degraw and Douglas Streets. In the end, the Gallo Wars accounted for twelve murders, mostly of men from the Gallo camp. By 1963, the fighting had petered out, as Albert and Larry Gallo were arrested and Joey went to prison for extortion.

While they were alive, the Gallo brothers streaked through the world of the Mafia like meteors. Larry died in 1968 of cancer. Joey was gunned down in one of the Mafia's most memorable hits in 1972, outside Umberto's Clam House in Manhattan. Joey's wake was in a Brooklyn funeral home at 440 Clinton Avenue, and the scene was enough to give a person chills.

"Blood on the street! Blood on the street!," Gallo's mother Mary could be heard wailing from inside the funeral parlor. Minutes before the wails, Mary had cried out "My Joey, my Joey," before she fainted. The funeral mass was a somber affair at St. Charles Church in Brooklyn, heavily photographed by police. Joey's burial was at Green-Wood Cemetery, in a grave on a hillside next to his brother Larry. Cemetery workers told reporters that the Gallo family asked that a tent be put up beside the grave to block the view of surveillance cameras and anyone who "wished them ill."

After Joey Gallo was gunned down outside Umberto's Clam House in Manhattan, the Mafia was wracked by a series of killings in 1972. Most of the victims were Mob associates, and the motives for their killings remained murky. Police didn't make any arrests, which wasn't unusual for Mob hits. Since the day Joseph Colombo was shot in Manhattan in June 1971, and into the summer of 1972, there had been fourteen Mob-style killings in the city.

Thomas Eboli would become the fifteenth victim.

Eboli was a dapper gangster who dressed sharply and wore a signature snap-brim gray straw hat. Born in Italy, Eboli became an American citizen in 1960, and although he lived in Fort Lee, New Jersey, commuted into Manhattan where police said he acted as the overseer of the Genovese crime family's interests on the docks and in nightclubs. Eboli was well placed within the crime family since 1959, when he served as acting boss while the official boss, Vito Genovese, was in prison for a narcotics conviction. When Genovese died in 1969, Eboli and two other mobsters took on the duties of running the family as a ruling committee, until a heart ailment forced Eboli to take a backseat in that role. Still, Eboli remained a power in the crime family.

In his younger days, Eboli managed boxers and used the named "Tommy Ryan" in that job. Among his fighters was Vincent Gigante, the man who shot at Mob boss Frank Costello. Eboli's temper would sometimes get the best of him. During one prizefight in 1952 he jumped in the ring and assaulted a referee who had ruled against his boxer. When Eboli testified before investigative committees, he seemed to be irrational, a fact that wasn't overlooked by other mobsters.

But on the night of July 16, 1972, Eboli didn't seem to be under any specific threat, nor did he face problems in the Genovese family. That evening Eboli and his chauffeur had driven in a blue Fleetwood Cadillac to Crown Heights in Brooklyn to see his girlfriend. According to an account given to police by the chauffeur, Eboli got out of the car on Lefferts Avenue and told his aide to come back to pick him up at 1:00 a.m. At that time, Eboli was walking back to the Cadillac, which was parked in front of **388 Lefferts Avenue,** when someone shot at him. Eboli was hit with five .32 caliber rounds in the left side of his head. By the time police arrived, Eboli was dead.

The account given to police by the chauffeur, a man named Joseph Sternfeld, was questionable. Sternfeld said that Eboli was returning to the car when a truck suddenly drove up and there were gunshots. Sternfeld said he didn't see the shooter because he had ducked down under the dashboard of the Cadillac when the shooting started. Seeing his boss dead, Sternfeld told police he had decided to drive the car back to New Jersey, rather than wait for police to arrive.

Sternfeld was indicted for perjury after Brooklyn district attorney Eugene Gold said Sternfeld knew much more than he had testified to before a grand jury about the Eboli slaying. Police pointed out that the Cadillac that Sternfeld had been driving had blood on the passenger seat, which indicated that Eboli would have been in the car when he was wounded, and not outside, as the chauffeur had claimed.

But despite the perjury charge, Gold's staff and the police were never able to get to the bottom of the Eboli slaying. Police believed that Eboli had been lured to the spot where he died, something that was unlikely, because he was visiting a girlfriend there. In any case, the killer or killers knew enough about Eboli's movements to plan the ambush.

A few people did profit from his demise. As pointed out by Mob historian Selwyn Raab in *Five Families*, Eboli's old boxer client Gigante took over his gambling operations. Another mafioso named Frank "Funzi" Tieri suddenly found himself anointed the new boss of the Genovese borgata.

CHAPTER SIXTEEN

A LATE LUNCH—BONANNO STYLE

Brooklyn district attorney Eugene Gold was busy dealing with more than just Mafia homicides in 1972. For months, NYPD detectives and those assigned to Gold had been watching a trailer in a junkyard at **5702 Avenue D** in the Canarsie section, the place of business of Paul Vario, a high-ranking member of the Lucchese crime family. A twenty-five-year-old undercover detective had posed as a corrupt cop and hung out around the junkyard and collected bribes. Not only was the detective outfitted with a recording device, but police had also surreptitiously entered the trailer on a night when the guard dogs slept soundly and installed a surveillance device, which transmitted hundreds of hours of conversations of Mob associates. From a vantage point in Nazareth High School across the street, detectives also took tens of thousands of still photographs and lengthy movie film of activity at the trailer and junkyard.

The so-called "Gold Bug," which the district attorney proudly displayed at a news conference when the operation was completed, was one of the first significant uses of electronic surveillance in the borough against the Mob. It turned out to be a bonanza for law enforcement. In a secret operation carried out early one morning in October 1972, hundreds of plainclothes cops and detectives assembled at Gold's office in downtown Brooklyn and were given envelopes containing grand jury subpoenas and information about the people who were to be served. If anyone offered them a bribe to toss out the subpoena, the person was to be arrested. About six hundred people, including Mafia members and associates, were on the list of targets, and over the course of a few days most were given the subpoenas.

As a result of the grand jury probe, prosecutors indicted a number of high-level Mafia figures, including Lucchese crime boss Carmine Tramunti, his captain Paul Vario, some police officers, and others who frequented the junkyard trailer. Also charged were two Long Island politicians. Not surprisingly, the investigation showed that hundreds of businesses were linked to mafiosi. Trying to get the most mileage out of what was a big investigation for his staff, Gold said that the probe had dealt a major blow against the Mafia, and hinted that the Mob was on the ropes.

History would prove otherwise.

■ ■ ■

New York State court officer Albert Gelb left his job in downtown Brooklyn at the criminal court in the early-morning hours of March 11, 1976. He had just come off the late shift at night court (6:00 p.m. to 1:00 a.m.), where he served as the "bridge man," calling out the order of cases, handing out papers, and keeping order in the room.

The twenty-five-year-old court officer had developed a flair for making arrests. In one episode at a diner in Queens, he had noticed Mob associate Charles Carneglia with a gun; after a confrontation and a scuffle, Gelb arrested him. Carneglia, the troubled brother of Gambino crime-family captain John Carneglia, bitterly remembered the incident. Gelb would also never forget it, because he began receiving strange and threatening telephone calls afterward.

New York State court officer Albert Gelb, who had a run-in with Gambino crime-family associate Charles Carneglia in a Queens diner, an incident that got Carneglia hit with a weapons charge. PHOTO COURTESY US ATTORNEY'S OFFICE, EASTERN DISTRICT

Gelb left the courthouse around 1:30 a.m. that March night, and after escorting Judge Richard Brown to his car—this was done as a usual precaution, because judges were often the target of angry people—went to his own vehicle and began the drive to his house on **109th Street** in the Richmond Hill section, a community that straddled Brooklyn and Queens. Gelb was being followed home by fellow court officer David Vartian, as both men planned to do a bit of Bible study at Gelb's home. Although he was born a Jew, Gelb had turned to the Bible later in life, finding that studying it gave him solace and purpose in life. When Charles Carneglia had made angry telephone calls to him, Gelb had told

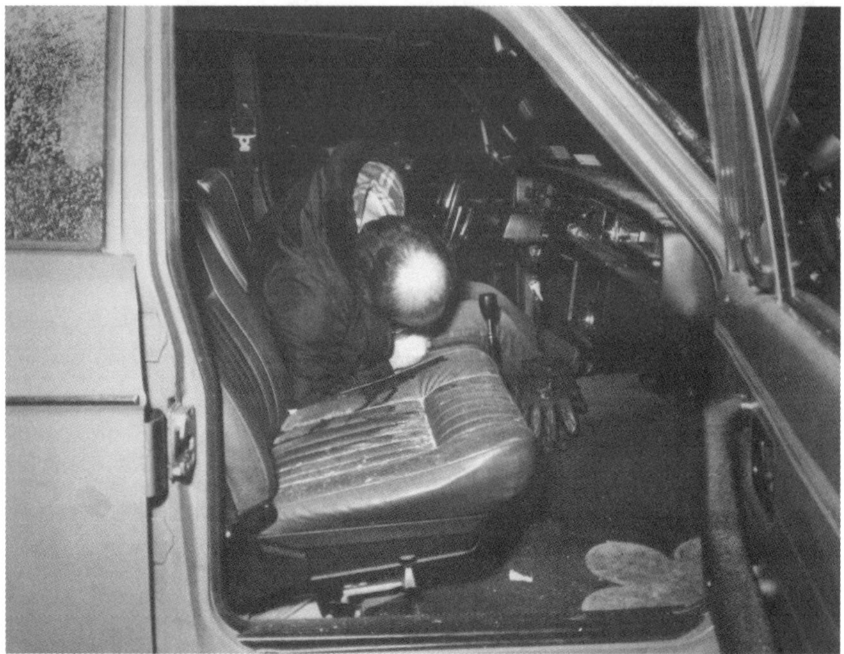

Crime-scene photo of the killing of Albert Gelb, March 11, 1976, in Queens, a case that officially remains unsolved. PHOTO COURTESY US ATTORNEY'S OFFICE, EASTERN DISTRICT

him to find peace in the Scriptures—something that Carneglia was incapable of doing at that point.

Vartian was a few blocks behind Gelb's car and was stopped by a light when he heard what sounded like firecrackers, followed by the squeal of tires. After the light turned in his favor, Vartian turned onto 109th Street and noticed Gelb's car in the street, double-parked, but without Gelb at the wheel. Vartian at first thought his friend was making a quick visit to a neighbor's house, but grew concerned when ten minutes passed and he had not returned. Walking up to Gelb's car, Vartian made a terrible discovery: Gelb was slumped on his right side in the front seat. He had seven bullet wounds in his body, and he was dead.

Gelb's murder had all the earmarks of a Mob hit, and Dennis Quirk, head of the court officers' union, thought he had a pretty good idea of who did it. The killer was either Charles Carneglia or someone very close to him, as retaliation for the way Gelb had brought law enforcement heat on the Gambino associate. A few days after Gelb was killed, a couple of men showed up at the home of Gelb's father. A relative remembered that the gentlemen looked out of place—they certainly weren't Jewish; in fact, they seemed Italian. They had a message for Gelb's father that seemed like an apology for a tragic mistake. The message: Whatever had happened to Albert Gelb, no one in the underworld approved of it. The strangers never gave their names and walked away, leaving Gelb's family with its grief and a mystery that would never be solved.

■ ■ ■

Joe and Mary's Italian-American Restaurant at **205 Knickerbocker Avenue** in Brooklyn was one of those Italian restaurants with a rear patio where patrons could eat alfresco next to some tomato plants used for salads and sauce. Some of the Bonanno crime family crowd liked it for its homey style. There were some cheap art reproductions on the walls, including a copy of Leonardo da Vinci's *The Last Supper*. Around lunchtime on July 12, 1979, Carmine Galante, one of the men vying for leadership in the Bonanno family, entered the establishment with his bodyguards, Baldassare Amato and Cesare Bonventre. The three men took seats in the patio area. They were there for a bon voyage lunch for restaurant owner Joseph Turano, who was leaving for Italy.

Galante was an old Bonanno hand who had done serious prison time for a federal heroin conviction. When he got out of jail, so the legend goes, Galante announced his freedom by blowing up the door of the cemetery vault of Frank Costello. A foul-tempered thug, Galante had been trying to wrest control of the Bonanno family from its official boss, Philip Rastelli. Giving muscle to Galante's faction were Sicilian immigrants known as "zips" who helped him in his heroin operations. The Sicilians were tough characters, and, emboldened by them, Galante had started to covet the operations of the other Mafia families, particularly in Atlantic City. The other bosses were not going to let this go any further.

Bonanno crime family member Baldassare Amato, originally from Sicily, was one of two bodyguards who accompanied Carmine Galante to a luncheon where he was shot dead on July 12, 1979. Amato and cohort Cesare Bonventre escaped unharmed. PHOTO COURTESY US ATTORNEY'S OFFICE, EASTERN DISTRICT

It was around 2:45 p.m. on that July 12 afternoon, minutes after Galante and company had sat down at Joe and Mary's Restaurant, that three

Cesare Bonventre, one of the Sicilian bodyguards for Bonanno mobster Carmine Galante, who accompanied him to the fateful lunch in July 1979.
PHOTO COURTESY US ATTORNEY'S OFFICE, EASTERN DISTRICT

masked men got out of a car in front of the eatery and rushed toward the patio. All carried firearms, including shotguns, witnesses later recalled. Before Galante had time to react, a shotgun blast hit him in the chest while another struck him in the head, blowing his left eye out of its socket. Another friend of Galante's was shot dead, and Turano was wounded, as was his seventeen-year-old son, John. Bonventre and Amato were unharmed.

The assassination of Galante was done with a touch of the old brazen Mafia style, seen with the killings of Masseria and Maranzano in the old days of the Castellammarese Wars. With Galante out of the picture, Rastelli was now the undisputed boss of the Bonanno family, acting through surrogates on the street because he was in prison. Galante's allies had been earmarked for death as well, but they were demoted in rank instead. Given a big boost in power and elevated to the rank of captain was an ambitious Rastelli loyalist named Joseph Massino, who had ferried messages to and from the imprisoned boss.

■ ■ ■

The hit on Galante clarified the leadership of the Bonanno family for a while. But by 1981, competing forces were once again at work, setting the stage for more bloody intrigue. Not everyone was happy with Rastelli. Three crime-family captains in particular—Dominick "Big Trin" Trinchera, Alphonse "Sonny Red" Indelicato, and Philip Giaccone—thought Rastelli was a bum, and said so. Massino heard through the Mob grapevine that the three captains were plotting to take over the crime family, but his hands were tied. The ruling Mafia Commission, informants said, had told the Bonanno crowd to work out their problems without any bloodshed.

With the Commission's admonition, things remained peaceful. But Massino picked up some disturbing intelligence that Trinchera, Indelicato, and Giaccone had been stockpiling weapons and planning a coup d'état. At that point Massino turned to his friend Paul Castellano, head of the Gambino crime family, and the leaders of the Colombo family. Their advice to Massino was simple: Do what you need to do to protect yourself.

Massino's plan was to get the three captains to agree to a meeting at a Brooklyn social club on May 5, 1981, to sort out the crime-family problems. It was actually the third such meeting to take place, and according to protocol, Trinchera, Indelicato, and Giaccone showed up at the club located in the vicinity of **6709–6721 Thirteenth Avenue** without guns. Massino was also there, as well as some other crime-family veterans.

For a few moments things were peaceful and convivial, but this ended in a deadly instant. Four armed men wearing masks burst out of a closet. Two of them raced to block an escape through the rear door.

Bonanno crime-family gangster Joseph Massino helped arrange for the murders of three rival crime captains in May 1981, an act which led to his eventually ascension to boss of the family. PHOTO COURTESY US ATTORNEY'S OFFICE, EASTERN DISTRICT

Bonanno crime captain Philip Giaccone, who, along with Dominick Trinchera and Sonny Indelicato, was slain in a crime-family power struggle in May 1981. PHOTO COURTESY US ATTORNEY'S OFFICE, EASTERN DISTRICT

Bonanno crime captain Dominick Trinchera, one of the three men slain on May 5, 1981, in a power struggle within the crime family. PHOTO COURTESY US ATTORNEY'S OFFICE, EASTERN DISTRICT

"Don't anybody move—this is a holdup," said one of the masked men, Canadian gangster Vito Rizzuto.

The three captains tried to react and defend themselves, but it was a lost cause. Rizzuto and fellow Canadian mobster Gerlando Sciascia began firing away with shotguns and pistols. Trinchera, an obsese man, lost a good part of his abdomen in one blast. Giaccone and Indelicato were killed almost instantly. For good measure, Sciascia put a final bullet in Indelicato's head.

Almost as soon as the shooting started, it was over. The only person to escape was Frank Lino, who had accompanied the three captains to the meeting and had the presence of mind in his panic to run out of an unguarded rear door. The three bodies on the floor lay in blood and viscera. Some Bonanno family men, alerted by a walkie-talkie message, entered the club and helped wrap up the bodies for disposal in an empty lot in Queens (see chapter 18).

■ ■ ■

One of the main allies for Joseph Massino throughout the Bonanno family power struggle was Dominick "Sonny Black" Napolitano. Although he was a killer, Napolitano had a fondness for racing pigeons, a pastime that was once a big sport in Brooklyn but had been steadily dying out since the end of World War II. Napolitano kept his pigeons in a coop that he had built on the roof of **420 Graham Avenue,** site of the Motion Lounge, his base of operations in the Williamsburg section of Brooklyn. The area around the lounge was—and still is—an area populated by a significant Italian-American population. Gangsters like Napolitano gravitated to such areas, and the lounge was his home of sorts.

In the late 1970s a new face appeared at the Motion Lounge. Donny Brasco had blown onto the scene by showing up at social clubs on the Lower East Side of Manhattan and earning a reputation for being able to move stolen property for the Mob. Brasco had a lot of luck moving the stolen stuff because he had a very eager recipient—the Federal Bureau of Investigation. Brasco was really FBI agent Joseph Pistone, and as part of his operation, he would turn the stolen property over to the government, receiving some marked cash to give his new wiseguy friends in the Mob.

Pistone was able to impress Bonanno crime-family members like Benjamin "Left Guns" Ruggiero, who was a close associate of Napolitano's. It was only a matter of time before the undercover agent was able to get close to Napolitano and become a regular at the Motion Lounge. Pistone did such a good job of getting into Napolitano's good graces that the mobster considered him a brother, trusting him enough to commission the undercover agent to seek out Anthony "Bruno" Indelicato, the son of one of the three slain captains, and kill him.

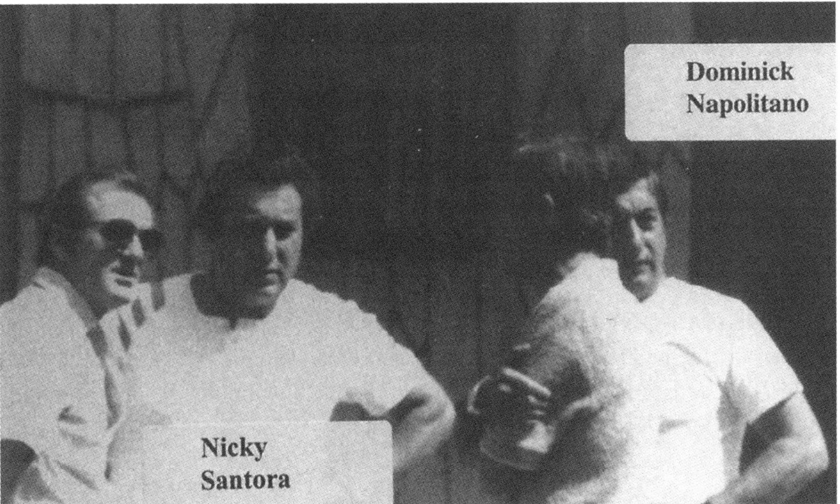

FBI surveillance photo showing Sonny Napolitano in a hastily called meeting outside his Motion Lounge with his Bonanno crime-family crew, after learning that FBI agent Joseph Pistone had infiltrated their group. PHOTO COURTESY US ATTORNEY'S OFFICE, EASTERN DISTRICT

Napolitano also wanted to have Pistone inducted into the Mafia. While this would have been a law enforcement coup, it would have led to some sensitive legal issues, not the least of which was what would have happened had Napolitano kept pressing to have Pistone kill someone, or commit another serious crime.

So, with a lot of other mobsters disappearing and things getting tense, the FBI pulled Pistone from his undercover role on July 30, 1981. This was also the day that Napolitano learned how Pistone had deceived him. Three FBI agents—Doug Fencl, Jim Kinne, and Jerry Loar—paid a visit to the Motion Lounge building and rang the bell for Napolitano's apartment on the second floor. The mafioso invited the agents up and was told that the man he knew as Donny Brasco was, in fact, FBI agent Joseph Pistone. To make the point, the agents showed Napolitano a photo of Pistone posing with fellow agents.

As he spoke with the agents in his apartment at the corner of Withers and Graham, Napolitano kept calm and said he didn't know Pistone. But inside his head Napolitano was reeling from the shock of the disclosure.

After the agents left, Napolitano called Ruggiero and some others. A surveillance photo shows all of them meeting outside the lounge for a quick conference, the sense of urgency and their discomfort clearly revealed in the picture. Later, Napolitano retreated to the pigeon coop on the room roof of the building, where he often retreated to be alone and think. The surveillance camera captured him looking grim, his brow furrowed with worry lines. Once the Mafia bosses learned of how he had been hoodwinked so effectively by Pistone, his future in the Mob—indeed, his very life—would be on the line.

■ ■ ■

The Mafia leadership would hold Napolitano accountable for the way he allowed his crew to be infiltrated by the FBI. But during this period many other Mob bosses were also being indiscreet, lulled into a false sense of security when they met and talked.

FBI surveillance technology had advanced greatly over the years, and the agents who planted bugging devices and cameras were experts at what they did. Once the agents found out where mobsters liked to eat and talk, it was just a matter of time before listening devices were planted in those locations.

Such was the case one day in December 1982, when a team of FBI agents made a surreptitious entry before dawn at the Casa Storta Restaurant at **186–88 Twenty-First Street** in the Bensonhurst section of Brooklyn. The bureau had picked up firm intelligence that a top Colombo crime-family captain named Gennaro Langella would be holding court there that day, taking his meals at a rear table. The bug was positioned in an area nearby so that it would pick up Langella's conversations and relay them to an FBI listening post a few blocks away.

The fruits of the Casa Storta bug were delicious for the FBI. Conversations at the restaurant revealed that a Colombo soldier named Ralph Scopo was a union official with the concrete workers council. Scopo and Langella talked about the way the Mob had created a so-called "concrete club," in which large construction contracts over $2 million were fixed in a cartel-like arrangement. The Mob got a cut of the contracts, with payments going to four of the five Mafia families.

The Casa Storta wasn't the only location bugged by the FBI at this time. A bug was also planted in the home of Gambino boss Paul Castellano, which not only revealed specific details of crimes, but also the salacious side of the crime boss's life. The device picked up firm indications—no pun intended—that he was having an affair at home with his Colombian maid. He boasted of his sexual prowess that was further enhanced by a penile implant (see chapter 20).

Another bug was placed in the Palma Boys Social Club, and picked up the conversations of Anthony Salerno, the street boss of the Genovese family (see chapter 12). A roving bug was installed by investigators of the New York State Organized Crime Task Force in the Jaguar of Anthony "Tony Ducks" Corallo, picking up Corallo's discussion of Mafia business as he was chauffeured around by his driver, Salvatore Avellino.

All of the surveillance bugs provided the FBI with hundreds of hours of conversations, which, over time would mesh into a massive web of evidence. This led to the momentous 1986 federal trial against the Mafia Commission, and the imprisonment of the old guard leadership of four of the five crime families.

■ ■ ■

While the FBI and NYPD, as well as other law enforcement agencies, worked together to go after the Mob, there were a few cops who crossed the line, selling their souls to the Mafia in quest of a quick buck. Among them were Louis Eppolito and Stephen Caracappa, who became known as the "Mafia Cops." Both men had become highly regarded NYPD detectives, working primarily out of Brooklyn precincts and the major case squad. Eppolito was the son of Gambino soldier Ralph Eppolito, and had a few other relatives who were members of the Mob, or associates. Caracappa had a family history that was unremarkable. The detectives began to work together, and around 1985, began secretly working for the Lucchese crime family, receiving up to $75,000 from acting family boss Anthony Casso, through businessman Burton Kaplan, who agreed to act as intermediary.

Former NYPD detective Stephen Caracappa, one of the two deadly "Mafia Cops" who helped kill for the Lucchese crime family, shown leaving Brooklyn federal court. *NEWSDAY* LLC, 2006

Former NYPD detective Louis Eppolito, the other half of the deadly duo known as the "Mafia Cops," who killed for the Mob. *NEWSDAY* LLC, 2006

As would later be revealed in their federal racketeering trial, Eppolito and Caracappa not only took the payoffs in exchange for information, but also did murders for the Mob.

One of the first unfortunate souls to be killed by Eppolito and Caracappa was jeweler Israel Greenwald. A devout Jew who was married and had two daughters, Greenwald seemed at first to be an unlikely target for the Mafia. He made frequent trips to Europe for business. It was prior to one such trip in 1985 that another jeweler asked Greenwald to deposit a US T-bill bond overseas. The bond had been stolen—apparently unbeknownst to Greenwald—and after it was cashed in London, the FBI got wind of it and demanded to know how he had come to possess it.

Greenwald cooperated with the FBI and gave the agent the name of the jeweler who had asked him to deposit the T-bill. Greenwald said the jeweler had told him the T-bill was an asset someone was trying to hide in a divorce case—a lie, as it turned out. However, Greenwald's friend tipped off the men behind the stolen bond scam, one of whom happened to be Burton Kaplan. Fearful that he would be arrested, Kaplan used his underworld contacts to get in touch with Eppolito and Caracappa, who agreed to take care of the unsuspecting Greenwald.

On February 10, 1986, Greenwald was pulled over by Eppolito and Caracappa as he drove in Brooklyn. The detectives told the jeweler that he had been identified as a motorist involved in a hit-and-run, and that he had to go to the precinct to clear up the matter. Greenwald agreed to go. Eppolito and Caracappa would use this traffic-stop ruse more than once in their murderous career.

Instead of taking Greenwald to the station house, the two cops took him to a garage at **2232 Nostrand Avenue,** which consisted of a number of parking sheds. Caracappa and another Mob associate then took Greenwald into the garage, where he was bound and shot twice in the head. Greenwald was wearing his yarmulke when he died. The Mob associate who helped the detectives and did the shooting, Frank Santoro, then coerced the man who worked at the garage to dig a grave and bury Greenwald, throwing some lime into the pit to speed up decomposition. Greenwald's body would remain buried for nearly twenty years, until investigators finally got a firm lead and unearthed his remains as part of the federal investigation of Eppolito and Caracappa.

Brooklyn became the favored hunting ground for the Mafia Cops. After killing Greenwald, they targeted a number of other people, including one innocent man who was murdered in a case of mistaken identity. The tragic mix-up came with the Christmas Day 1986 murder of twenty-six-year-old Nicholas Guido, who had the additional misfortune of having the same name as a reputed Gambino crime-family associate. Anthony Casso, acting Lucchese boss, wanted the Mob-linked

"Nicholas Guido" hit after Guido allegedly took part in the October 1986 attempt to murder Casso, and the contract went out to the Mafia Cops to get information about the victim's home address. Then, in a colossal blunder, the two corrupt detectives did a records check and identified the wrong Nicholas Guido as the target, passing along the information to the Mob hit team. The slayers stalked the innocent Guido and killed him as he got into his car by his house on **Seventeenth Street,** in the Windsor Terrace section of Brooklyn.

Another Brooklyn murder done by the Mafia Cops was that of Gambino captain Edward Lino, whose cardinal sin had been his involvement in the planning of the murder of Paul Castellano, whom Casso had viewed as a friend. What seemed to push Casso personally over the edge was when he learned that Lino had been involved in the earlier plot to kill him. The night of November 6, 1990, Caracappa and Eppolito followed Lino as he drove in his Mercedes from his home on Long Island into Brooklyn. Once again using the ruse of a traffic stop, the Mafia Cops pulled Lino over and had him drive off the **Belt Parkway Service Road, at a spot close to Abraham Lincoln High School.** The cops then shot Lino in the head.

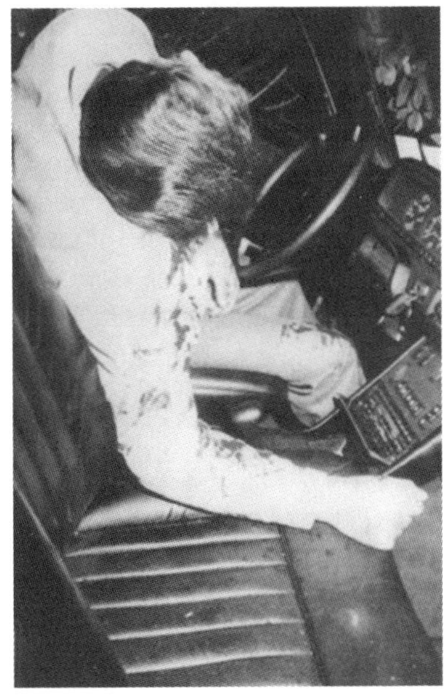

Gambino crime-family captain Edward Lino was gunned down as he drove in his car in Brooklyn by Mafia Cops Louis Eppolito and Stephen Caracappa, the night of November 6, 1990.
PHOTO COURTESY US ATTORNEY'S OFFICE, EASTERN DISTRICT

Yet another target of the Mafia Cops in Brooklyn was Bruno Facciolo of the Lucchese family. Facciolo's murder stemmed from out-of-control Mob paranoia, when the then acting head of the Lucchese clan, Vic Amuso, suspected Facciolo of being an informant, even though there was no evidence to support this suspicion.

In August 1990, after Carracapa and Eppolito tipped off Caso that Facciolo might be an informant, some Lucchese mobsters lured Facciolo to a Brooklyn auto body shop and overpowered the doomed mafioso as he tried to escape. Facciolo was shot and stabbed to death after his assailants denied him the opportunity to call his daughter to say goodbye. Facciolo's body was found in the trunk of a car in Brooklyn. He had a dead canary in his mouth, a sign that he was an informant.

Facciolo may not have been an informant, but John "Otto" Heidel certainly was. Allied with a bunch of burglars known as the Bypass Gang, because of the way they got around alarm systems, Heidel was able to provide the FBI and the NYPD with information about the gang's activity. Heidel's problem was that Burton Kaplan, the businessman who served as the Mob's point of contact with the Mafia Cops, began to suspect that Heidel was an informant. Kaplan asked his police contacts about Heidel, and they said that the young burglar had been working for the government as a snitch. Anthony "Gaspipe" Casso put out a contract on Heidel, and on October 8, 1987, he was dead. Heidel had tried to flee from his gun-wielding assailants, running north in a panic on **Thirty-Fifth Street, at Avenue U.** It was no use, as Heidel, wounded with a couple of shots in his buttocks and back, was caught and shot numerous times. The killer shot was a final round directly into his chest.

■ ■ ■

Around the same time that Eppolito and Caracappa were launching their new careers as hit men, John Gotti was coming to the fore as the new power of the Gambino family after having engineered the assassination of Castellano. But while Gotti had intimidated his own crime-family members into accepting him, there were others in the Mafia world who never forgave him for the way he had killed off Castellano.

On April 13, 1986, Gotti had planned to visit some of his crime-family members at the Veterans and Friends Social Club at **1468 Eighty-Sixth Street,** Bensonhurst, Brooklyn. The club was a base of operations for the aging but powerful captain, Jimmy Failla, who held sway in the trash-hauling industry rackets. Failla had been close with Castellano, and his allegiance to the Gotti regime would be crucial.

But Gotti never made the trip to Failla's club. Gotti's change of plans meant that his underboss Frank DeCicco would have to drive away alone from the club, and meet the crime boss in Manhattan. DeCicco never got in the car. A remote-controlled bomb exploded as DeCicco stood by his car, killing him instantly. The explosion made a two-foot-wide crater in the street and shook nearby buildings. Another mobster who was talking with DeCicco was seriously hurt, while a woman pedestrian was slightly injured. Bombings were rare in the Mafia, although they had been done by the old Black Hand extortionists in the early part of the twentieth century. The bombing was believed by many investigators to have been meant for Gotti, although it was never proven who had carried out the plot.

About a year later, FBI agents warned Gotti that they had picked up credible intelligence that the Genovese crime family, in the person of Vincent Gigante, had wanted him dead. Warned that his life was in danger, Gotti changed his driving and travel habits, even resorting to having his car frequently inspected for explosive devices.

■ ■ ■

The Mafia hadn't seen an old-fashioned war since the days when the Gallo brothers battled with crime boss Joseph Profaci in the 1960s. Mob hits since then had been either in retribution for some transgression, like stealing money from the rackets, or something more trivial, like an insult—such as the time John J. Gotti had Louis DiBono killed for not showing up to meetings. But beginning in 1991 and continuing until mid-1993, Brooklyn was rocked by a bloody battle for control of the Colombo crime family. On the one side were those loyal to imprisoned boss Carmine Persico, who, although incarcerated after his conviction in the Commission case, still ruled the family through intermediaries that visited him in prison. Opposing Persico was a smaller faction led by Victor Orena, a Long Island gangster who had actually been anointed by Persico as the acting street boss of the family.

Mafia bosses who were in prison needed acting bosses to handle things for them on the street. But the sudden authority vested in the acting bosses, along with the money they handled from the rackets, sometimes went to their heads. "Once Orena got the taste of honey, he not only took things over, he stopped the flow of tribute to the Persico faction," one investigator told a reporter.

Persico put out a directive from prison: Kill Orena. But a June 1991 attempt to hit Orena failed when he spotted the gunmen near his Long Island home and fled. Both factions tried to negotiate a truce, but couldn't, and the bullets started flying. From late 1991 through October 1993, the Colombo family war roiled Brooklyn, leaving at least twelve men dead and seven people wounded, including some innocent bystanders. One man killed turned out to be a member of the Genovese crime family, who had the misfortune of going into a social club targeted by Persico's men.

In the beginning the war went badly for Persico's side. On November 18, 1991, Persico captain Gregory Scarpa Sr. was shot by armed men in a car who had tailed him as he drove with some associates. The two groups engaged in a gun battle, but no one was hurt. Six days later on November 25, Henry Smurra, a Persico loan shark, was shot dead as he sat in his car in **Sheepshead Bay,** outside a donut shop. Then on December 5, 1991, in another case of errant gunfire, an elderly Colombo crime-family member visiting the Belvedere Socal Athletic Association Club at **985 Sixty-Third Street** in Bensonhurst was killed by gunfire as he played cards. Seventy-nine-year-old Rosario Nastasi was a bookmaker who was part of the Persico wing of the crime family. Joel Cacace, a fifty-one-year-old Colombo captain, fared a bit better after he was shot in front of the Party Room Social Club at **2112 East Fourteenth Street** in the Sheepshead Bay section on February 26, 1992. Cacace was shot at at least fourteen times and hit once in a fusillade fired from a station wagon. Cacace fired back and later recovered from his wounds after undergoing surgery.

All of the shoot-outs forced Brooklyn district attorney Charles J. Hynes, whose job it was to help protect the citizens of the borough, to convene a special grand jury investigation in late 1991 to compel the mobsters to put down their weapons. For a few weeks things quieted down. But then on January 7, 1992, Nicholas Grancio, a captain in the Colombo family, and part of the Orena faction, was shot in the head and killed as he sat in a car at the intersection of **McDonald Avenue and Avenue U** in the Gravesend section. Clearly, sitting in a car was proving to be risky business for anybody in the Colombo clan.

Hynes pressed his investigation, and got federal and state officials to agree to go after Colombo family rackets and to ramp up surveillance of the other crime families in an effort to get the Mob to pressure the Colombo group. Yet, the killings and shootings continued. In one of the biggest incidents of the entire war, Scarpa himself was ambushed for the second time early on December 29, 1992. Scarpa had left his home near Twelfth Avenue in Brooklyn and was a passenger in the front seat of a car that was driven to **1358 Eightieth Street,** near Thirteenth Avenue. A group of gunmen attacked, firing so many shots at Scarpa's vehicle that it was riddled with holes, its rear window blown out.

Police later found at least twenty-five shell casings for bullets from nine-millimeter and .25 caliber weapons. With that much firepower, clearly the assailants wanted to be sure they didn't blow their chance for a killing. But while Scarpa was shot in the face and lost his left eye, he survived the attack, and got himself to a nearby hospital.

Federal officials finally brought indictments against some of the Colombo family leaders in May 1993, and by then, the war had petered out. It had been a nonsensical battle, taking lives and bringing intense law enforcement scrutiny.

As a postscript, Scarpa died in 1993 while under indictment for murder and racketeering. He had contracted AIDS from a blood transfusion and suffered for years, winning over $150,000 in a legal settlement over the fatal contamination. It was later revealed that Scarpa had for years worked as an informant for the FBI. The relationship the mobster had with his FBI handler, Special Agent R. Lindley DeVeccio, caused the G-man problems, and placed him under suspicion that he had been working with Scarpa by providing him information used to set up homicides. DeVeccio was later cleared in an internal investigation. The Brooklyn district attorney's office attempted to prosecute DeVeccio for complicity in some Mob murders, but the case fell apart and was dismissed in November 2007.

While the Colombo war was over in 1993, the crime family still surfaced in connection with the shocking slaying of a police officer on August 26, 1997. Officer Ralph C. Dols, a twenty-eight-year-old New York housing cop, was gunned down execution-style after returning from work to his home in Sheepshead Bay. Dols was wounded three times in the stomach and twice in the arm before he had time to get out from behind the wheel. Sadly, he died on the operating table at Coney Island Hospital.

Investigators soon learned that Dols's wife, Kim T. Kennaugh, had an interesting marital pedigree that had earned her the sobriquet "Black Widow." Her first husband had been murdered ten years earlier as he sat in his parked car in South Brooklyn. Kennaugh later lived with Joel Cacace, the Colombo crime-family captain who had been wounded during the bloody war. She then left Cacace and took up with Dols, marrying him in 1995 and having his daughter about three months before the shooting. It would take a decade before federal investigators developed evidence that Dols may have been killed on orders from the Mob. Turncoats from the Colombo family alleged that Cacace had apparently been angry that Dols had married his old girlfriend, and had ordered the cop's killing in retribution. Cacace would later be cleared of that charge, as would Thomas "Tommy Shots" Gioeli and alleged hit man Dino Saracino.

■ ■ ■

With the end of the Colombo war, the only Mob killings New York City would see in the coming years were solitary acts of violence, either done in fits of anger, or as a way of enforcing discipline. Take the case of Randolph Pizzolo, a Mob wannabe, who had his own anger management issues. Pizzolo had tried to ingratiate himself with members of the Bonanno crime family as a way of seeking induction into the borgata. But Pizzolo had a way of irritating people, becoming obnoxious in nightclubs and loose with his mouth when talking about the Bonanno family. In a visit to one Queens bar, Pizzolo bragged that he was tougher than anyone in the Bonanno group, and was the only one who knew how to kill. It's also said that he alienated Vincent "Vinny Gorgeous" Basciano, an up-and-coming captain in the Bonanno family.

On the night of November 30, 2004, Pizzolo drove his BMW to **Monitor Street,** an industrial road in the Greenpoint section of Brooklyn. The street was adjacent to the polluted Newtown Creek, which served as the dividing line between Brooklyn and Queens. Pizzolo was waiting for Ace Aiello, another

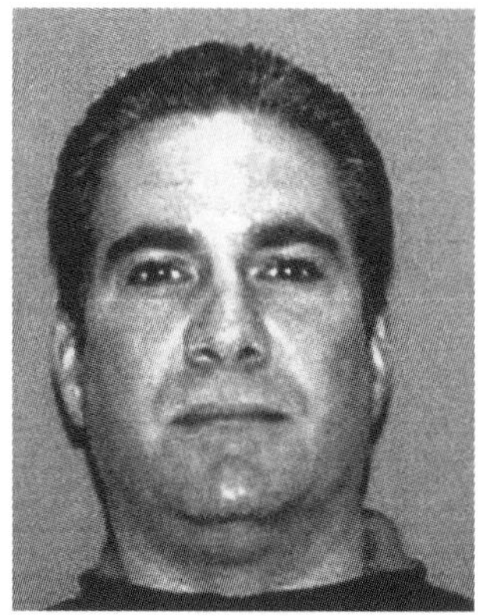

Bonanno crime-family associate Randolph Pizzolo aspired to become a member of the crime family, but irritated a lot of gangsters with his brash and impulsive behavior. PHOTO COURTESY US ATTORNEY'S OFFICE, EASTERN DISTRICT

Bonanno family member, whose neck seemed to merge with his head. Aiello soon drove up in another vehicle, and Pizzolo walked around the front of his car and extended his hand to greet him. Instead of reciprocating with a handshake, Aiello pushed Pizzolo away, pulled out a Luger, and started shooting.

A worker at a nearby lumberyard found Pizzolo's body early the next morning at the edge of Monitor Street, the motor of his BMW still running. The dead man still had over $1,000 cash in his pocket, proving that the slaying was clearly not a robbery gone awry. In 2008 Aiello would plead guilty to charges stemming from the killing, and in 2011, a federal jury would convict Vincent Basciano of plotting to kill Pizzolo. He escaped the federal death penalty but was sentenced to life in prison, which he was already serving for an earlier conviction.

The body of Bonanno crime-family associate Randy Pizzolo was found near his still-running BMW on Monitor Street in Brooklyn, the morning of December 1, 2004. PHOTO COURTESY US ATTORNEY'S OFFICE, EASTERN DISTRICT

CHAPTER SEVENTEEN

A BOROUGH TO DIE FOR

The Bronx is the smallest borough of the five that make up New York City, but at least in the formative days of the Mafia, it loomed large. Located north and slightly east of Manhattan, the Bronx was for a long time a quiet backwater of the city, with miles of woodlands and open spaces. Its beaches and waterfront communities on the East River and Long Island Sound evolved as vacation and resort areas in the early twentieth century. The land attracted homeowners who needed space for what was considered elaborate residences.

One of those who called the Bronx home was Gaetano Reina, a wealthy ice merchant. In the days before electric home refrigerators were widely available, icemen would roam the city to sell ice to residential and commercial properties. Ice was a lucrative business and organized along cartel lines, with territories divided up among the more powerful, and prices set by agreement. Reina played a pivotal role in that cartel, a position that was enhanced by his being part of the Mafia operation of Joseph Masseria, the man considered to be the top Mob boss in New York, at least in 1930.

But as was shown in detail earlier in this book, Masseria's heavy-handed tactics and greed alienated a number of his subordinates, including Charles Luciano. Instead of keeping his men happy, Masseria treated them with treachery. Apparently, Masseria wanted Reina to give up some of his ice-racket profits.

Reina's home was at **3183 Rochambeau Avenue,** where he lived with his wife and children. However, Reina also had a relationship with a widow at an apartment at **1521 Sheridan Avenue,** some three and a half miles away from his official home. The Sheridan Avenue apartment was listed under the names "Mr. and Mrs. James Ennis."

The evening of February 26, 1930, Reina left the Sheridan Avenue apartment house and was hit with ten slugs from a shotgun wielded by one of two men who accosted him in front of the building. Police found the weapon under a parked car. Had he been able to react more quickly, Reina might have been able to defend himself. Police found a legal handgun on Reina, along with $804 in cash.

Reina's death is considered the first major killing in what became known as the Castellammarese War, the battle among the Mob bosses that ultimately led to Masseria's own demise. Like many of the murders in this fight, there was all sorts of double-crossing going on. John Pinzolo, an associate of Masseria's, took over command of Reina's group, but that only added to the intrigue and bloodletting. Pinzolo was himself shot dead in his Manhattan office at 1487 Broadway.

The killings that erupted during the fabled Castellammarese War following Reina's murder eventually led to Masseria being killed in the famous restaurant assassination on April 15, 1931, in Coney Island (see chapter 15). With Masseria out of the way, the younger members of the Mafia who had chafed under his rule pledged their allegiance to Salvatore Maranzano, the more-erudite boss who saw the Mob as some kind of extension of the old Roman Empire in terms of the way things were to be organized, with himself as a "Little Caesar."

To solidify his position and set the rules, Maranzano called a historic meeting in the Bronx at a large banquet hall. The location, according to informant Joseph Valachi, was on Washington Avenue. Valachi didn't describe an exact address, but later research seemed to put the hall at the intersection of **187th Street and Washington.** The setting took on the air of a religious event, with saintly pictures on the walls and a large crucifix over the platform where Maranzano spoke, recalled Valachi.

The meeting was a pivotal one in the history of the American Mafia. Maranzano said that the war had to be forgotten, and that those who had lost friends in the battle had to forgive and move forward. To do otherwise could lead to fatal consequences. Maranzano then anointed himself the top boss, the boss of all bosses, or *capo di tutti i capi*. The underworld was to be divided up into five borgatas, or families, led by men Maranzano had hand-picked: Charles Luciano, Gaetano "Tom" Gagliano, Vincent Mangano, and Joseph Bonanno. Maranzano would be the fifth family boss. Each of the bosses were to work through underbosses and lieutenants. Chosen as underboss for Luciano was Vito Genovese, Mangano was backed by Albert Anastasia of Brooklyn, while Gagliano had as his underboss Thomas Lucchese.

The banquet hall conclave is remembered in Mob history as the place where the basic structure and lineage of the New York Mafia's Five Families was set. As the years passed, the names Genovese, Bonanno, and Lucchese stuck with those families, while the Mangano family became known as the Gambino clan. While Philadelphia has its Independence Hall as a place to commemorate the founding of the United States, the old hall where the modern New York Mob was born has—as far as anyone can tell—disappeared. The area of the Bronx is very near the old Italian neighborhood of **Arthur Avenue,** which is still a tourist mecca noted for its good cuisine. But the neighborhood has gone through a great deal of change and renewal, which means that the old hall has been lost to history.

Maranzano didn't live long enough to see his great plan for the Mafia come to fruition. On September 10, 1931, as described in chapter 8, Maranzano was himself assassinated in his Manhattan office by four gunmen. The date of his death is significant because it has been described as the beginning of a great purge with the Mafia known as "The Night of the Sicilian Vespers." Mob folklore has it that as many as ninety gangsters who were allied with Maranzano were killed in a coordinated series of murders that supposedly took place in several American cities in the weeks following his death. Assiduous research by crime historians has shown the Vespers story to be just that—a tall tale.

Less than a handful of murders in which the victims were connected to Maranzano could be found. However, one of them happened in the Bronx, not far from where Maranzano had his big banquet hall meeting. On September 10, 1931, the same day Maranzano died, one James Lepore took his two daughters—ages four and six—to a barbershop at **2400 Arthur Avenue** for haircuts. The shop wasn't very busy, and Lepore, who had a reputation as a Mob "muscle man," was standing in the doorway at about 5:45 p.m. after chatting with two of the barbers. Lepore's role with the Mob was what was known as the "grape racket," likely referring to an extortion scheme among grape sellers centered in the Webster Avenue area of the Bronx. The weather had been unusually hot, and Lepore was mopping his face with a handkerchief when witnesses remembered hearing several shots and then the sound of a car racing away. In the doorway Lepore lay dead. His daughters were unharmed.

Prosecutors in the Bronx couldn't make any headway in talking with the barbers who were present in the shop when Lepore was killed. To force them to testify, the Bronx prosecutors charged the recalcitrant witnesses with conspiracy. Among those indicted was the barbershop proprietor, Salvatore Caruso. Nevertheless, the Lepore murder was never solved. The old barbershop is now a popular Italian pastry store. In his talks with the government many years later, Joseph Valachi related how Vito Genovese explained the simple truth behind Lepore's murder: He had been a Maranzano loyalist, and hence, had to die.

■ ■ ■

If James Lepore was murdered because he backed the wrong Mafia boss, the motive for the slaying more than sixty-five years later of Bonanno crime-family captain, Gerlando "George from Canada" Sciascia, was a bit more complicated. Sciascia was part of a group of Canadian gangsters who traveled between

Bonanno crime-family captain Gerlando "George from Canada" Sciascia was part of a group of Canadian mobsters aligned with the New York Mafia. PHOTO COURTESY US ATTORNEY'S OFFICE, EASTERN DISTRICT

Montreal and New York in a long-running criminal career. A handsome, fair-haired man, Sciascia was involved in some pretty ugly Mafia business. In May 1981, Sciascia was one of three men hiding in the closet of a Brooklyn social club who suddenly came out and ambushed the three Bonanno captains who were locked in a bitter dispute for control of the crime family. Sciascia's job in the murder was to run his fingers through his hair, the signal for the other gunmen to jump out of the closet and start shooting.

About a year after the murder of the three captains, Sciascia was arrested in a large Mafia drug case that had ensnared Gene Gotti, the brother of the future Gambino boss John Gotti, and John Carneglia. But after a long trial, mistrial, and subsequent second mistrial, Sciascia was acquitted. However, Gene Gotti and Carneglia were convicted and given fifty-year prison sentences.

Free from the heroin case, Sciascia was deported back to Canada, but was able to legally return to the United States in 1997, at which time he promptly started overseeing the illegal activities of the Canadian wing of the Bonanno family. Sciascia's status put him in constant contact with Bonanno boss Joseph Massino, and for a while the two had a good relationship. But not long after Sciascia returned to the United States, he started to have problems with Massino. The common wisdom in the Mob was that Sciascia was angering Massino by badmouthing crime captain Anthony Graziano, calling him an unreliable drug abuser. "Every time I see this guy he is stoned," Sciascia once said. Sciascia also got under the skin of other Bonanno members by threatening them, and after a while, Massino decided that Sciascia had to be killed.

But the real reason may have been different than the conventional stories that had been floating around the Mob about Sciascia's demise. In 2011 Massino, who by then had become a federal witness, testified that he had ordered Sciascia killed because he had once killed the son of a made Mafia member. Massino wasn't specific about who Sciascia killed, but he did relate how he had farmed out the murder of the Canadian to a crew of Bonanno crime-family members in the Bronx. Massino wanted Sciascia killed in such a way that it would appear the murder took place over a drug deal. Sciascia's body was to be dumped in the street.

On March 18, 1999, police found Sciascia's body on **Boller Avenue** in the Eastchester section of the Bronx, a backwater of single-family homes. He had been shot numerous times and his face was bloodied. As a way of steering suspicion away from the Bonanno family, Massino at the time ordered that his high-ranking members show up at the wake for Sciascia. That ruse didn't fool some of Sciascia's Canadian associates, who immediately suspected that Massino and company were involved. It would take law enforcement several more years to learn the truth.

Gerlando Sciascia was shot dead in the Bronx on orders from Bonanno crime-family boss Joseph Massino around March 18, 1999. PHOTO COURTESY US ATTORNEY'S OFFICE, EASTERN DISTRICT

Another Bonanno crime-family murder took place in February 2001 in the quiet neighborhood of Throggs Neck. The reasons were more personal. The local crime-family captain who held sway in the area was Vincent "Vinny Gorgeous" Basciano, who got his name from a beauty salon he once owned, called "Hello Gorgeous," and his own good looks.

With his pompadour hair and his perpetual tan, Basciano had a presence about him that many adored. He was also hot-tempered and had a reputation for violence.

Sometime in early 2001, informants said Basciano got wind of a threat made by a Mob associate who allegedly wanted to kidnap one of the Vinny Gorgeous's four sons. The idea was said to have been the brainchild of Frank Santoro, a Throggs Neck man who was constantly getting into legal trouble and had developed a nasty drug habit.

Vincent "Vinny Gorgeous" Basciano was an ambitious Bonanno crime-family captain whose base of operations was in the area of East Tremont Avenue in the Bronx. PHOTO COURTESY US ATTORNEY'S OFFICE, EASTERN DISTRICT

On February 15, 2001, Santoro decided to take his pet Doberman pinscher for a walk around the neighborhood prior to having dinner with his wife and son. Santoro swung around the neighborhood with the dog and was yards from his front door at **4212 Throggs Neck Expressway** when he was cut down by shotgun blasts. Santoro never had a chance. One blast cleaved the top of his skull, allowing his brain to be partially exposed. He was found by his wife, Maria, in a small verge by the side of the road, his eyes staring wide open into space and bits of his brain tissue on the ground.

At a later federal trial, government witnesses described how Basciano, his close associate Dominick Cicale, and others had stalked Santoro during that final perambulation with his dog. In 2006 a jury convicted Basciano of engineering the murder of Santoro, something he continued to deny. Basciano was sentenced to life in prison.

■ ■ ■

Murder is the way the Mafia polices its ranks. But shakedowns and other rackets are the way it makes its money. The Gambino family, as well as any of the other Mafia groups in New York, knew how to try and squeeze businesses for cash. The trick was for the Mob to acquire a secret interest in a company, usually through extortion, and then take out money through no-show jobs, bankruptcy bust-outs, or other methods.

In March 2005, the FBI unveiled one of its boldest undercover operations into La Cosa Nostra since agent Joseph Pistone had penetrated the Bonanno family two decades earlier. For more than two years, FBI agent Joaquin "Jack" Garcia, a big man who looked the part of a head-breaking gangster, wormed his way undercover to get close to some of the leaders of the Gambino crime family. Since John Gotti had died and the rest of his relatives were neutralized, power in the Gambino family had devolved to acting street boss Arnold Squitieri and another old captain.

Posing as "Jack Falcone," Garcia got to know the owner of a now-defunct strip club at **4139 Boston Post Road** in the Bronx, who in turn introduced him to Gregory DePalma, a captain in the Gambino family who Garcia had learned had a secret interest in the business. DePalma took a liking to Garcia, who provided him and other mafiosi with flat-screen television sets, jewelry, and other items that were allegedly stolen, but were provided to the undercover agent by the FBI. DePalma, known for his hair-trigger temper, was the kind of mobster who loved consorting with big-name celebrities. He had spent time with Frank Sinatra and baseball legend Willie Mays, and had gone on golf outings with comedian Dean Martin.

Gambino crime-family captain Gregory DePalma (left) with the late singer Frank Sinatra in a detail from a larger photograph taken at the Westchester Premier Theater and used by federal prosecutors during a trial. FEDERAL BUREAU OF INVESTIGATION

DePalma was also a crafty mobster. During the course of many months, Garcia discovered that DePalma held Mob meetings at the hospital bedside of his comatose son, Craig, who had been in a vegetative state since a suicide attempt in 2002. The son had attempted to hang himself after testifying in a Mob trial. DePalma spent most of his time eating, taking meetings for breakfast, lunch, and dinner at various restaurants in Westchester County, before ending up with Garcia in the Bronx at **City Island,** a place known for its seafood. With so much eating, Garcia gained eighty pounds during the investigation.

Strip clubs are easy marks for gangsters, and the club in the Bronx made a nice shakedown target. While the Gambino family had its hooks into the strip club, a group of Albanian gangsters tried to get a piece of the action as well. To fend off the Albanians, the club paid a Gambino-family soldier $5,000 a month in protection money, according to a former law enforcement official. DePalma, who years earlier had a secret interest in the club, reclaimed it as his territory, and had Garcia working as a part owner, the former official said.

With Garcia secretly tape-recording his interactions with DePalma and acting family boss Arnold Squitieri, the result was predictable. DePalma, Squitieri, and several other reputed members and associates of the Gambino family were indicted on racketeering charges in 2005. Among the allegations were that

DePalma and others extorted the owners of Bronx nightclubs, including the strip club. Prosecutors charged that the Gambino family pulled in over $30 million from its various shakedowns and other rackets.

Squitieri pled guilty in April 2006 to extorting construction companies, but DePalma elected to go to trial, and lost. When it came time for sentencing, a then-ailing DePalma asked the judge for lenciency by saying "Give me one more shot." The court wasn't swayed, and gave DePalma a twelve-year sentence. While in prison DePalma's health deteriorated further, and in late 2009, he died in a federal prison hospital at the age of seventy-seven. His son died after eight years in a coma in 2012, at the age of forty-four.

Squitieri was released from prison in 2012. One thing he certainly wasn't doing was watching the hot flat-screen television set he had received from Garcia. It seems that early in the investigation Squitieri had watched an episode of *The Sopranos* on HBO, which featured a gangster who got in trouble when it was discovered that he had been using a stolen television. Unnerved by the plotline, Squitieri got rid of the set. Of course, by then the FBI had so much other evidence against him that it didn't matter.

CHAPTER EIGHTEEN

A QUIET PLACE TO DINE, DRINK, AND DIE

Queens is the largest borough in New York City, with about 120 square miles, and it has some of the largest expanses of green space in the metropolis. Among the many parks in the borough is Juniper Valley Park, a fifty-five-acre expanse of athletic fields and lawns adjacent to the community of Middle Village. This park has the strangest history of any of the city's recreational spaces, thanks to the finagling of mobster Arnold Rothstein.

Gangster and gambler Arnold Rothstein was behind a strange development of flimsy homes in the old Juniper Swamp area of Queens. The homes are shown here being torn down in the 1930s. PHOTO COURTESY ROBERT F. HOLDEN

Back in the 1920s, when he was in his heyday as one of the great minds of organized crime, Rothstein acquired a large section of what was known as the Juniper Swamp, a soggy area of peat about three blocks from the Lutheran Cemetery at **Juniper Avenue.** Rothstein, who took greater interest in real estate later in his life, constructed a group of buildings that comprised 143 houses in two large clusters, which appeared to resemble apartment buildings.

But after Rothstein was gunned down in Manhattan in 1928, officials discovered that the structures were uninhabitable and cheaply made. The development—if it could be called that—had no streets connecting it to the nearby community, although sewer lines had been laid. In 1929, Fiorello H. LaGuardia, the Republican fusion candidate for mayor, made what became known as the "phantom village" an election issue. LaGuardia charged that Rothstein never intended the flimsy buildings to be inhabited, and put together the project because it was close to property owned by some Queens and Tammany Hall politicians. LaGuardia suspected that Rothstein's plan was to have the city condemn the property at some point and take the land by the process of eminent domain for parks or some other public purpose. The result would be a nice payment of city money to Rothstein and his cronies, LaGuardia suspected.

"There is more to the Rothstein case than 'Who shot Rothstein?'" said LaGuardia.

LaGuardia didn't win the 1929 election, losing to the flamboyant incumbent Democrat Jimmy Walker. In the 1930s, New York City acquired the acreage from Rothstein's estate for about $400,000, at the cost of $5,700 an acre—considered a bargain, because some realtors said it was worth $10,000 an acre. The Rothstein buildings were torn down, and eventually the parkland was developed into an expanse of athletic facilities, including tennis courts, a wading pool, basketball courts, bocce courts, and soccer and

Juniper Valley Park in Queens, site of Arnold Rothstein's old "phantom village." AUTHOR'S COLLECTION

baseball fields. Juniper Valley is considered by the city to be one of Queens' most beloved parks, and is located at **Juniper Boulevard,** between **Lutheran Avenue, Seventy-First Street, and Dry Harbor Road.**

Nothing is left of the old Rothstein phantom village, but for those looking for a tangible piece of old history, the Pullis Farm Cemetery, dating back to the 1840s, still remains in the park, at **81st Street and Juniper Boulevard North.** The city also got another benefit from the Rothstein deal: The extensive deposits of peat in the ground, estimated to be worth $500,000, were dug up and reportedly used in landscape cultivation.

■ ■ ■

Anthony Carfano knew everybody who mattered in the heyday of the Mafia. A stocky man who earned his stripes in the Mob as an enforcer in Brooklyn, Carfano worked under the likes of Frankie Yale and later, in Chicago, Al Capone. Carfano—known by the nickname "Little Augie Pisano" among his Mob associates, and affectionately as "Gussie" among his grandchildren—worked for Capone as a salesman, but was essentially nothing more than an enforcer for the bootlegging operation in the Windy City. For his troubles early in his career on the street, Carfano got a long knife scar on his cheek, much like Capone. With all his connections, Carfano built up a web of associations among some of the Mafia's heaviest hitters, like Charles Luciano, Albert Anastasia, Frank Costello, Joe Adonis, and Michele Miranda.

Carfano seemed to be in the middle of everything that was going on in the Mob, and navigated his way among the top mafiosi of the day. Even though he was indicted three times for murder, he was able to see the charges dismissed. When Albert Anastasia was slain in a Manhattan barbershop, Carfano was questioned by police but never charged. A high roller, Carfano was always flush with cash, some of which apparently came from union welfare fund fraud, a crime for which the charges were dismissed on a technicality.

When Luciano was deported to Italy after World War II, Carfano remained close to Frank Costello, who was the presumed boss of the crime family Luciano had left behind. From Italy Luciano would contact Carfano by telephone at his Long Island home as a way of staying in touch with the Mob in New York. After Costello escaped death when he was shot at in Manhattan, he retired and left Vito Genovese with a free hand to run the crime family. With many of his friends either dead, out of the country, or in retirement, Carfano was on the outs with the new leadership of the family.

On the evening of September 25, 1959, Carfano drove in his Cadillac into Manhattan with a wad of cash and headed to the Copacabana at 10 East Sixtieth Street, the nightclub of choice for all of the wiseguys, for the simple reason that Frank Costello had been the secret owner. With its Brazilian and Latin theme, the Copa was a popular club. Its headliners over the years included Frank Sinatra, Dean Martin, Jerry Lewis, and Harry Belafonte. At the Copa on this particular night, Carfano met up with Janice Drake and her friend Madeline Unger. The trio then left for dinner at Marino's Italian Restaurant at 716 Lexington Avenue.

At some point in the evening, Carfano reportedly received a telephone call, and by about 9:30 p.m. he and Drake, who was the blonde wife of television comedian Allan Drake, and the mother of a thirteen-year-old son, drove to the Travelers Hotel near LaGuardia Airport. Carfano and Drake stayed until about 10:30 p.m., when they again got in his car and drove away. Minutes later, witnesses said they heard shots. Carfano's car was found with its engine running and its front wheel on the curb in front of **24–50 Ninety-Fourth Street.** Inside, slumped against the passenger-side front door, was Drake, with a bullet wound to the head. Carfano lay slumped to his right with his head in Drake's lap, also with a bullet wound to his head.

Initially, police believed that Carfano was killed because he had shown disrespect to Genovese, refusing to come to a meeting the Mob boss had called in the days after he became boss of the family. Investigators surmised that the killer or killers hid in the backseat of Carfano's Cadillac, something the dead man's family viewed with skepticism. About four years later, Mob turncoat Joseph Valachi reiterated that Genovese had indeed ordered Carfano killed because of his disrespect. Drake may have died as result of being in the wrong place at the wrong time, although some considered her a go-between for mobsters.

Decades later, Carfano's grandson, attorney Frank Bari, claimed in a book that he had learned his grandfather died because he had tried to open up new rackets in Florida. In planning such a move, Carfano ran afoul of two powerful Florida mobsters, Meyer Lansky and Santos Trafficante, the latter being the Mob boss of Tampa. Bari claimed, without naming a source, that Lanksy had asked Genovese to get rid of Carfano. Bari asserted that his own father, a war veteran who changed his name to Murray Zimmerman, had warned Carfano about a hit contract on his life, but that the elderly man thought he wouldn't be harmed. (Despite numerous investigations over the years, no one was ever prosecuted for Carfano's murder.)

In a city with some high-publicity Mob hits, the murders of Carfano and Drake made for big headlines. Adding to the intrigue was the reported fact that it was Drake who had dined with Anastasia the night before he was killed in 1957.

Carfano didn't have a big funeral, and for a couple of years he was buried in unconsecrated ground, because the Catholic Church wouldn't allow his burial in an archdiocese cemetery. But eventually Carfano was reportedly reinterred in the vault of the politically connected DeSalvio family, in the Old Calvary Cemetery in Queens, **49–02 Laurel Hill Boulevard.** Carfano's wife, Lillian, was a member of the DeSalvio family. The crypt is right next to the cemetery chapel.

■ ■ ■

Mobsters know that the dinner table is a good place to do business—assuming a hit doesn't turn a meal into the Mafia version of the Last Supper. But in a city packed with Italian restaurants, it was a bit surprising that some of the Mafia bigwigs from around the country chose to gather at the small and out-of-the-way La Stella Restaurant, **102–11 Queens Boulevard,** on the afternoon of September 22, 1966. Granted, the place got a two-star review from *New York Times* food critic Craig Clairborne, who liked the antipasti and all of the pasta dishes. The place had a loyal clientele, and the owners did the cooking.

Around 2:30 p.m. police burst into La Stella and broke up a luncheon for thirteen Mafia members. These weren't just any mobsters. At the table were Thomas Eboli, the acting boss of the Genovese family, Carlos Marcello of New Orleans, Mob boss Carlo Gambino, and a couple of his loyal underlings. Also present was Joseph Colombo and Michele Miranda, a powerful Genovese captain. The cops took all thirteen men into custody and put them into patrol cars for the trip to a local precinct. The raid was done so quickly that the mafiosi neglected to pay the check before they were taken away.

From the looks of things, the police seemed to think that the fact all the gangsters looked well-fed and had on $300 suits was a sign they were up to no good. Chief Inspector Sanford Garelik called the raid the "biggest since Apalachin," referring to the Mafia conclave upstate in 1957. Some of those picked up in La Stella had even attended the Apalachin meeting. At the precinct the mobsters had to strip down to their underwear and had their cash confiscated—just in case the government had any claim on it.

All of the men made bail and were asked to appear before the grand jury, at which time they invoked their Fifth Amendment rights against self-incrimination. During a break in the grand jury proceedings, Marcello led some of the others back to La Stella for a reprise of the aborted luncheon. News photographers were on hand and recorded the event. In the months that followed, the Mafia leaders and their attorneys would accuse Queens County prosecutors of carrying out the raid as an election campaign publicity stunt. Even the New York Civil Liberties

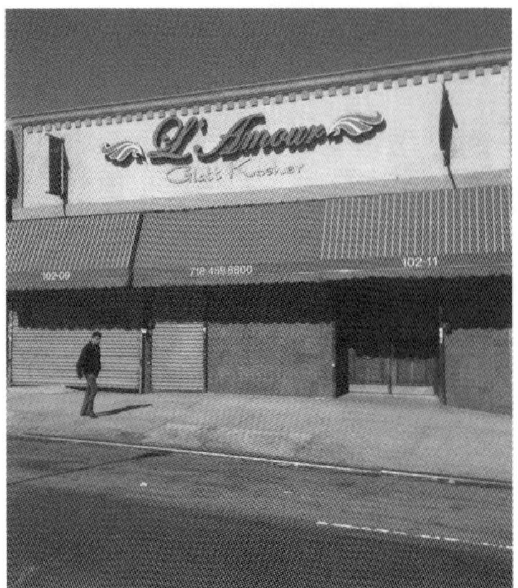

Address in Queens of the old La Stella Restaurant, scene of the September 22, 1966, luncheon attended by numerous Mafia bosses and associates. AUTHOR'S COLLECTION

Union joined the outcry, saying the arrests and treatment of the witnesses had violated their rights

So why did thirteen of the nation's top mafiosi gather at La Stella? The police believed that the meeting was called because of problems within the family of Joseph Bonanno, and a potential struggle for the control of the Genovese family after boss Vito Genovese was imprisoned on a federal heroin conviction. There was also the question of what was to be done with the leadership of the Lucchese family, because namesake Thomas Lucchese was ill with cancer. All of these were possible reasons for such a get-together. It is more likely, however, that any business these mobsters had to discuss was dealt with earlier, and elsewhere. A late lunch at a public restaurant was not the place to deal with the Mafia's matters of state. The criminal contempt cases against the men fizzled away. In a nod to ethnic change in Queens, La Stella closed in 1992. In 2014 the location was home to a Bukharian Jewish reception hall known as L'Amour Glatt Kosher, serving the large Bukharian population that has migrated to Queens since the 1980s.

■ ■ ■

Mafiosi not only came to Queens to eat but also as a place of final repose. A few miles from Queens Boulevard and the old location of La Stella is St. John Cemetery, **80–01 Metropolitan Avenue,** in Middle Village, one of the leading burial grounds of the Catholic Church in the city. Farther west is Calvary Cemetery, **49–02 Laurel Hill Boulevard, Woodside.** Calvary opened in 1848 and is the oldest and largest Catholic cemetery in the city. Both have become favorite burial places for mafiosi who leave this world either by natural causes or by the barrel of a gun. For the first *Godfather* film, director Francis Ford Coppola used Calvary for the burial scene for the main character, played by Marlon Brando. In the 1960s real Mob funerals were happening with frequency, as the old namesakes of some of the five Mafia families started to die off.

The first of the big dons to go was Joseph Profaci. Stricken with liver cancer, Profaci passed away on June 7, 1962, at a Long Island hospital. At the time of his death, Profaci had been maneuvering his way through the Gallo Wars and had survived with his crime family relatively intact and under his control. Perhaps one of the more Christian of the Mafia leaders, Profaci is said to have had a small altar in his Brooklyn home. Not skimping on things when Profaci died, his family had him interred at St. John in a family mausoleum near the Cloisters building. The name "Profaci" is engraved on the front above a bronze door.

Mafia boss Joseph Profaci, an observant Catholic, was buried in a family mausoleum at St. John Cemetery in Queens after his death in June 1962. AUTHOR'S COLLECTION

Thomas Lucchese died five years after Profaci, on July 13, 1967, after a long battle with brain cancer. But unlike some of his predecessor in Mob life, Lucchese had a low-key funeral, with only about thirty mourners showing up at the church. Carlo Gambino, whose son Thomas had married Lucchese daughter Frances, was one of those who attended the wake earlier on Long Island. The family had tried to keep details of Lucchese's burial secret, but it became apparent to police that the crime boss would be buried at the **New Calvary Cemetery,** an offshoot of the original Calvary Cemetery. In contrast to big spectacles like the funerals of Joseph Masseria or Frankie Yale, that of Lucchese only required a single flower car and nine limousines. His grave is marked by a simple upright stone on which is carved the name "Lukhese."

Imprisoned Vito Genovese was the next of the big Mob names to die. Genovese passed away on February 14, 1969, of a heart attack at the federal medical center for prisoners in Springfield, Missouri, where he had been serving a fifteen-year term for his narcotics conviction. Genovese's funeral was actually in New Jersey, where he had lived, and where his daughter Nancy taught grade school. Only about one hundred people attended the funeral service in a church that could hold about five hundred. But among those in attendance were thirty fifth-grade pupils of Genovese's daughter, who sang the responses during the mass. If there were any mobsters in the pews, the police didn't spot any. Genovese was laid to rest at St. John's in a grave with a simple stone, about three hundred yards from the mausoleum where his predecessor in crime, Charles Luciano, reposes.

■ ■ ■

Although James Plumeri ended up at St. John's, he wouldn't have the chance to die in his bed like some of his contemporaries. A trusted lieutenant to Thomas Lucchese, Plumeri had a number of businesses in the Manhattan garment district, and found himself getting in and out of trouble for most of his life, beginning as a juvenile delinquent at the age of ten. His arrest sheet showed suspicion of homicide, burglary, and income tax evasion. On Seventh Avenue, the home of the garment industry, Plumeri was known as a loan shark, gambler, and bookmaker. He seemed to regard union pension and welfare funds as a personal piggybank, and was accused of trying to get his share of kickbacks for arranging loans. Plumeri was the uncle of garment district racketeer John "Johnny Dio" Dioguardia.

Early on the morning of September 17, 1971, an off-duty NYPD narcotics officer found Plumeri facedown on a grassy area in front of **60–11 Fifty-Fourth Avenue** in the Maspeth section of Queens. Plumeri had a silk tie pulled tight around his neck and a plastic bag covering his head. When asked about Plumeri's cause of death, a police officer with a wry sense of humor remarked: "Let's say it was lack of air."

Cops figured that the dumping of Plumeri's body on a public street was a way for his killers to send a message. Despite some early speculation that Plumeri died because of some friction between Mafia families, police never came up with a good explanation, and his killing remained unsolved. Plumeri's funeral was relatively private, with a small graveside service at St. John's.

■ ■ ■

Joseph Massino was one of those Queens Mob associates who worked the area around the trucking terminals and warehouses of Maspeth, near the Newtown Creek. Although Massino made his legitimate money from a coffee and sandwich truck that catered to drivers and warehouse workers, he became an adept hijacker. In the early 1970s, Massino was becoming closely allied with Philip Rastelli and the Bonanno crime family, a group he was later destined to lead. Hijacking led to a foray into cigarette smuggling with Joseph "Doo-Doo" Pastore, a habitué of strip clubs who often met with Massino in an apartment above the latter's sandwich store, located at the time at **58–14 Fifty-Eighth Avenue,** to divide up cash and talk about business.

But Massino had grown suspicious of Pastore and wanted to get rid of his business partner. Turning to his friend Carmine "Tootie" Franzese, a member of the Colombo crime family, Massino was able to lure Pastore to the Fifty-Eighth Avenue apartment where he was killed. It was a bloody scene, and it fell to Massino's brother-in-law Salvatore Vitale to clean up the blood, which was all over the kitchen. There was one problem: Pastore's body wasn't in the apartment. It had been placed unceremoniously in a dumpster around the corner on **Rust Street,** a risky move, because detectives might have been able to trace Pastore's movements in the neighborhood back to the apartment.

Fortunately for him, Joseph Massino was leading a charmed life. Even though he had worked with Pastore, police weren't able to tie Massino to the murder of his old business associate in the early days of the investigation. The Pastore killing would be just one of several Massino committed or set up, which helped to solidify his stature in the Bonanno family and eventually pave the way to his leadership role.

■ ■ ■

Of all of the accidental deaths that ever happened in New York City, the tragic loss of twelve-year-old Frankie Gotti as he drove on a motorized bike in Howard Beach, Queens, was one that would have the most grim and far-reaching repercussions in Mafia lore. Gotti was the precocious son of Gambino mobster John Gotti, who in early 1980 was a steadily rising star in the Mob. Gotti and his wife, Victoria, had five children, and Frankie, born in October 1967, was described by his siblings as a well-adjusted, quiet, and somewhat shy boy who had no problems in school. His sister Victoria called him "Curly-Q" because of his dark curly hair.

As spring approaches, the afternoon sun is sometimes so low in the sky that drivers can find themselves facing unaccustomed glare if driving in a westerly direction. The bright sun can obscure road conditions, and care has to be taken when driving. John Favara, a rug salesman who lived in the same neighborhood as the Gotti family, wasn't too careful as he was driving through the intersection of **157th Avenue and Eighty-Seventh Street** in Howard Beach, late on the afternoon of March 18, 1980.

The Howard Beach, Queens, intersection where twelve-year-old Frankie Gotti, the son of Gambino crime-family boss John Gotti, was accidentally struck and killed by a car driven by John Favara. AUTHOR'S COLLECTION

According to authors Jerry Capeci and Gene Mustain in their book *Mobstar*, a dumpster being used in the renovation of a home obscured Favara's vision at the intersection. As Frankie Gotti was riding a motorized bike loaned to him by a slightly older Kevin McMahon, Favara's car struck Frankie and dragged him along the street. The youngster was alive, but just barely, as his mother rushed to the scene and tried to comfort him. A short while later Frankie Gotti died from his injuries in the hospital. It fell to John Gotti himself to tell his wife that their son had perished.

The death of the child put Gotti, his wife, and their entire family into a tailspin of depression and rage. Gotti would sit alone and cry. His wife would walk the streets at night and visit local ball fields to look for Frankie. Although the child's death was an accident, Favara didn't help his cause with the Gotti family when he held a noisy party, which provoked Victoria Gotti to beat his car with a baseball bat. Favara's friends urged him to move away.

In July 1980 Favara was in a parking lot near his workplace on Long Island when a group of men abducted him and tossed him into a van. He was never seen in public again.

Some law enforcement officials believe Gotti, seeing how devastated his family was by the death of Frankie, ordered that Favara be killed. Another theory is that Gotti's underlings, such as his old friend Angelo Ruggiero, took matters into their own hands to satisfy the crime boss. In 2009, federal officials developed evidence from cooperating witnesses that Favara was not only killed, but his body dissolved in acid for disposal. The gruesome task, the witnesses told investigators, was done by Gambino soldier Charles Carneglia, possibly at his auto junkyard at **651 Fountain Avenue,** or one of his other properties on Pine Street. Both locations were technically in the East New York section of Brooklyn, but very close to the Queens border. To prove he had carried out the macabre task, Carneglia allegedly dropped some of Favara's finger bones in a bowl of soup Ruggiero was eating in the Lindenwood Diner at **2870 Linden Boulevard,** also in Brooklyn.

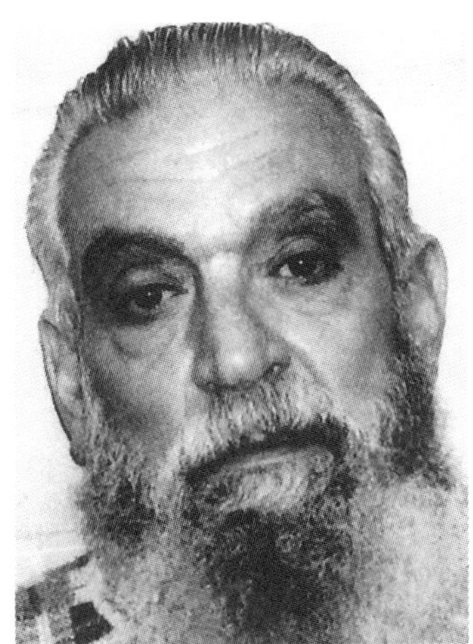

Gambino crime-family member Charles Carneglia was, according to federal court testimony and records, the man responsible for disposing of the body of John Favara, the motorist who accidentally ran over and killed the twelve-year-old son of Mob boss John Gotti in March 1980. PHOTO COURTESY US ATTORNEY'S OFFICE, EASTERN DISTRICT

■ ■ ■

The Mafia used the more conventional method of burial to get rid of other victims' bodies in the early 1980s. When the Bonanno crime family and Joseph Massino killed the three captains in May 1981, the corpses had to be disposed of quickly. To do that, Massino contacted his neighbor and fellow mobster John Gotti, who agreed to have members of his crew bury the bodies of Dominick Trinchera, Philip Giaccone, and Alfonse "Sonny Red" Indelicato, in an out-of-the-way lot in Queens, off Ruby Street.

The area of the burial was a place at **Ruby Street and Blake Avenue,** astride the border between Queens and Brooklyn, in the East New York area. Overgrown with weeds and surrounded by dilapidated buildings, the place made an ideal burial ground, if the grave diggers knew what to do. Gotti's men picked up the three bodies in a van that the Bonanno cleanup crew had left at the corner of **Cross Bay Boulevard and 160th Street.** The digging was done at night to lessen the chance of inadvertent discovery by the police. The bodies of Trinchera and

In October 2004 a team of FBI agents excavated an empty lot on Ruby Street, an area in Brooklyn very close to the Queens border, for the remains of slain Bonanno captains Dominick Trinchera and Philip Giaccone. *NEWSDAY*, LLC, 2004

Giaccone were planted the deepest. Indelicato's body was closer to the top of the pit.

If Massino's intention was to have the bodies buried so that they wouldn't be discovered, he failed. A few days after the burial, on May 5, 1981, a bunch of children playing in the empty lot noticed a human hand sticking out of the ground. After police arrived, they unearthed Indelicato's corpse, and, figuring that he was the only victim, didn't look any further. Some twenty years later, after Massino became a government cooperating witness and revealed where the other two bodies were, the FBI used backhoes to unearth the remains of Trinchera and Giaccone. Formal identification was made through DNA analysis, although there were enough identification papers with the remains that the agent had a pretty good idea right away whose bones they had collected.

The murder of the three captains was orchestrated by Massino, with the help of the Bonanno family's Canadian subsidiary. The planning and the execution of the plot were well-kept secrets in the Mafia. But the FBI had some hints that something

Ten years after an FBI excavation had uncovered the bodies, the old burial ground for the three Bonanno captains, slain in May 1981, had become a construction site and parking area for vehicles. AUTHOR'S COLLECTION

had happened. The day after the murders, pen register devices used by the federal agents to record incoming and outgoing calls from particular telephones started to act up, making chirping sounds as they were activated. A lot of calls were being made between telephone numbers of the various Bonanno wiseguys.

■ ■ ■

The nondescript doorway at **98–04 101st Avenue** in Ozone Park may not have seemed like much to passersby. The building was a simple two-story attached brick structure in a neighborhood that was largely Italian-American, and there was no sign on the door or in the window. But over the years the Bergin Hunt and Fish Club had become the central place in Queens for the crew of John Gotti.

In his early gangster days, Gotti was part of the crew of the Fatico brothers, Carmine and Daniel. The Faticos worked out of the area of East New York, technically in Brooklyn, but really on the border with Queens. The brothers operated out of a social club on Fulton Avenue, and Gotti became a reliable operative in their hijacking operation. Eventually, the Fatico brothers tired of the worn-down area of East New York and moved their operation to the new location, on 101st Avenue in Queens. The name "Bergin" used for the club was likely a spelling error, since it may have been meant to refer to Bergen Beach, a neighborhood in Brooklyn. In any case, misspelled or not, the name Bergin Hunt and Fish Club stuck. The location was also closer to John F. Kennedy International Airport, a main target of Mafia hijackers.

After the Faticos faded from the scene—they had substantial legal problems late in their lives—Gotti continued to use the Bergin club as his place, while his mentor Aniello Dellacroce gravitated to the Ravenite club in Manhattan. As it turned out, Gotti used another unmarked storefront next to the Bergin as a private office setting. He also had a barber chair installed so he could get his daily hairstyling and shave.

It had become routine that Mafia social clubs like the Bergin were targeted for police and FBI surveillance, which made it easy for law enforcement to spot who was associated with the Gambino crime family as they trooped to the South Ozone Park location. Surveillance devices were also placed in the Bergin, sometimes by law enforcement agencies who didn't know that each had secured eavesdropping warrants from different judges. The bugs picked up useful intelligence but never led to significant criminal cases. Meanwhile, Gotti conducted business as usual,

Gambino crime-family boss John Gotti held court in his heyday at the Bergin Hunt and Fish Club at 98–04 101st Avenue in Ozone Park, in what is now a row of neighborhood businesses. AUTHOR'S COLLECTION

and the Bergin became part of neighborhood folklore. Residents told reporters that the area was safe, indicating that Gotti's presence had made it so. On the Fourth of July, Gotti held celebrations on the block with food and fireworks, in direct defiance of the police, who seemed to turn a blind eye to things.

When Gotti took over as head of the Gambino family following the death of Castellano, he gradually spent more of his time at the Ravenite club on Mulberry Street in Manhattan. The move proved to be the key to his undoing. Gotti required his captain to show up at least once a week at the Ravenite, something which made it easy for the FBI to get surveillance photos. When Gotti started using an apartment upstairs from the Ravenite as a secret meeting place, the FBI developed intelligence that allowed the placement of a bug, which proved fruitful. It was Gotti's own words picked up on this bug that helped to sink him.

After Gotti was arrested for the final time in late 1990, the Bergin crew kept up a pretense of business as usual. The group even sponsored a final fireworks spectacle for the Fourth of July in 1991. But something went woefully wrong that night, and the fireworks prematurely detonated, injuring a few people. The accident seemed a fitting symbol for the way Gotti's power had started to fizzle with his arrest. After Gotti, the location of the Bergin was used as a dog-grooming salon and later an Italian ice and sandwich store. Apart from some old-timers' memories, there is nothing left to recall the old days of the Mob.

■ ■ ■

Of all of the cop killings to have happened in New York City, the death of Detective Anthony J. Venditti on January 21, 1986, would prove to be the most vexing. Venditti and his partner, Detective Kathleen Burke, were working undercover as part of an organized-crime investigation when they got into a wild confrontation outside of a diner in Ridgewood, Queens. The two undercover cops were working with federal investigators on members of the Genovese crime family, and in particular were focused on the movements and dealings of Federico "Fritzy" Giovanelli, a captain in the crime family.

Venditti and Burke, who was only assigned to the case temporarily, because Venditti's regular partner was unavailable, eventually picked up information that Giovanelli had some business out in Ridgewood. On the evening of January 21, the two detectives stopped by Castillo's Restaurant at **54–55 Myrtle Avenue,** close to the intersection with St. Nicholas Avenue. It turns out Giovanelli was also in the area, and pulled up into the diner parking lot with associates Carmine Gualtieri and Steven Maltese.

What happened next remains murky, and has never been established to the satisfaction of three juries, much less the police and FBI. Burke had actually been circling the block in a car and pulled into the diner parking lot as Venditti was getting ready to exit the building. Burke had noticed Giovanelli at the location and was trying to get to her partner to tell him. But in an instant, Burke had fired her gun, sustained a wound to the chest, and Venditti was mortally wounded. A civilian witness stated—and later recanted—that he saw Giovanelli with brass knuckles asking his cohorts, "What are we going to do with this fucking guy?," and then shots were fired as the mobster and his friends came face-to-face with Venditti.

Giovanelli and his two associates were quickly arrested on second-degree murder charges. But the case proved anything but routine. Evidence of what happened was muddled by Burke's account of what had transpired, an account riddled with inconsistencies and contradicted by statements of other eyewitnesses. As one commentator noted, the police also didn't establish a motive as to why Giovanelli would have wanted Venditti harmed, given that there was evidence he knew he was being followed by the detectives.

Twice prosecutors with the Queens District Attorney's Office tried but failed to win convictions in the murder of Venditti. Federal prosecutors in the office of then Manhattan US Attorney Rudolph Giuliani won a conviction under the racketeering laws, but the murder element of the case was overturned on appeal. Nevertheless, Giovanelli, who was a top lieutenant to crime-family boss Vincent Gigante, remained a target of law enforcement, and in 2004 was convicted on conspiracy charges. He eventually was released from prison in 2011.

In October 2011 during a ceremony in Queens, attended by his family, clergy, and the likes of NYPD commissioner Ray Kelly, Venditti was memoralized with the rededication of a park in his name. Within the small parcel of land at the intersection of **St. Nicholas and Myrtle Avenues** is a plaque inscribed with a quote from Raymond Chandler's 1950 collection of short stories, titled *The Simple Art of Murder*:

> "Down these mean streets a man must go who is not himself mean: who is neither tarnished nor afraid."

CHAPTER NINETEEN

TALES OF THE OLD AND NEW MOBS

The Astoria section of Queens has become the focal point for the Greek population in New York City. A trip down any of the main streets in the neighborhood reveals numerous Greek restaurants, travel agencies, family associations, and Orthodox churches.

In the 1980s a wily gambler named Spyredon "Spiros" Velentzas, who ran a travel agency in Astoria, saw the benefits of protecting his operation in the Greek community by allying with the Mafia. The Greek men who immigrated to New York in the 1960s and '70s had a penchant for certain games of chance played in their local *kafeneio*, or coffeehouse. Velentzas ran illegal dice games known as "barbout" or "barbat" among the Greeks, and, as a necessary offshoot, loaned money at usurious rates. Illegal horse-betting parlors were also part of Velentzas's organization.

Velentzas, who was also known by the nickname "Sakafias," could never be as big as the Mafia, but he saw the wisdom in using the Italians, specifically the Lucchese crime family, for protection. He was only too glad to pay on average about $10,000 a month to stay in the good graces of La Cosa Nostra. Although Velentzas had competitors, he sometimes bought them off or enticed them to cooperate with his ring.

One man who was something of a competitor with Velentzas was Samuel "The Arab" Nolo, a part-time burglar who owned a popular Middle Eastern restaurant in Manhattan frequented by Mafia members and celebrities alike. Nolo was not a small-time burglar, and in 1972 was arrested on charges he and others took part in the widely publicized heist at the Pierre Hotel in Manhattan, which reportedly victimized actress Sophia Loren. For that crime Nolo received a seven-year state prison sentence.

On October 26, 1988, Nolo showed up at Olympic Travel, Inc., at **Thirty-First Street and Ditmars Boulevard** in Astoria, a business partly owned by Velentzas. Both men were to have a meeting, and before Velentzas was to show up, Nolo picked up the telephone at the travel agency to talk with him. Distracted by the telephone conversation, Nolo didn't see an armed man come into the store and fire at him with a handgun. When police showed up, Nolo said "Spiros had this done to me," and again, a few minutes later, just before he died, said "Spiros Velentzas" when the officers asked him again who had shot him.

Four years later, Peter Chiodo, an obese man known appropriately as "Big Pete" and "Fat Pete," admitted to the FBI and in federal court testimony that Lucchese acting boss Vic Amuso had ordered him to shoot Nolo, to help Velentzas. Chiodo became a government witness when he saw that his future with the Mob was going to be terribly short-lived; this was after he was shot twelve times while working on his car at a Staten Island gas station. His 500-plus-pound weight contributed to his survival, said doctors. What also convinced Chiodo to talk were threats made against his wife.

Obese Mob associate Peter Chiodo is shown here leaving a Brooklyn funeral home. Chiodo finally decided to cooperate with the FBI after he was shot numerous times in an assassination attempt. Chiodo's testimony was instrumental in convicting Greek Mob boss Spiros Velentzas on federal racketeering charges in 1992. PHOTO COURTESY US ATTORNEY'S OFFICE, EASTERN DISTRICT

After Velentzas and a number of his associates in the Greek organization were indicted in 1991, Chiodo repeated his allegation during the trial—that the Nolo hit was ordered to help Velentzas. The jury convicted Velentzas in June 1992, and he is currently serving a life term in federal prison, where he continues to protest his innocence.

■ ■ ■

Michael Pappadio was one of the many garment industry businessmen who profited handsomely from his ties to organized crime. His brother Andimo, a captain in the crime family of Thomas Lucchese, was considered by federal investigators to have been a major narcotics operative for the Mob until his murder at the age of sixty-two in 1976, on Long Island. Michael amassed interests in a number of garment trucking and manufacturing businesses, which for decades had been infiltrated by organized crime. He did it while cementing ties to a number of major Mafia figures, notably Joseph "Joe Stretch" Stracci and Anthony Corallo, the man who took over as boss after Thomas Lucchese died in 1967. Police surveillance reports stated that Michael Pappadio would meet most days with Mob figures in Manhattan's garment district restaurants.

Pappadio became ill in the late 1980s and as a result wasn't active on a day-to-day basis in his various businesses, relying instead on other family members. He could have simply lived out the rest of his days at his large house at **2450 Little Neck Parkway** in the Bayside area of Queens and counted his money, some of which he shared with his bosses in the Lucchese crime family.

But things are never that simple when the Mafia has its hooks into a cash cow like the garment business. The Lucchese family had broken down into two factions: the Brooklyn crowd, led by Victor Amuso and Anthony "Gaspipe" Casso, as well as the more-traditional East Harlem group, with which Pappadio was aligned. Eventually, Casso and Amuso assumed the overall leadership and wanted to make sure the crime family was getting its cut of the garment industry rackets.

For years Pappadio had been close with Sidney Lieberman, a Mob-connected garment district trucking executive who seemed to have as many lives as a cat. Lieberman was a Jew who with the help of his Mafia ties became a power in the garment trucking business. He had a duplicitous streak; according to FBI reports which later surfaced, Lieberman was secretly telling Amuso and Casso that Pappadio was making enormous amounts of money from garment businesses he had kept secret from the crime family. Pappadio denied hiding any businesses, but that didn't matter, as the Lucchese bosses ordered him to stay away from the garment area in Manhattan and to turn over his business records. Pappadio turned over the records, but according to law enforcement reports, he didn't stay away from the garment district, and for that, the Mob ordered his death.

There was nothing quick or merciful about the way Michael Pappadio died. In fact, it was all quite sadistic. Details of Pappadio's demise on May 13, 1989, are known because Al D'Arco, one of the participants in the hit, became a government cooperating witness and told the FBI what happened. According to D'Arco, on the fateful day Pappadio was told to come for a meeting at a bagel store known as Crown Foods, at **123–11 Rockaway Boulevard.** Waiting for Pappadio along with D'Arco were at least two other men. When Pappadio arrived and went to the office in the store, Carmine Avellino blurted out a signal.

"Surprise—look who's here," said Avellino, according to D'Arco.

Armed with a bludgeon, which was nothing more than a length of cable wrapped in blue tape, D'Arco started hitting Pappadio over the head. To everyone's surprise, Pappadio remained standing and told D'Arco to stop hitting him. Another assailant who D'Arco identified to the FBI as George Zappola fired a .22 caliber pistol at Pappadio, but the round apparently ricocheted off his head.

Zappola then pulled out a larger-caliber handgun and fired again into Pappadio's skull. Pappadio remained standing for a moment and then sank to the floor, bleeding profusely from the head wound.

With Pappadio dead, Avellino pulled a wad of cash from the dead man's pocket, recalled D'Arco. Then, Pappadio's corpse was placed in a body bag. To keep any blood from getting on the floor of the trunk of the car being used to transport the body, Zappola took a plastic sheet hanging on a stack of bagel trays, promising to return it to the store. D'Arco and Zappola then drove away with Pappadio's body in the trunk, to a street behind a Roy Rogers restaurant off Woodhaven Boulevard and Metropolitan Avenue. They left the car in a secluded area near the intersection of **Alderton Street and Trotting Course Lane,** where a Mob associate from Long Island came to take it away, according to the FBI report.

Pappadio's wife, Frances, thought her husband was going to buy some fruit and other supplies for a family barbecue when she had dropped him off the day of his disappearance, at the Great Bay Diner at the corner of **Bell Boulevard and Thirty-Fifth Avenue.** She came back in an hour as planned and did not find him, thinking that perhaps one of her children had already picked him up. But Pappadio was nowhere to be found. Even his brother Fred had no clue as to where he was, and eventually stopped contacting his sister-in-law, she told the FBI. To this day, Pappadio's remains have never been found.

■ ■ ■

Michael Pappadio represents the kind of businessman who plays with the Mafia to make himself and his Mob controllers millions of dollars. In the end it cost him his life. Union officials also forged corrupt deals in New York City with organized crime. In terms of labor racketeering, it was the rank and file be damned. With the Mafia involved, union benefit and pension funds were looted and contracts not enforced, all to the detriment of the union membership. Some businesses were protected from the unions, and others managed to use non-union workers even if they were technically union shops. By playing cozy with the Mafia, union leaders who were corrupt gave themselves lucrative kickbacks.

But by the late 1980s and early '90s, the Mafia was feeling the pressure of labor racketeering investigations by the FBI and local district attorneys. Organized crime's leadership was getting paranoid. If a union official weakened and decided to turn into a cooperative witness, the Mob bosses could be brought down like dominoes.

The Lucchese crime family not only used the garment district as a cash cow, but they had also worked out arrangements with the union for painters, which extorted millions for contractors anxious to have labor peace. James Bishop had been head of the painters' union from 1973 to 1989 when he was reportedly forced out by the crime-family bosses.

Anthony Casso, one of the acting bosses of the Lucchese family, became concerned that Bishop might prove to be weak in the face of burgeoning investigations of the painting industry. To find out if his fears were justified, Casso contacted two NYPD detectives who were on the payroll, and who had done contract killings for the Mob. The detectives, Louis Eppolito and Stephen Caracappa, the infamous "Mafia Cops" discussed in chapter 16, confirmed that the sixty-year-old Bishop was cooperating with an investigation led by Manhattan district attorney Robert Morgenthau.

The morning of May 17, 1990, Bishop left his girlfriend's apartment at Cryder Point, a six-story complex at **162–01 Powells Cove Boulevard** in Whitestone, Queens. The building was close to the East River, in a choice residential area with a vista that overlooked the Throggs Neck Bridge. As Bishop prepared to back his Lincoln sedan out of his parking space, witnesses said a man approached and fired about eight .380 caliber rounds through the closed car window. Bishop desperately put the car in forward gear and drove about 150 feet before striking a fence. He died on the way to hospital.

The murder of Bishop was quickly labeled a Mob hit, and led to a number of arrests. In January 1996, two Lucchese crime-family captains were indicted in Brooklyn federal court for Bishop's slaying.

■ ■ ■

As far as anyone could tell, the Mob didn't do any murders at the social club next to the public library at **6970 Grand Avenue** in Maspeth, Queens. The club was down an alley adjacent to a small office building at 6964 Grand Avenue, and Salvatore Vitale, underboss of the Bonanno crime family, liked using it as his meeting place during the time he was street boss while official boss Joseph Massino was in prison. If need be, mobsters could use the public telephone in front of the library, but that didn't last long, as by 1990 the FBI eventually got wise to the location.

Using a vantage point across the street from the alley where the club was located, FBI surveillance teams, as part of an investigation known as the "Grand Finale," began to photograph all of the mafiosi who visited the location. The gatherings made Grand Avenue seem like a block party. Agents parked their cars some distance away as a precaution and spent many hours from 1990 to 1992, photographing Vitale and other Bonanno captains like Louis Restivo, Anthony

Urso, Michael Cardiello, and Gerlando Sciascia. Other crime-family members like Patrick DeFilippo, Louis Tartaglione, and Vincent Basciano were also caught on film.

Agents also got a court order for a tap on the public telephone in front of the library. The tap didn't catch any incriminating calls involving Vitale, but eventually the FBI was able to make a case against a few of the Bonanno family members, notably Michael "Mickey Bats" Cardello, who pled guilty to a racketeering charge. But once Massino got out of prison in 1992, he ordered that all of the social clubs, including Grand Avenue, be closed as a way of thwarting surveillance. Why make it easy for the FBI to get photographs, said Massino.

■ ■ ■

Mobsters rarely go after journalists in the United States. There have been exceptions, notably the acid blinding of columnist Victor Riesel and the bombing of Arizona reporter Don Bolles in 1977. But nothing compared to the brazen assassination on March 11, 1992, of the Cuban-born Manuel de Dios Unanue, a Spanish-language reporter.

Manuel de Dios Unanue was a Cuban-born Spanish-language journalist who was shot dead on March 11, 1992, on orders of a Colombian drug cartel. *NEWSDAY* LLC, 1989

De Dios was sitting at the bar in Meson Asturias Restaurant in Elmhurst, Queens, when a man approached him from behind and shot him twice in the head, killing him instantly. De Dios, who had once served as editor of the Spanish-language daily, *El Diario-La Presna*, had long been a thorn in the side of the Latin American drug cartels, with his reporting in New York. Through two magazines he founded, *Cambio XXI* and *Crimen*, he revealed the identities of suspected drug dealers, and even ran their photographs. He had also written a book titled *The Secrets of the Medellin Cartel*, and named drug dealers on a radio show he hosted. It was a risky business, and when de Dios was killed, suspicion immediately fell on the drug cartels.

For years, the Colombian drug syndicates had loomed large in terms of their impact in New York City. The cartels were the source of much of the cocaine reaching the five boroughs, and over time would diversify and provide a key source of heroin. Cocaine was also marketed as crack-cocaine, which fueled the rising homicide rate in New York, pushing murders up to the historic level of 2,245 in 1990. The cartels themselves had no hesitation about using violence, and drug murders made up a significant part of the killings in the city as a way of controlling members and territory, and assuring market share. By his news coverage, de Dios had been threatening the cartel operations in substantial ways.

The murder of de Dios was a stealthy, convoluted operation that involved a number of operatives. Evidence later developed by the federal Drug Enforcement Administration and the FBI determined that José Santacruz Londoño, a Colombian cartel leader, had put the murder plot in motion by hiring cartel associate John Mena to kill the journalist. The actual shooting was repeatedly subcontracted until an eighteen-year-old illegal immigrant named Wilson Alejandro Mejia-Velez agreed to pick up the contract for $7,000. De Dios was a creature of habit and regularly visited the Meson Asturias, a fact that the assassins quickly discovered. After using photographs to confirm the identity of de Dios, the conspirators gave Mejia-Velez the gun he used to kill the journalist.

The killing of de Dios rocked the city, and a reward was posted for $70,000. Federal investigators pressed an investigation, which a year later led to the arrest of Mena and Mejia-Velez. Mena turned into a cooperating witness and testified against Mejia-Velez, who was convicted of killing de Dios in 1994. Londoño, the cartel boss who had instigated things, was himself killed by Colombian police in March 1996. The Meson Asturios eventually closed, to be replaced by a Mexican restaurant specializing in tacos, with free delivery. In 1995, the city designated a small triangle of land on **Eighty-Third Street, between Baxter and Roosevelt Avenues,** as Manuel de Dios Unanue Triangle.

■ ■ ■

Either Thomas and Rosemary Uva thought the middle-aged and geriatric men who frequented Mafia social clubs were too stuffed with linguine and calamari to put up much of a fight, or the couple was just plain stupid. In any case, the decision the Uvas made to target the clubs for robbery was one that would lead to notoriety and death—their own. With Thomas armed with an Uzi submachine gun, and his wife driving the getaway car, the couple set about robbing a number of clubs used by members of the Bonanno and Gambino crime families. The pair, who earned the nickname "Bonnie and Clyde," didn't just rob the club patrons of their cash and jewelry; they also humiliated them by having them pull down their trousers.

With two crime families victimized by the Uvas, the couple soon had a contract placed on their heads. If they knew they were targets, the Uvas didn't seem to care, and openly drove around the Ozone Park area. On Christmas Eve Day of 1992, around 8:30 a.m., the couple was flush with $1,000 cash and jewelry, and may have been planning some holiday shopping as they were stopped at the intersection of **Woodhaven Boulevard and 103rd Street,** not far, as it turned out, from the old social club used by John Gotti's crew. Suddenly someone came up and shot them both in the head. Their vehicle, now driverless and carrying two corpses, rolled into the intersection and struck another vehicle. The Uvas' short run as bandits was over.

Both the Gambino and Bonanno family had people who claimed credit for the hit. The matter of who had bragging rights was settled in 2007, when Dominic Pizzonia, a Gambino crime-family member, was convicted in a federal racketeering trial of conspiring to kill the couple, although there was very little evidence of his involvement. Thomas Uva was dead at the age of twenty-eight, and Rosemarie, at thirty-one. But their story gained them a bit of immortality, serving as the basis for the 2014 film, *Rob the Mob*.

■ ■ ■

When Congress liberalized the nation's immigration laws to make it easier for Russians and other citizens of the Soviet Union to emigrate to the United States, the unintended result was that numerous Eastern European gangsters found an easy way to start a new life in a land rich with illegal opportunities.

Settling at first among the Soviet diaspora in the Brighton Beach section of Brooklyn, and later in parts of Queens, Russian gangsters created a series of loosely connected organizations that for years would show a level of criminal enterprise that rivaled other crime groups. The Russian groups, known as brigades, would come together for temporary alliances to make the most of the opportunities that arose. The Russians extorted their fellow immigrants with abandon; ran gigantic credit-card scams; defrauded the Medicare, Medicaid, and welfare systems; made tens of millions of dollars with Mafia families in a gasoline racket; and trafficked in women for prostitution.

When necessary, the Russian brigades would kill. In 1985, Evsei Agron, considered one of the early bosses of the Russian Mob in Brighton Beach, was gunned down in an unsolved homicide as he was leaving his apartment building. That same year Elia Zelster was shot dead in an office in the Sheepshead Bay section of Brooklyn. But nothing seemed to underscore the reckless lengths the Russian brigades would go to more than the destructive arson fire that ravaged a block of small businesses at **92–01 Sixty-Third Drive** in the Rego Park section of Queens. The fire caused extensive damage to several businesses, including a two-week-old gourmet food store popular with immigrants, which was the main target of the attack.

The investigation into the arson attack eventually uncovered the involvement of Mani Chulpayev, an immigrant from Uzbekistan who became a cooperating witness for the FBI. Chulpayev's cooperation turned out to be of great importantance in the fight against Russian brigades. Not only did Chulpayev admit to his involvement in the Rego Park fire, but he is also said to have provided information about as many as ten brigades of Russian criminals operating along the East Coast. He also provided information about the Russian and Eurasian gang ties to the Lucchese and Colombo crime families.

Because of his cooperation with federal investigators, Chulpayev avoided a possible lengthy prison sentence, and eventually wound up in Florida, where he started an auto dealership. But in 2013, Chulpayev, who earned a reputation in his earlier prison days for loving philosophy, was arrested and charged with taking part in the murder a year earlier of an Atlanta rapper known by the stage name of Lil Phat. The murder case was still pending as of this writing.

■ ■ ■

Usually, the Mafia and smaller ethnic crime groups like the Greeks were able to arrive at mutually beneficial relationships, which assured a steady cash flow from the rackets. This happened in the years that the Velentzas organization was active in Astoria. But by the mid-1990s a new group of Albanian gangsters started to assert itself, and decided to throw the old rules out the window. The Mafia was no longer considered by these new Eastern European interlopers as worthy of any respect. Feeling brash and powerful, the Albanians showed disrespect to the traditional Mafia families like the Lucchese and Gambino groups. The Albanians also weren't shy about reminding people of their cultural tradition of vendettas, which kept feuds alive for decades. It was a recipe for trouble.

One man who harnessed the Albanians into a powerful combination was Alex Rudaj, an immigrant from Montenegro who worked for a time as a busboy at Central Park's Tavern on the Green in Manhattan, and had dreams of making his crew a new "Sixth Family" to rival the traditional Five Families of La Cosa Nostra. The late Joey Gallo had his own fantasy of making his crew a sixth family in the 1970s. But Rudaj was operating outside the traditional code of conduct of the Mafia, and had no hesitation about getting in the face of powerful Italian gangsters. In one incident, Rudaj and an associate beat up an elderly reputed Gambino soldier on Arthur Avenue in the Bronx, stripped him down to his underwear, and took his wallet.

Gambling in Queens was the big moneymaker for the ethnic crime groups, and Rudaj's Albanian organization was not going to be denied its cut of the racket. This was made clear when the Albanians announced they were going to take over gambling in Astoria, and that there was nothing the Italians could do about it. Arnold Squitieri, the acting boss of the Gambino family at the time, called Rudaj to a meeting at a gas station to sort out their differences, but things didn't go well. One of Rudaj's men pointed a shotgun at a gas pump and threatened to blow up the station. At that point, Squitieri got into a car at gunpoint and was driven around until he made a deal with Rudaj's crew.

Ethnic Albanian gangster Alex Rudaj, shown in a surveillance photo outside a bar. Investigators said Rudaj, who led a crew of Albanians, had aspirations to become as important as the traditional Mafia families. PHOTO COURTESY FEDERAL BUREAU OF INVESTIGATION

Emboldened by the way the Gambino family had backed down, Rudaj's organization started to get tough with the Greek gambling operations around Astoria in an effort to stop them from competing with Albanian clubs. (Greek crime boss Spyredon Velentzas was in prison at this point, and no longer a factor.) In one infamous incident on August 2, 2001, at a Greek club called Soccer Fever, **26–80 Thirtieth Street,** Rudaj and at least six other men stormed the location and beat the club owner with a pistol. They chased patrons away, effectively shutting down the operation, which had been under the protection of the Lucchese family. More brazen acts took place under Rudaj's command, with Mafia members and associates sometimes being beaten or threatened, usually over gambling disputes.

Rudaj's men agreed with the Lucchese family to compensate the Italians with some $1,500 a week for lost revenue, a small sum given the millions estimated to have been generated by the gambling operations taken over by the Albanians. But after several months the Albanians stopped making the payments, with no apparent repercussions.

Clearly, the Albanian organization had in many ways supplanted the Mafia in Queens, an amazing turn of events, but one which underscored the changing times for organized crime. The appearance of newer, emerging ethnic crime groups mirrored what had taken place in the Italian-American community decades earlier. The Rudaj organization spread its wings and got involved in stolen cars; sold weapons; and, when needed, shook down businesses in Astoria, the Bronx, and Westchester. They also worked out deals with the Bonanno crime family.

But the Albanians got involved in crime at a time when the FBI had perfected its ability to go after criminal enterprises, and controlled an impressive stable of cooperating witnesses and informants. For the Rudaj organization, the end result was predictable. In 2004 Rudaj and several of his associates were indicted by a Manhattan federal jury. After a jury trial, Rudaj and his men were convicted in 2006, and given lengthy prison terms.

■ ■ ■

The infamous Lufthansa heist at John F. Kennedy Airport took place on December 11, 1978, but has been reverberating in New York City's popular culture for decades, mainly through the Martin Scorcese film *Goodfellas*. The cash and jewelry grabbed by a crew of criminals under the leadership of James Burke amounted to a value of about $6 million at the time. The gang had really only expected about $2 million when they hit the Lufthansa cargo area at the airport. The extra cash was spread around some of the higher-ups in the Bonanno and Lucchese crime families.

But while Burke and his sidekick Henry Hill got some of the loot that didn't go to the bosses, the heist amounted to a death sentence for a lot of the people involved, beginning with the hapless Steven Edwards, the driver who was supposed to immediately take the van used in the heist to a junkyard in New Jersey, but instead spent the time getting high at the home of his girlfriend. Because of Edwards's dawdling, police immediately found the van and were able to get fingerprints from the vehicle, quickly reinforcing suspicion that Burke's crew was somehow involved. For his transgression, Edwards was shot dead at his house at Ozone Park homes at **109–16 120th Street** by homicidal Mob associate Thomas DeSimone. A month later, DeSimone, whose character in *Goodfellas* was played by Joe Pesci, was killed, and disappeared, as punishment for the earlier killing of a made member of the Gambino crime family.

Paranoid of potential informants and fearful of being linked to the heist, Burke engineered a killing spree in which a number of his accomplices were murdered. One of his victims was Martin Krugman, a Queens hair salon owner who had first tipped off Burke to the Lufthansa cash, but angered Burke by constantly demanding his cut of the haul. Krugman was killed and his remains reportedly buried under the basement floor of the Roberts Lounge, a bar at **114–45 Lefferts Boulevard** used by Burke and his Mob mentor, Paul Vario. In June of 1980, police excavated the basement and uncovered some human bones.

The only significant conviction from the Lufthansa case was that of Louis Werner, a Lufthansa cargo agent who was found guilty of giving Burke's gang some important inside help to pull off the heist. Burke, whose character was played in the Scorcese film by Robert De Niro, was never convicted for the Lufthansa caper, but instead was sent to prison for a murder, and for playing a role in the Boston College basketball point-shaving case. He died in 1996 in prison from lung cancer.

Excavation in the basement of a Queens home in which the remains of Mob associate Paul Katz were found in 2013, about forty years after he disappeared. PHOTO COURTESY US ATTORNEY'S OFFICE, EASTERN DISTRICT

But the specter of Burke and the Lufthansa case has lingered. In June 2013, FBI agents, based on a tip from a cooperating witness, began digging under the basement floor of a house at **81–48 102nd Road** in Ozone Park, a residence owned by Burke's daughter Catherine. Agents found the remains of Paul Katz, a former associate of James Burke. According to court records, in the 1960s Katz had a warehouse in Richmond Hill that Burke and then Bonanno crime-family associate Vincent Asaro used to store stolen property. But after a police raid, Burke, perhaps through information provided by corrupt NYPD officers, believed Katz was an informant. Both Burke and Asaro then allegedly strangled Katz with a dog chain, federal court records stated.

In February 2014, Asaro, a captain in the Bonanno family, was indicted on charges he took part in the Katz murder. The indictment also accused Asaro of helping Burke with the Lufthansa heist by giving some of the loot to Joseph Massino, as tribute to the Bonanno crime family. As of this writing, the case against Asaro, who has been described as a hopeless gambler, is pending in Brooklyn federal court. Given Asaro's advanced age of seventy-eight, and the long prison sentence he faces if convicted, he is expected to roll the dice and go to trial for a crime many Mafia buffs have long thought was dead and buried.

CHAPTER TWENTY

PRINCELY PALACES AND UNMARKED GRAVES

Staten Island is the least densely populated of all of New York City's five boroughs and encompasses both open and secluded spaces. Certainly for those reasons alone, the island has been favored by mobsters seeking solitude in their private lives and secrecy in the way they do some of their dirty deeds.

In the summer of 1981, Dominick "Sonny Black" Napolitano was not in a good frame of mind. While he had backed the winning side in the Bonanno crime-family war, which culminated in the death of the three captains in May, Napolitano was soon hit with the bombshell disclosure that his friend Donnie Brasco was actually undercover FBI agent Joseph Pistone. Napolitano had been so taken in by Pistone that the mafiosi had even been prepared to recommend him for membership in La Cosa Nostra.

But with the public revelation that Pistone had been working undercover, Napolitano knew that he was in trouble. So, when in August 1981 Napolitano got a call that he was to go to a meeting with some other crime-family captains, he seemed resigned to a fate he couldn't change. He had a final drink at a Brooklyn bar, left some jewelry with the bartender, and drove off to the parking lot of the old Hamilton House restaurant in Bay Ridge. It was there that Napolitano got into a car with Bonanno captains Frank Lino and Steven Cannone and drove across the Verrazano-Narrows Bridge to Staten Island.

Once at a house off **Annandale Road,** Napolitano went inside and saw some old familiar faces, including that of the portly Frank Coppa, another Bonanno captain. For a moment, seeing so many old associates, Napolitano might have just believed he was going to walk out of the meeting alive. But when he went to go to the basement, Napolitano stiffened when he sensed trouble. He was pushed down the steps by Lino. Someone fired a shot, and then the gun jammed. Sensing imminent death, Napolitano had one last request.

"Hit me one more time, and make it good," Lino would later remember Napolitano saying just before he died.

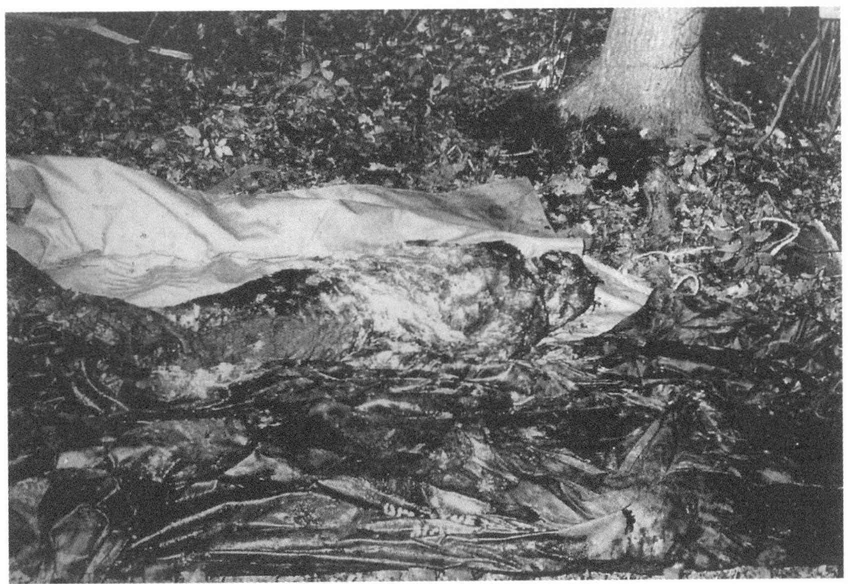

The badly decomposed corpse of Bonanno crime-family captain Dominick "Sonny Black" Napolitano was found in a wooded area of Staten Island about a year after he was killed by fellow mobsters. PHOTO COURTESY US ATTORNEY'S OFFICE, EASTERN DISTRICT

Napolitano's body was bundled into a body bag Lino had gotten from a friend who worked at a funeral parlor and taken to a secluded wooded area. Lino expected to find a grave already dug, but when he got to the area, found nothing. So, Napolitano's body was left in an area of wooded growth by a stream near the intersection of **South Avenue and Bridge Street.**

A year later, on August 12, 1982, a police officer from the 122nd Precinct responded to a call of human remains found in a wooded area.

The corpse was badly decomposed, and there was an indication animals may have gnawed at the fingers. At the morgue, X-rays revealed numerous bullet fragments in what was left of the brain. After more tests and analysis, Napolitano's remains were identified in November. The FBI had long suspected that Napolitano had been dealt Mob justice for the way Pistone had infiltrated his circle. Now there was proof.

■ ■ ■

As a businessman and boss of the Gambino crime family, Paul Castellano was a wealthy man. His poultry operations were successful, and the Gambino rackets were pulling in wads of cash weekly. Castellano's greed may not have endeared

Gambino crime boss Paul Castellano made millions of dollars from both his legitimate businesses and the Mob, living in style, with a palatial home in the Todt Hill section of Staten Island. AUTHOR'S COLLECTION

him to his subordinates, but he had been the boss ever since his cousin Carlo Gambino had died in 1976. So, by late 1983, Castellano had become a prime target for the FBI's special Gambino squad led by agent Bruce Mouw.

Castellano lived in a palatial home at **177 Benedict Road** in the tony Todt Hill section of Staten Island. The house reeked of privilege, and was girded by a tall fence and electronic security devices. For good measure Doberman pinschers guarded the grounds as well.

The story of the way Mouw and his FBI team penetrated the home would become the stuff of legends. Two special FBI technicians devised a plan in March 1983 to cause problems with Castellano's cable television hookup, and then, under the guise of correcting the problem, made repeat visits during which they planted bugs in the "White House," as the home was known. The signals were then picked up in a special apartment rented by the FBI to monitor the surveillance.

One of the crucial bugs was placed in a lamp over the kitchen table. It was there, said an informant, that Castellano often conducted business. The well-positioned device picked up numerous conversations crucial to the FBI understanding of the Gambino crime-family operations. The bugs also picked up an unanticipated bonus. Castellano was having a sexual relationship with his housemaid, a Colombian woman named Gloria Olarte. The tapes captured Castellano in some intimate moments, including one in which he bragged about his penile implant device.

■ ■ ■

By 1984 the FBI had so many bugs and wiretaps around the Mafia leadership that it was inevitable agents would get a line on where and when the fabled Commission, the leadership panel of the Mob, would be meeting. Since the days of Lucky Luciano the New York families, as well as Chicago, had a body of overseers to resolve disputes and set policy among the Mafia groups. Eventually, the five New York families alone composed the Commission, and meetings took place on a haphazard schedule and surrounded by great secrecy, because the bosses were paranoid about all being found in the same place at the same time. The incident at La Stella Restaurant in Queens in 1966, not to mention the infamous Apalachin conclave in 1957, showed how vulnerable the Mob was if a meeting was discovered by the police.

A fortuitous tip by an informant gave the FBI a crucial lead that the Commission was set to meet on May 15, 1984, at a house on Staten Island. Agents with video surveillance cameras positioned themselves in the vicinity of a house at **34 Cameron Avenue,** and as later shown in evidence submitted in the so-called Commission Trial, got unprecedented camera coverage of some of the nation's top Mob bosses trooping into the building.

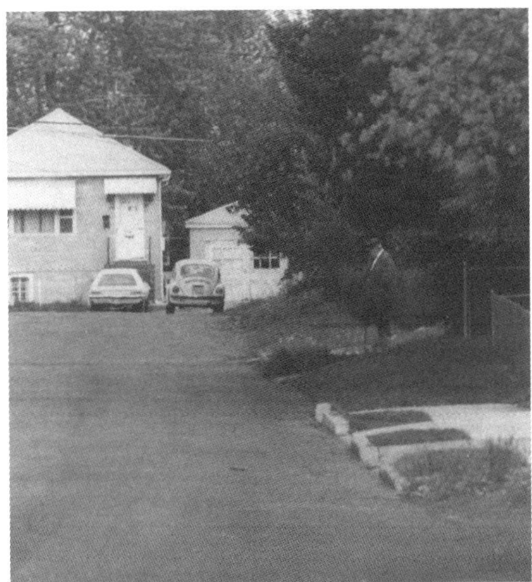

Genovese crime-family boss Anthony "Fat Tony" Salerno exits a home on Cameron Avenue in Staten Island after attending a 1984 meeting of other bosses who were part of the Mob's ruling Commission. The photo was used in evidence in a federal racketeering trial. PHOTO COURTESY PATRICK MARSHALL

Among the first to show up with his driver was Anthony Salerno. He was soon joined by Gambino captain Frank DeCicco and

Jerry Langella, the emissary of the Colombo family. The Lucchese family was represented by Neil Migliore and Salvatore Santoro. Eventually, Gambino boss Paul Castellano showed up, driven by his faithful acolyte Thomas Bilotti.

Knowing that the location had been used for a Commission meeting, the FBI later planted a bug inside the Cameron Avenue address, but never got any useful information, because the bosses never used it again. But the photographs and videos of the various Mob bosses proved to be crucial evidence in the Commission trial of a conspiracy among the Mafia families. As a result, Salerno and a number of his confederates were convicted and given what amounted to life sentences.

■ ■ ■

Thomas Pitera earned the nickname "Tommy Karate" after he learned martial arts to defend himself as a child growing up in Brooklyn. With a high-pitched voice, Pitera was often the butt of jokes and picked on by schoolmates—hence, the need to defend himself. But as an adult mobster with the Bonanno crime family, Pitera also picked up another sinister sobriquet: "The Butcher."

Once affiliated with the Bonanno borgata, Pitera quickly earned a fearsome reputation as a contract killer. He was initially allied with the three captains, the ones murdered in the 1981 power struggle within the crime family. Eventually, Pitera worked within the crew led by Anthony Spero, the Bonanno captain who held down the Brooklyn wing of the crime family and was suspected of ripping off drug dealers.

What set Pitera apart from most in the Mob was the way he seemed to relish killing his victims and disposing of their bodies. Sometimes the killings were for business, but other times they were intensely personal, such as what occurred after his girlfriend Celeste died of an accidental drug overdose. Celeste overdosed in the presence of her friend Phyllis Burdi, and Pitera, overcome with grief and anger, made it his mission to make Burdi pay for his loss. In September 1987, Burdi, a pretty woman described as a Cindy Crawford look-alike, had been having sex and doing drugs with Frank Gangi, when Gangi nonchalantly answered the telephone and told Pitera that Burdi was with him. Pitera then arrived at the apartment, shot a sleeping Burdi, and dismembered her body in the bathtub.

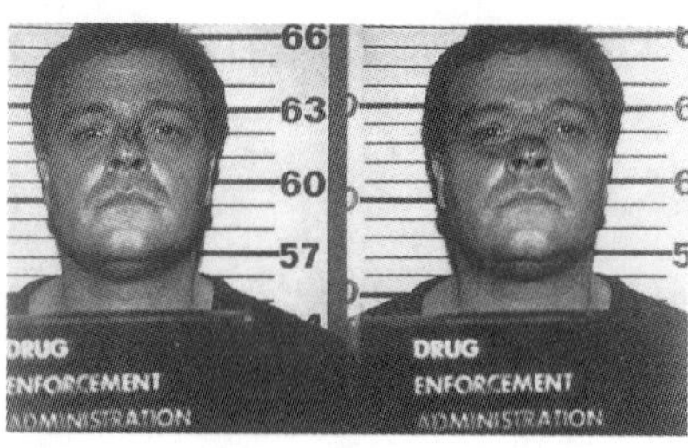

Bonanno crime-family member Tommy Pitera earned the nickname "The Butcher" for the way he dismembered his murder victims. PHOTO COURTESY DRUG ENFORCEMENT ADMINISTRATION

Pitera relished the idea of killing and dismembering his victims. When federal Drug Enforcement Administration agents raided his home they found it stocked with books about killing and dismembering bodies. The late author Philip Carlo, who wrote a biography about Pitera, said that when the mobster wanted to cut up a body, he would strip down and neatly fold up his clothes before he got in the bathtub and began removing his victim's limbs and head. After doing the deed, Pitera would wash out the tub, shower, and get dressed, said Carlo.

Pitera found his own personal cemetery for disposing of his murder victims, many of whom were cut into pieces. The 311-acre William T. Davis Wildlife Refuge is located in the western part of Staten Island, by the intersection of **Travis and**

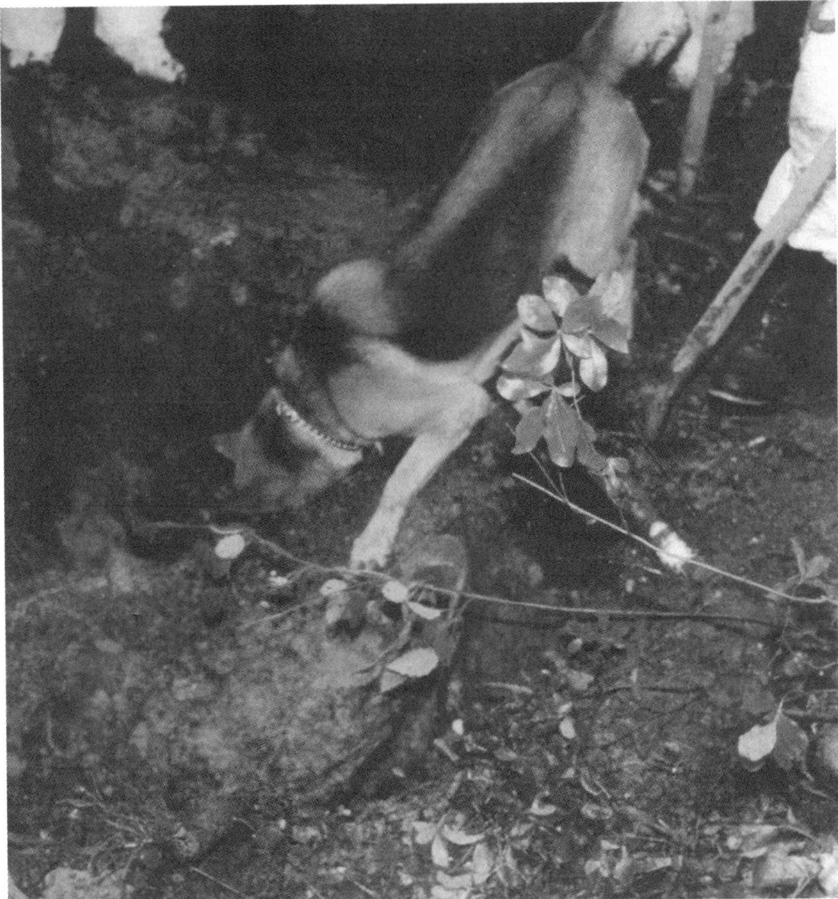

Cadaver dogs were used by federal agents to locate the bodies of Tommy Pitera's victims, buried within the William T. Davis Wildlife Refuge on Staten Island. PHOTO COURTESY DRUG ENFORCEMENT ADMINISTRATION

Richmond Avenues. As its name indicates, the refuge attracts a wide variety of waterfowl. It is far from the big-city crowds—a perfect place to plant a body, which is what Pitera did there in the belief that the damp soil would hasten decomposition. Investigation revealed that Pitera would wrap up the body parts in plastic or suitcases and then dig a deep grave in an effort to thwart any attempts by police to use dogs to find the remains. The heads were disposed of at different locations.

In April 1990, Gangi decided to cooperate with the DEA agents and told them about the burial ground used by Pitera. Two months later, federal agents and the NYPD excavated the area and found numerous sets of human remains.

The evidence was used in Pitera's federal racketeering murder trial, at which he was convicted in June 1992 of six murders and drug trafficking. Although he was a brutal killer, Pitera was spared the federal death penalty, and is serving a life sentence. The wildlife refuge is said to be a way station for about 117 species of migratory birds, as well as home to everything from field mice to raccoons. Given that it is likely Pitera wasn't the only killer to think of the refuge as a burial ground, it is likely many more bodies of Mafia victims are hidden within.

■ ■ ■

About five and a half miles southwest of the wildlife refuge where Tommy Pitera buried his victims is the Kreischer Mansion. The Victorian-style building at **4500 Arthur Kill Road** has a wraparound porch and an odd turret that makes it resemble something out of *The Addams Family*. It overlooks the Arthur Kill, the narrow body of water that separates Staten Island from New Jersey. The mansion was built around 1885 by wealthy brick manufacturer Balthasar Kreischer as one of two similar homes he had planned for his sons Edward and Charles. But things didn't go well for the Kreischer family. One of the homes mysteriously burned down, and after years of success the family business started to falter. At one point the factory also burned down, although it was rebuilt.

The bad luck continued. In June 1894, Edward Kreischer, the junior member of the family business, died under mysterious circumstances. After leaving his home the morning of June 5 in what was described as a "cheerful frame of mind," he went to the factory and then to a nearby wharf. He never returned. A worker discovered Kreischer's body, and next to the corpse was a revolver with one chamber empty. Kreischer had a bullet in the brain, and the conventional wisdom was that he took his own life. The main reason given for Kreischer's suicide was that he despaired over trouble he had with his eldest brother, George, as well as William Landeroth, the superintendent of the brick factory.

Over the decades, given the terrible events surrounding the home, stories arose that the remaining Kreischer mansion was haunted, with tales of apparitions, slamming doors, and strange noises. The home was even featured on the Biography Channel's *Haunted Encounters: Face to Face*, in which investigators of the paranormal taped what they believed were voices from the past.

But in 2005, the macabre tales turned very real at the mansion. Robert McKelvey, an associate of the Bonanno crime family, had been boasting about the group's crimes. To punish him, on March 29, 2005, Bonanno soldier Gino Galestro lured McKelvey to the Kreischer house, where associate Joseph Young worked as a caretaker. As was later revealed in Brooklyn federal court testimony, Young stabbed McKelvey as he entered the mansion, and after the victim tried to run away, tackled him and drowned McKelvey in a garden pool in the front of the house. Young had carried out the murder in exchange for $10,000, investigators said.

With a corpse on their hands, Young and three associates dismembered McKelvey's body with hacksaws, burned the remains in the mansion furnace, and disposed of the ashes and bone fragments in the septic tank system, according to trial evidence. Investigators later found the bone fragments as well as samples of McKelvey's blood from the stairs leading to the mansion basement. Faced with such damning evidence, Young was convicted of the killing. Young testified on his own behalf at trial, but didn't help his cause when he admitted that he had dismembered the corpse, even though he pinned the murder on someone else. This bit of nuanced testimony didn't impress the jury.

What also didn't endear Young to the jury was his answer to one particular question asked of him by the prosecution. When questioned about what occupation he listed on his MySpace page, of all the things he could have said, McKelvey had one word: "Death."

EPILOGUE

Back in the day when Charles Luciano, Albert Anastasia, Frank Costello, and other top Mafia bosses were getting arrested, one thing you could always say about them from the photographs that survived was that they dressed well. News photographers invariably captured them in expensive suits, ties, and overcoats, as well as those ever-present and popular fedoras. They also seemed to live very well from their spoils, which were substantial. Luciano stayed in luxury hotels, Anastasia had a large home above the Palisades in New Jersey, and Costello had an estate on the expensive North Shore of Long Island, where he spent his retirement cultivating orchids.

Modern police booking photos and news photographs portray a different image of today's New York mafiosi. They show coarse, overweight, and poorly dressed men with a preference for sweatpants and athletic shirts, for which health clubs and athletic fields are foreign territory. If it ever entered their minds to do something about negative stereotyping, they might have thought about getting some tips from watching a few episodes of *What Not to Wear*. The way Mob life has been in recent years, it's unlikely many of them could afford wardrobe makeovers. In the 1980s and '90s mobsters in New York could spend $250,000 to $500,000 on legal expenses for trial without spilling their espresso. But by 2010 lawyers were bemoaning the fact that the Mob money was gone. More and more of the remaining mafiosi were known by the pejorative of "brokester," meaning someone who lived hand to mouth and scrambled to make rent. More often than not, they needed to be represented by court-appointed lawyers because they didn't have enough cash for private counsel.

Another sign of the way the Mafia has changed is seen in the caliber of cases brought by police and prosecutors. Somebody like Joseph Massino was charged with seven murders in his 2004 racketeering trial and was convicted of all of them. When it came time for Massino to forfeit his ill-gotten gains, the FBI tallied up $10 million in gambling income, Mafia tribute, and other rackets and sent him a bill. He could have written a check to cover it. Massino was able to pay by dipping into his hoard of cash, secreted over the years inside his Howard Beach home.

But many of the Mob cases brought in 2013 through mid-2014 in New York City were relatively small beer, a hodgepodge of extortion allegations involving no more than $100,000 in loans and illegal peddling of erectile dysfunction drugs like Viagra and Cialis. The big rackets of yesteryear are simply no longer bringing in the big money, with one exception noted below: narcotics. The most recent murder charge in the 2014 indictment stemming from the Lufthansa heist involved a death forty-five years earlier of a victim identified through DNA technology.

The unceasing federal and state investigations of the Mafia in New York have no doubt contributed to the current paucity of members in the crime families. The bench of Mafia talent no longer seems to be there. The Bonanno family alone has been ransacked by FBI investigations, leading to scores of convictions and prison terms for its members, as well as the defection of old bosses like Massino and his former underboss and brother-in-law, Sal Vitale. Both the Colombo and Lucchese families have been on life support for years. The Gambino family has also been hurt by a wave of indictments, but its Sicilian wing seems to have gained control, pushing the family into drug dealing. Only the Genovese family seems to be relatively unscathed, its leadership crafty and well insulated.

The Mafia may not be what it was in New York City, but that doesn't mean it is extinct, or that it still doesn't pose a problem in certain areas. Extortion remains a fact of life for small businesses, and the Mob will always remain involved in gambling and labor racketeering. February 2014 indictments in Brooklyn federal court have alleged that New York Mob associates attempted to link the Gambino family with Italy's powerful N'drangheta organization, to traffic in cocaine and heroin through legitimate shipping companies. One of the elements of the alleged conspiracy called for the transportation to Italy of cocaine in frozen fish. Seasoned federal investigators and FBI agents know that local mafiosi are trying to cement ties with their Italian counterparts, who seem to have more extensive international narcotics ties, as well as more money.

But the inescapable fact in the modern era is that the Mafia is no longer preeminent among criminals. History, as depicted in *Gangland New York*, has illustrated how newer ethnic crime groups and combinations have in some ways supplanted the New York Mafia.

Latin drug operations have generated more money than the Cosa Nostra has seen in a long time. Traditional Mob families, shown up by the drug cartels, have realized the profits to be made from narcotics, and have for years ignored the old ban on drug dealings. Gambling, once under the thumb of the Mafia all over the city, has been increasingly overseen by Eastern Europeans. Albanians have developed their own niche for smuggling marijuana and painkillers like oxycodone, as seen by some February 2014 guilty pleas in Brooklyn federal court.

Mexican and Asian criminals have exploited the human smuggling and trafficking operations, which remain important links in the flow of illegal immigrants.

Of course, there are also the cocaine and heroin pipelines from Central and South America. It helps to keep perspective to note that while mobsters of old amassed fortunes in the millions of dollars, they were nothing compared to what modern white-collar criminals can steal. Bernard Madoff made an extraordinary fortune, dwarfing anything an individual mafioso could ever hope to accumulate. Madoff's crooked Wall Street enterprise was a $17 billion-plus Ponzi scheme, named after the Italian immigrant criminal Charles Ponzi, who, in the 1920s, defrauded his old countrymen. Like Ponzi, Madoff actually got started as an *affinity* con artist, meaning he exploited his ties to various Jewish friends, charities, and organizations before branching out to a wider international pool of victims. In a way, Madoff was like the old Black Hand criminals and early mafiosi of Mulberry Street in Manhattan: He victimized his own crowd. In the process, Madoff may have destroyed as many lives as the Mafia did. His investors lost fortunes, businesses, and homes, and for years have been wracked with the fear and anxiety that comes with such losses.

Although his name will forever live in infamy as Wall Street's biggest con man, Madoff thought himself a cut above the Mafia as he consorted with the habitués of Palm Beach and the French Riviera. In terms of the money they controlled—while they had it, anyway—Madoff's people put him in a world far beyond what the modern mafioso knows.

But there is a strange symmetry with the tales in *Gangland New York* and Madoff's story. As he entered Manhattan federal court on June 9, 2009, on his way to prison, Madoff needed to run a gauntlet of reporters and photographers so he could pass through a set of polished bronze doors facing north toward Columbus Park. His last walk as a free man was over the pavement at the old Five Points.

As of this writing, in the late spring and early summer of 2014, it is impossible to say what the next round of investigations will reveal about the history of the Mob in New York, and what there might be to add to the crime archaeology of *Gangland New York*. In a city that is constantly changing, and where excavations are always taking place, new things are likely to emerge. Aging gangsters, anxious to clear their consciences before dying, may reveal where some bodies are buried. We will just have to wait and see what more the city gives up.

HISTORIC ROLL CALL

SELECTED LIST OF CHARACTERS IN GANGLAND NEW YORK

Nicky Barnes (Harlem drug lord): After becoming a cooperating witness while in prison, Barnes was released in 1998, and is part of the federal witness protection program.

Vincent Basciano (acting Bonanno boss and captain): Following his second conviction for racketeering murder in May 2011, he was sentenced to life without parole to the federal supermax prison, formally known as ADX Florence, in Colorado.

Charles Becker (NYPD lieutenant): Following his execution in July 1915 at Sing Sing, Ossining, New York, Becker was buried at Woodlawn Cemetery in the Bronx.

Joseph Bonanno (Bonanno family boss): After spending years in exile from the New York Mob scene, Bonanno died in May 2002 in Tucson, Arizona. He is buried at Holy Hope Cemetery and Mausoleum in Tucson.

Louis Buchalter (Jewish gangster): Executed at Sing Sing in March 1944, Buchalter is buried in Mount Hebron Cemetery, Queens.

Stephan Caracappa (NYPD detective): Following his conviction in the Mafia Cops trial in 2006, Caracappa was sentenced to life in prison without parole. He is currently in Coleman-II US Penitentiary. He was seventy-two as of this writing.

Anthony "Little Augie Pisano" Carfano: After his murder in September 1959 with Janice Drake, Carfano was initially buried in Westchester County, but he was reportedly moved to the DeSalvio family mausoleum in Calvary Cemetery, Queens.

Charles Carneglia (Gambino family soldier): Convicted of racketeering murder offenses in March 2009, Carneglia was sentenced to life without parole, and is serving his time at Canaan US Peniteniary. He was sixty-seven as of this writing.

John Carneglia (Gambino captain): Convicted in 1989 on federal heroin charges, he was sentenced to fifty years in prison. He is currently in Allenwood Federal Correctional Complex, Allenwood, Pennsylvania, and is due for release in August 2018. As of this writing he was sixty-nine.

Paul Castellano (Gambino family boss): Murdered on December 16, 1985, he is entombed in an unmarked area of the main mausoleum at Moravian Cemetery in New Dorp, Staten Island.

Michael Chen (Chinatown gang leader): Murdered on March 13, 1983, in Chinatown, his place of burial is unknown.

Vincent "Mad Dog" Coll (Irish Mob assassin): Murdered in Manhattan on February 8, 1932, at the age of twenty-three, Coll is buried in Saint Raymond's Cemetery in the Bronx.

Joseph Colombo (Colombo family boss): After being shot in June 1971, Colombo remained paralyzed. He died in May 1978 at the age of fifty-four, and is buried in St. John's Cemetery, Queens.

James Coonan (leader of Irish Westies): Convicted of federal racketeering offenses in 1988, Coonan is serving a seventy-five-year prison term at Schuylkill FCI, and is due for release in 2030. As of this writing he was sixty-seven.

Frank Costello (Mafia boss): Died on February 18, 1973, at the age of eighty-two, and is entombed in a mausoleum at St. Michael's Cemetery, Queens.

Salvatore D'Aquila (Mafia boss): Murdered in Manhattan on October 10, 1928, at the age of fifty. He is buried at St. John Cemetery, Queens.

Frank DeCicco (Gambino family captain): After his murder at the age of fifty-one by a car bomb in April 1986, DeCicco was interred at Moravian Cemetery on Staten Island.

Aniello Dellacroce (Gambino family underboss): Died in December 1985 at the age of seventy-one. He is entombed in the Cloisters at St. John Cemetery, Middle Village.

Thomas Dewey (Manhattan district attorney): Died in March 1971 at the age of sixty-eight, and is buried in the town cemetery of Pawling, New York.

Daniel Driscoll (leader of Whyos Gang): Following his execution at The Tombs in January 1888, he was buried at Calvary Cemetery in Queens.

Mock Duck (Chinatown Tong leader): Known also as Sai Wing Mock, he died on July 23, 1941, and is buried in Cypress Hills Cemetery, Queens.

Monk Eastman (leader of gang): Murdered on December 26, 1920, at the age of forty-five. He was buried with military honors at Cypress Hills Cemetery, Queens.

Louis Eppolito (NYPD detective): Following his conviction in the Mafia Cops trial in 2006, Eppolito was sentenced to life in prison without parole, and is incarcerated at Tucson US Penitentiary. As of this writing he was sixty-five.

Antonio Flaccomio (early victim of Italian criminals): Murdered on October 14, 1888, in Manhattan. His place of burial is unknown.

Arthur Flegenheimer (Jewish gangster and gambler): Murdered in Newark, New Jersey, on October 23, 1935, at the age of thirty-four. A convert to Catholicism, he is buried at Gate of Heaven Cemetery in Valhalla, New York.

Tommy Gagliano (Mafia boss): The boss of what became the Lucchese crime family is believed to have died in 1951, although the exact date is uncertain. His approximate age at death was sixty-one. Gagliano is buried in Woodlawn Cemetery in the Bronx.

Carmine Galante (Bonanno family gangster): Murdered on July 12, 1979, in Brooklyn at the age of sixty-nine. He is buried in St. John Cemetery in Middle Village.

Carlo Gambino (Gambino family boss): Died on October 15, 1976, at the age of seventy-four. He is entombed in the Cloisters at St. John Cemetery in Middle Village.

Vito Genovese (Genovese family boss): Died on February 14, 1969, at the federal medical center for prisoners in Springfield, Missouri, at the age of seventy-one. He is buried at St. John Cemetery in Middle Village.

Vincent "The Chin" Gigante (Genovese family boss): Died on December 19, 2005, at the age of seventy-seven, in the federal medical center for prisoners in Springfield, Missouri. He was cremated at Green-Wood Cemetery in Brooklyn.

John J. Gotti (Gambino crime boss): Died on June 10, 2002, at the age of sixty-one in the federal medical center for prisoners in Springfield, Missouri. He is entombed in the Cloisters at St. John Cemetery in Middle Village. His son Frank, who died in 1980, is also entombed in the same space.

Sammy "The Bull" Gravano (former Gambino family underboss): Received lengthy federal and state prison sentences for drug trafficking in 2002, and is in custody. As of this writing he was seventy.

Nicholas Howlett (river pirate): Following his execution in The Tombs in January 1853, he was buried at what was described as a "Catholic cemetery in Williamsburg," likely Calvary Cemetery in Queens.

Thomas Hyer (Manhattan pugilist): Died of heart trouble in June 1864 at the age of forty-five. He is buried at Green-Wood Cemetery, Brooklyn.

Paul Kelly (leader of Five Pointers gang): Died in April 1936 at the age of sixty. He is buried at Calvary Cemetery in Queens.

Bow Kum (Chinatown murder victim): After her murder in August 1909, Bow Kum was buried in Cypress Hills Cemetery in a section used by a Chinese fraternal organization for interring its members. As was the custom of the time among Chinese immigrants, her remains were dug up about ten years later and sent back to China.

Gennaro "Jerry" Langella (Colombo family): Died on December 15, 2013, at the federal medical center for prisoners in Springfield, Missouri, where he was serving a lengthy prison term. He is is buried at Green-Wood Cemetery in Brooklyn.

Joseph "Socks" Lanza (Waterfront crime boss): Remained one of organized crime's powers on the New York waterfront until his death in October 1968. He is buried at Calvary Cemetery in Queens.

Tom Lee (Chinatown Tong leader): Known as the "Mayor" of Chinatown, Lee died in January 1918 at the age of seventy-six. He was interred at Cypress Hills Cemetery, Queens.

Zelig Lefkowitz (Jewish gangster): After his murder in October 1912, he was buried in Washington Cemetery, Brooklyn.

Frank LoCascio (Gambino family consigliere): Serving a life sentence at the federal medical center, Devens, in Massachusetts. As of this writing he was eighty-one.

Frank Lucas (Harlem drug dealer): As of this writing, Lucas was believed to be eighty-four years old and is no longer in prison.

Thomas Lucchese (Lucchese family boss): Died of natural causes at the age of sixty-seven in July 1967, and is buried at Calvary Cemetery, Queens.

Charles Luciano (Mafia boss): Died in Naples of a heart attack at the Capodichino Airport in January 1962 at the age of sixty-five. He is buried in a family mausoleum at St. John Cemetery, Middle Village, Queens.

Ignazio "The Wolf" Lupo (Mafia leader): Died on January 13, 1947, at the age of sixty-nine. He is buried at Calvary Cemetery, Queens.

Daniel Lyons (leader of Whyos gang): Died in August 1887 at the age of twenty-eight from a gunshot wound he suffered at a saloon in the Five Points. His burial place is unknown.

Owen "Owney" Madden (Irish gang leader): Died at the age of seventy-three in April 1965 in Hot Springs, Arkansas, of natural causes.

Vincent Mangano (Mafia boss): Vanished at the age of sixty-three on April 18, 1951. His remains have never been found.

Salvatore Maranzano (Mafia boss, murder victim): Murdered on September 10, 1931, at the age of forty-five in New York City. He is buried in St. John Cemetery, Middle Village, Queens.

Joseph Masseria (Mafia boss, murder victim): Murdered on April 15, 1931, at the age of forty-five in Coney Island, Brooklyn. He is entombed in the family mausoleum in Calvary Cemetery, Queens.

Joseph Massino (former Bonanno family boss): His life sentence was commuted to time served, about twelve years, in July 2013. He is currently in the federal witness relocation program, and at this writing is seventy-one years old. Massino may testify for the government in *US v. Vincent Asaro* (USDC EDNY).

Frank Matthews (Harlem drug lord): Matthews has been a fugitive from justice since 1973. His whereabouts are unknown.

Giuseppe "Pete" Morello (early Mafia leader): Murdered on August 15, 1930, at the age of sixty in New York City. He is buried at Calvary Cemetery, Woodside, Queens.

John Morrissey (pugilist and gang member): After leaving his boxing and gang careers behind him, Morrissey entered politics and served terms in the US House of Representatives and the New York State Senate. He died of pneumonia at the age of forty-seven on May 1, 1878, and is buried outside Troy, New York.

Hugh Mulligan (West Side Irish gangster): Died in July 1973 at the age of sixty-two. His place of burial is unknown.

Gallus Mag Perry (Pirate woman): Known as Mag (Margaret) Perry, she was married to dance-hall owner Jack Perry, and based on newspaper stories is believed to have lived to around 1875. Her place of burial is unknown.

Alphonse "Allie Boy" Persico (Colombo family): Died of cancer at the age of sixty-one, September 12, 1989, while serving a twenty-five-year sentence at the federal medical center for prisoners in Springfield, Missouri. He is entombed in Green-Wood Cemetery, Brooklyn.

Carmine "The Snake" Persico: The brother of Alponse, he is currently serving a federal sentence at FCI Butner, North Carolina. His release date is March 2050. As of this writing he was eighty years old.

Joseph Petrosino (NYPD detective, murder victim): Murdered while on official NYPD business in Palermo, Sicily, on March 12, 1909, at the age of forty-eight. He is buried at Calvary Cemetery, Queens.

Joseph Profaci (Profaci family boss): Died of cancer on June 8, 1962, at age sixty-four. He is entombed in the family mausoleum at St. John Cemetery, Middle Village.

Gaetano Reina (Mafia boss): Murdered at the age of forty, on February 26, 1930, in the Bronx. He was buried at Woodlawn Cemetery in the Bronx.

Abe Reles (Jewish gangster): Died at the age of thirty-five in a fall from the Half Moon Hotel in Coney Island on November 12, 1941, while supposedly under police guard as a witness. He is buried in the Old Mount Carmel Cemetery in Glendale, New York.

Herman Rosenthal (gambler, murder victim): Murdered in Manhattan on July 16, 1912. He is buried at Washington Cemetery in Brooklyn.

Arnold Rothstein (Jewish gangster, murder victim): Murdered in Manhattan on November 6, 1928, at the age of forty-six. He is buried at Union Field Cemetery in Ridgewood, Queens.

Alex Rudaj (Albanian crime boss): Currently incarcerated at FCI, Fort Dix. His release date is May 2028. As of this writing he was forty-seven years old.

Stephanie "Queenie" St. Clair (Harlem numbers operator): Died in Harlem in 1969. She is reportedly interred at Trinity Church Cemetery and Mausoleum in Manhattan.

Anthony "Fat Tony" Salerno (acting Genovese family boss): Died in July 1999 at the age of eighty in the federal medical center for prisoners in Springfield, Missouri. He is entombed in the family mausoleum at Saint Raymond's Cemetery, the Bronx.

Gerardo Scarpato (restaurant owner, murder victim): The owner of the restaurant where Joseph Masseria was killed in April 1931, Scarpato was found dead, wrapped in burlap in the back of a car in Brooklyn, on September 11, 1932. His age at death and place of burial are unknown.

Mickey Spillane (West Side Irish gangster): Murdered in Queens on May 13, 1977, at the age of forty-four. He is buried in Calvary Cemetery, Queens.

Joseph Valachi (Mafia turncoat): Died in federal custody on April 3, 1971, of a heart attack. He was sixty-seven. Valachi is buried at Gate of Heaven Cemetery, Lewiston, New York.

Spyredon "Spiros" Velentzas (former Greek crime boss): Incarcerated and serving a life sentence in FCI Schuylkill. As of this writing he was seventy-nine.

Joseph Watts (Gambino family associate): Incarcerated at FCI McDowell in West Virginia, with a release date of March 2022. As of this writing he was seventy-two.

Frankie Yale (Mafia figure): Murdered in Brooklyn on July 1, 1928, at the age of thirty-five. He is buried in Holy Cross Cemetery in Brooklyn.

Max Zweifach (Jewish gangster): Sometimes refered to by the surname of "Zweibach," he was murdered in Coney Island, Brooklyn, on May 14, 1908, at the age of twenty-four. He is buried at Mount Zion Cemetery in Queens.

ACKNOWLEDGMENTS

Doing research for *Gangland New York* was often a solitary task. Much of the work was done by mining online newspaper archives, principally those available through the Library of Congress digital newspaper collection. The New York Public Library microfilm section, as well as the City Hall library in New York City, was also useful in making available newspapers and books about the old days of crime in the city.

Five former FBI agents—Pat Marshall, Phil Scala, Bruce Mouw, Joaquin "Jack" Garcia, and Charles Rooney—have been helpful over the years, and I want to acknowledge them here. At the US Attorney's Office in Manhattan, chief spokesman Jim Margolin provided help in my research of many of the cases in this book when he was a spokesman for the FBI. The same holds true for Robert Nardoza, retired spokesman for the US Attorney's Office in the Eastern District of New York (Brooklyn), and office paralegal Samantha Ward. Also providing information about some notable federal drug prosecutions were Jim Hunt and Erin McKenzie-Mulvey of the New York office of the Drug Enforcement Administration.

From the defense attorney side, Murray Richman was again a treasure trove of old stories, particularly about the Bronx. Attorney James Kousouris of Manhattan provided research assistance for the cases dealing with Albanian crime. Theresa LaBianca was also helpful in some critical areas of research about the legendary William Poole. Queens attorney Andrew Fatos was generous with his time in giving perspective about the Greek community. Robert Holden of the Juniper Park Civic Association, Inc., and Pepper Salter Edmiston, granddaughter of Mike Salter, and her family also provided important photographs.

Journalists whose articles and/or books I consulted include Russ Baker, Meyer Berger, Bill Berkeley, Howard Blum, Ralph Blumenthal, Celestine Bohlen, Brendan Browne, Leonard Buder, Edward C. Burks, Jerry Capeci, Alfred E. Clark, John Darton, Norman Davies, Robert C. Doty, Joseph P. Fried, Nicholas Gage, Cindy Galli, Charles Grutzner, Joseph O. Haff, Anemona Hartacollis, Marlene Jensen, Peter Kihss, Francis X. Klines, Arnold H. Lubasch, Leslie Maitland, John Marzulli, Alexandra Kathryn Mosca, Michael Norman, Rocco Parascandola,

Emanuel Perlmutter, Julia Preston, Selwyn Raab, Edward Ranzal, William Rashbaum, Christina Santucci, Greg Smith, Gay Talese, Joseph B. Treaster, Juan M. Vasquez, and Murray Weiss. I also have to tip my hat to the many unsung writers who toiled away in anonymity and without bylines in the many early New York City newspapers. Their work really did bring many of these stories to life.

Newsday editor Deborah Henley and assistant managing editor Maryann Skinner are again to be thanked for getting me approval to write this book, and in helping me to obtain archival photographs that ran in *Newsday*. Monica Quintanilla, my immediate *Newsday* editor, also deserves thanks for putting up with my requests for time off. Cathy Mahon, *Newsday*'s permissions coordinator, was instrumental in securing me a number of historic photographs.

Of course, I want to thank my agent, Jill Marsal, and my Lyons Press editors Lauren Brancato, James Jayo, Holly Rubino, and Keith Wallman for seeing something special in this wide-ranging, historical look at New York City crime.

NOTES

Chapter One: The Rise and Fall of the Five Points (1800 to 1895)
The current physical layout of the old Five Points area, Columbus Park, and environs came from the author's personal observations of the areas. The history of the Five Points and the Collect Pond (Fresh Water Pond) comes from a variety of sources: Herbert Asbury's *The Gangs of New York*, Tyler Anbinder's *Five Points*, James D. McCabe Jr.'s *Lights and Shadows of New York Life: Or, the Sensations of the Great City*, David Valentine's *History of the City of New* York. Also consulted were articles in the *New York Times* and *The Sun*.

Chapter Two: The Sicilian Avengers
The early days of Mafia activity in New Orleans is derived in part from Jerry Capeci's *The Complete Idiot's Guide to the Mafia*, while Anbinder's *Five Points* has background on the Italian population of that area. The activities of Antonio Flaccomio and events surrounding his murder are described in a number of publications: *National Police Gazette*, *New York Herald*, *Evening World*, *The Illustrated American*, the *New York Times*, and *The Sun.*

Chapter Three: The Eastmans versus the Five Pointers
Books used in researching this chapter were Asbury's *The Gangs of New York*, Patrick Downey's *Gangster City: The History of the New York Underworld*, and Rose Keefe's *The Starker: Big Jack Zelig, the Becker Rosenthal Case, and the Advent of the Jewish Gangster*. Details of the Rivington Street shoot-out, the death of Monk Eastman, and the life of Paul Kelly are found in stories published in the *Evening World* and the *New York Times*. The website www.infamousnewyork.com was also consulted.

Chapter Four: Tales of Bloody Angle
Asbury's *The Gangs of New York* has many details about the early Tong wars and murders in Chinatown. Also consulted was Downey's *Gangster City* and Patrick Gilfoyle's *A Pickpocket's Tale: The Underworld of Nineteenth-Century New York.* The murder of Bow Kum, the trial of her suspected killers, and the various Tong fights are found in the *Evening World*, the *New York Times*, and *The Sun.* The

author also did extensive research into the Bow Kum murder at the City of New York Municipal Library and the New York Public Library.

Chapter Five: The Rise of the Jewish Gangster

Works consulted included Asbury's *The Gangs of New York*, Downey's *Gangster City*, and Keefe's *The Starker*. Newspapers extensively covered the events surrounding the trial of Lieutenant Charles Becker. The author principally relied on the *New York Times* and *The World*. The website of the Workmen's Circle, www.thecircle.org, was also consulted.

Chapter Six: "Mio Figlio!"

Works consulted for this chapter included Capeci's *The Complete Idiot's Guide to the Mafia*, Downey's *Gangster City*, and Thomas Reppetto's *American Mafia: A History of Its Rise to Power*. Newspapers that covered the events in the chapter, notably the cases involving Ignazio Lupo and Giuseppe Morello, as well as the kidnapping and death of Giuseppe Verotta, included *The New York Times* and the *New York Tribune*.

Chapter Seven: The War of the Bosses

Events leading up to and including the famed Castellammarese War have inspired numerous books and other published accounts. Books consulted were Capeci's *The Complete Idiot's Guide to the Mafia*, Alexander C. Hortis and James B. Jacobs's *The Mob and the City: The Hidden History of How the Mafia Captured New York*, Peter Maas's *The Valachi Papers*, Selwyn Raab's *Five Families: The Rise, Decline, and Resurgence of America's Most Powerful Mafia Empires*, Reppetto's *American Mafia*, and Tony Sciacca's *Luciano: The Inside Story of the No. 1 Godfather of Them All.* The author also consulted the *New York Times*.

Chapter Eight: The Rise of "The Combination"

As in chapter 7, the events of Lucky Luciano's rise to power, the assassination of Salvatore Maranzano, Luciano's downfall, and his deportation to Italy, have been extensively written about. Among the books consulted for this chapter were Capeci's *The Complete Idiot's Guide*, Maas's *The Valachi Papers*, Raab's *Five Families*, Reppetto's *American Mafia*, and Sciacca's *Luciano*. Stories published in the *New York Times* were used to supplement the book accounts.

Chapter Nine: "This Is for You, Frank"

This chapter dealing with period in the 1940s and '50s relied principally on Capeci's *The Complete Idiot's Guide*, Raab's *Five Families*, and Reppetto's *American Mafia.* News accounts used to flesh out the accounts of events were those printed in the *New York Times.* Also used was the 1958 report prepared by Arthur L.

Reuter for Governor Averell Harriman of New York, titled *The Activities and Associations of Persons Identified as Present at the Residence of Joseph Barbara Sr. at Apalachin, New York, on November 14, 1957, and the Reasons for Their Presence.*

Chapter Ten: "Blood on the Street"

Books relied upon for this chapter were Capeci's *Complete Idiot's Guide*, Peter Diapoulis and Steven Linakis's *The Sixth Family*, Tom Folsom's *The Mad Ones: Crazy Joe Gallo and the Revolution at the End of the World*, Raab's *Five Families*, Reppetto's *American Mafia*, Albert A. Seedman and Peter Hellman's *Chief!*, and Gay Talese's *Honor Thy Father*. The section dealing with the 1970s federal investigation of New York City's garment industry relied mainly on the author's stories printed in *Women's Wear Daily* in 1977. The chapter was also supplemented by accounts of events published in the *New York Times*.

Chapter Eleven: Paddy Whackers and Black Caesars

For the chapter's history of Irish organized crime in Manhattan in the twentieth century, particularly the gang known as "The Westies," T. J. English's book, *The Westies: Inside New York's Irish Mob*, provided a good deal of context. Details about the history of black organized crime were found in Ron Chepesiuk's book, *Gangsters of Harlem: The Gritty Underworld of New York's Most Famous Neighborhood*. Additional details were found in articles published in the *New York Times*.

Chapter Twelve: Bugs for Fat Tony—Bullets for Dai Lo

For details on the surveillance of Anthony Salerno's social club, this chapter relied on Raab's *Five Families*, and interviews with a former law enforcement official involved in the investigation of Salerno. Details of Chinatown gang warfare in the 1980s are described in various articles from the *New York Times*. The author also has personal knowledge of some of the events from previous reporting.

Chapter Thirteen: Gotti's Gamble

In detailing the planting of bugs in the Ravenite Social Club and environs, as well as the arrest of John Gotti in December 1990, this chapter relied on Howard Blum's *Gangland: How the FBI Broke the Mob*, Capeci's *Complete Idiot's Guide*, John H. Davis's *Mafia Dynasty: The Rise and Fall of the Gambino Crime Family*, Maas's *Underboss*, and Raab's *Five Families.* In addition, the author interviewed former law enforcement officials involved in the Castellano murder investigation and the Gotti racketeering case. Details about the murder of Louis DiBono and the Gambino crime-family involvement are found in the author's *Mob Killer: The Bloody Rampage of Charlie Carneglia, Mafia Hit Man*. The shooting at Rao's

Restaurant in 2003 was detailed in an article in *New York Magazine* by Steven Fishman. The Albanian Mob's attempt to strong-arm the restaurant was detailed in the author's *Vinny Gorgeous: The Ugly Rise and Fall of a New York Mobster* and the case file in *US v. Alex Rudaj, et al.* 03-cr-1110 (USDC-SDNY). The restaurant history can be found on its website.

Chapter Fourteen: The Dead Who Knew Brooklyn

The murder and funeral of William Poole in 1853 were described in detail in contemporary newspaper accounts, which were relied upon for this chapter, mainly the *New-York Daily Tribune* and the *New York Times*. Asbury's *The Gangs of New York* also has many details of the Poole murder. Al Capone's relationship with Brooklyn gangsters like Frankie Yale and details of the Adonis Club shoot-out are derived mainly from Laurence Bergreen's *Capone: The Man and the Era.* The demise of Frankie Yale was described in the *Daily News* and the *New York Times.* Murder Inc.'s exploits and those of affiliated gangsters are found in Downey's *Gangster City.*

Chapter Fifteen: The Last Lunch

Much of the information in this chapter about the Castellammarese War between Joseph Masseria and Salvatore Maranzano is derived from Capeci's *The Complete Idiot's Guide*, Downey's *Gangster City*, Raab's *Five Families*, and Reppetto's *American Mafia.* The Gallo Wars are detailed in *Five Families*, Diapoulos and Linakis's *Sixth Family*, and Folsom's *The Mad Ones*, as well as in stories from the *New York Times.* The demise of Abe Reles and Tommy Eboli are described in the *New York Times.*

Chapter Sixteen: A Late Lunch—Bonanno Style

The story of the "Gold Bug" was detailed in the *New York Times*. The author's *Mob Killer* is the source of information on the death of court officer Albert Gelb. Raab's *Five Families* and Capeci's *The Complete Idiot's Guide* provided details about the killing of Carmine Galante. The author's *King of the Godfathers* is the source for the section on the murder of the three captains and Dominick Napolitano. The placing of bugs in the Casa Storta and other Mob hangouts is detailed in *Five Families*. Guy Lawson and William Oldham's *The Brotherhoods: The True Story of Two Cops Who Murdered for the Mafia* is the main source for the section on the Mafia Cops killings, a trial that the author covered in 2006 for *Newsday*. *Five Families* provided information about the Colombo crime-family war of the 1990s, as did the *New York Times*. The *Times* was also the source for information on the murder of police officer Ralph Dols. The author's *Vinny Gorgeous* is the source for the section on the murder of Randolph Pizzolo.

Chapter Seventeen: A Borough to Die For

The killing of Gaetano Reina was described in the *New York Times*. The precise location of Salvatore Maranzano's meeting in 1931 is unknown, but Bronx criminal defense attorney Murray Richman, a veteran of many Mob cases, and a person familiar with the borough's history, provided a reasonable theory as to the location. Lepore's murder was also described in the *New York Times.* The author's *King of the Godfather* is the prime source of information about the murder of Gerlando Sciascia. The author's *Vinny Gorgeous* detailed the killing of Frank Santoro. Information about the case of undercover FBI agent Joaquin "Jack" Garcia is found in his book, *Making Jack Falcone: An Undercover FBI Agent Takes Down a Mafia Family*, as well as stories in the *The New York Times* and information provided by a former law enforcement official.

Chapter Eighteen: A Quiet Place to Dine, Drink, and Die

Information about Arnold Rothstein's "phantom village" in Queens, as well as his career and death, are found primarily in reports from the period published in the *New York Times*. In addition, information provided by Robert Holden, president of the Juniper Park Civic Association, was helpful in defining the area affected by Rothstein's venture. Anthony Carfano's death and the investigation of his murder were extensively detailed in the *New York Times*. Carfano's grandson Frank Bari also provided the author with information, and with author Mark Gribben wrote *Under the Willliamsburg Bridge: The Story of An American Family*. The famous La Stella lunch of mobsters was covered by the *New York Times* and other newspapers. The *Times* also covered the deaths of Joseph Profaci, Vito Genovese, Carlo Gambino, and Thomas Lucchese. The author also visited the cemeteries where the Mob bosses are buried or entombed.

The *Times* also covered the murder of James Plumeri. Details of the murder of Joseph Pastore are found in the author's *King of the Godfather*. Frankie Gotti's accidental death was covered in Capeci and Mustain's *Mobstar*, Victoria Gotti's *This Family of Mine: What It Was like Growing Up Gotti*. Details of the abduction, death, and disposal of the body of John Favara are found in *Mobstar* and the author's *Mob Killer.* The author covered the Ruby Street digging operation by the FBI for *Newsday*. Raab's *Five Families* details the operation and FBI surveillance of John Gotti's Bergin Hunt and Fish Club. The death of detective Anthony J. Venditti and the subsequent trials and ultimate acquittals of suspect Federico Giovanelli are described in the *New York Times* and Russ Baker's story of December 12, 1994, in *New York Magazine* titled "The Cop Out." The memorial service for Venditti was described in the October 11, 2011, edition of the *Times Ledger* newspaper.

Chapter Nineteen: Tales of the Old and New Mobs

Spiros Velentzas's federal criminal case is detailed in case file *91-cr-384* (USCD-EDNY), reported case 30 F.3rd 381, as well as reports in the *New York Times*. The *Times* also reported on the burglaries and other escapades of murder victim Sam Nolo. Michael Pappadio's murder is recounted in Capeci and Tom Robbins *Mob Boss: The Life of Little Al D'Arco*, and in FBI reports available online at www.smokinggun.com. The author had researched Pappadio's garment businesses while working as a reporter in the 1980s for Fairchild News Service. James Bishop's murder is detailed in the *New York Times* and Raab's *Five Families*. Details of the surveillance and investigation of Salvatore Vitale's club on Grand Avenue are found in the author's *King of the Godfathers*. The killing of Manuel de Dios Unanue was covered in the *New York Times* and the *New York Daily News*, as were the subsequent trials of those charged in his murder. The escapades and murder of Thomas and Rosemary Uva were detailed in the author's *King of the Godfathers*. The author also covered the trial of Dominick Pizzonia, who in 2007 was convicted in Brooklyn federal court of involvement in their murders. The ascent of Russian organized crime has been detailed over the years in articles in the *New York Times*. The author also covered a case in Brooklyn federal court in which Manny Chulpayev was a cooperating witness. Chulpayev's legal problems in 2013 and 2014 were detailed in a television report by ABC News correspondent Brian Ross. The criminal case involving Alex Rudaj and his Albanian gang is found in case file *US v. Alex Rudaj, et al.*, 03-cr-1110, (USCD-SDNY). Information about the dig for human remains in Queens in connection with the Lufthansa heist is found in case file *US v. Vincent Asaro, et al.* 14-cr-26 (USDC-EDNY).

Chapter Twenty: Princely Palaces and Unmarked Graves

Details of Dominick Napolitano's death and burial are found in the author's *King of the Godfathers*. The bugging and surveillance of the Staten Island home of Paul Castellano are detailed in Raab's *Five Families*. A former law enforcement official provided the author with details of the Mafia Commission meeting on Staten Island. Information on Tommy Pitera's gruesome career as a Mafia assassin are found in the *New York Times*, Phil Carlo's *Butcher*, and a Biography Channel special on Pitera. The bizarre Bonanno family murder at the Kreischer Mansion on Staten Island is detailed in the *New York Times* and the *New York Daily News*. The author also covered the trial of defendants charged in that murder case for *Newsday*. The history of the mansion is found on Wikipedia and other online resources.

Epilogue

Interviews in 2013 and 2014 with current and past members of law enforcement provided the author with perspective on the current state of the Mafia in New York. Details of the latest large narcotics case involving the Italian N'drangheta and alleged New York Mafia associates are found in the case file *Franco Lupoi, et al., 2014-cr-42* (USDC-EDNY).

BIBLIOGRAPHY

Books

Anbinder, Tyler. *Five Points: The 19th Century New York City Neighborhood That Invented Tap Dance, Stole Elections, and Became The World's Most Notorious Slum*. New York: Penguin Group, 2001.

Asbury, Herbert. *The Gangs of New York*. New York: Alfred A. Knopf, 1928.

Bari, Frank, and Mark C. Gribben. *Under the Williamsburg Bridge: The Story of an American Family.* Bloomington, IN: Trafford Publishing, 2009.

Bergreen, Laurence. *Capone: The Man and the Era*. New York: Simon & Schuster, 1994.

Blum, Howard. *Gangland: How the FBI Broke the Mob*. New York: Simon & Schuster, 1993.

Burrows, Edwin G., and Mike Wallace. *Gotham: A History of New York City to 1898*. New York: Oxford University Press, 1999.

Capeci, Jerry. *The Complete Idiot's Guide to the Mafia*. New York: Penguin Group (USA) Inc., 2004.

Capeci, Jerry, and Gene Mustain. *Mob Star: The Story of John Gotti*. New York: Penguin, 2002.

Capeci, Jerry, and Tom Robbins. *Mob Boss: The Life of Little Al D'Arco, The Man Who Brought Down the Mafia*. New York: Thomas Dunne Books, 2013.

Carlo, Philip. *Gaspipe: Confessions of a Mafia Boss*. New York: HarperCollins, 2008.

——. *The Butcher: Anatomy of a Mafia Psychopath*. New York: William Morrow Paperbacks, 2010.

Chepesiuk, Ron. *Gangster of Harlem: The Gritty Underworld of New York's Most Famous Neighborhood*. Fort Lee, NJ: Barricade Books, 2007.

Davis, John H. *Mafia Dynasty: The Rise and Fall of The Gambino Crime Family*. New York: HarperPaperbacks, 1993.

DeStefano, Anthony M. *King of the Godfathers: "Big Joey" Massino and the Fall of the Bonanno Crime Family*. New York: Kensington Publishing, 2008.

——. *Mob Killer: The Bloody Rampage of Charlie Carneglia, Mafia Hit Man.* New York: Kensington Publishing, 2011.

——. *Vinny Gorgeous: The Ugly Rise and Fall of a New York Mobster.* Guilford, CT: Globe Pequot Press, 2013.

Diapoulos, Peter, and Peter Linakis. *The Sixth Family*. New York: Bantam Books, 1977.

Downey, Patrick. *Gangster City: The History of the New York Underworld*. Fort Lee, NJ: Barricade Books, 2004.

English, T.J. *Paddy Whacked: The Untold Story of The Irish American Gangster*. New York: HarperCollins Publishers, Inc, 2006.

——. *The Westies: Inside New York's Irish Mob*. New York: G. P. Putnam's Sons, 1990.

Fentress, James. *Eminent Gangsters: Immigrants and the Birth of Organized Crime in America*. Lanham, MD: University Press of America, 2010.

Folsom, Tom. *The Mad Ones: Crazy Joe Gallo and the Revolution at the Edge of the World*. New York: Weinstein Books, 2008.

Garcia, Joaquin "Jack." *Making Jack Falcone: An Undercover FBI Agent Takes Down a Mafia Family.* New York: Pocket Star Books, 2009.

Gilfoyle, Timothy J. *A Pickpocket's Tale: The Underworld of Nineteenth-Century New York*. New York: W. W. Norton, 2006.

Gotti, Victoria. *This Family of Mine: What It Was Like Growing Up Gotti*. New York: Pocket Books, 2009.

Harlow, Alvin F. *Old Bowery Days: The Chronicles of a Famous Street*. New York: D. Appleton, 1931.

Hortis, Alexander C., and James B. Jacobs. *The Mob and the City: The Hidden History of How the Mafia Captured New York*. New York: Prometheus Books, 2014.

Keefe, Rose. *The Starker: Big Jack Zelig, the Becker Rosenthal Case, and the Advent of the Jewish Gangster*. Nashville, TN: Cumberland House Publishing, 2008.

Jacobson, Mark. *American Gangster and Other Tales of New York*. New York: Black Cat, 2007.

Lamothe, Lee, and Adrian Humphreys. *The Sixth Family: The Collapse of the New York Mafia and the Rise of Vito Rizzuto*. Mississauga, ONT: John Wiley & Sons Canada Ltd., 2006.

Lawson, Guy, and William Oldham. *The Brotherhoods: The True Story of Two Cops Who Murdered for the Mafia*. New York: Scribner, 2006.

Mass, Peter. *The Valachi Papers*. New York: G. P. Putnam's Sons, 1968.

——. *Underboss: Sammy the Bull Gravano's Story of Life in the Mafia*. New York: HarperCollins, 1997.

McCabe, James D., Jr. *Lights and Shadows of New York Life; Or, the Sensations of the Great City* (Facsimile Edition). New York: Farrar, Straus and Giroux, 1970.

Mosca, Alexandra Kathryn. *Green-Wood Cemetery (Images of America: New York)*. Mount Pleasant, SC: Arcadia Publishing, 2008.

Peterson, Virgil W. *The Mob: 200 Years of Organized Crime in New York*. Ottawa, IL: Green Hill Publishers, 1983.

Pietrusza, David. *Rothstein: The Life, Times, and Murder of the Criminal Genius Who Fixed The 1919 World Series*. New York: Carroll & Graf Publishers, 2003.

Raab, Selwyn. *Five Families: The Rise, Decline, and Resurgence of America's Most Powerful Mafia Empires*. New York: Thomas Dunne Books, 2005.

Reppetto, Thomas. *American Mafia: A History of Its Rise to Power*. New York: Henry Holt and Company, 2004.

Salerno, Ralph, and John S. Tompkins. *The Crime Confederation*. Garden City, NY: Doubleday, 1969.

Sciacca, Tony. *Luciano: The Inside Story of the No. 1 Godfather of Them All*. New York: Pinnacle Books, 1975.

Seedman, Albert A., and Peter Hellman. *Chief!* New York: Arthur Fields Books, 1974.

Sifakis, Carl. *The Mafia Encyclopedia: From Accardo to Zwillman*. New York: Checkmark Books, 2005.

Talese, Gay. *Honor Thy Father*. New York: Dell Publishing, 1981.

Valentine, David T. *History of the City of New York*. New York: G. P. Putnam and Company, 1853.

Van Pelt, Daniel. *Leslie's History of the Greater New York: Vol. 1, New York to the Consolidation.* New York: Arkell Publishing Company, 1899.

Walling, George W. *Recollections of a New York Chief of Police*. New York: Caxton Book Concern, 1887.

Court Documents and Cases

US v. Joseph Agate, et al., 08-cr-76, United States District Court for the Eastern District of New York.

US v. Vincent Asaro, et al., 14-cr-26, United States District Court for the Eastern District of New York.

US v. Vincent Basciano, et al., 03-cr-929, United States District Court for the Eastern District of New York.

US v. Vincent Basciano, et al., 05-cr-60, United States District Court for the Eastern District of New York.

US v. Louis Eppolito, et al., 05-cr-192, United States District Court for the Eastern District of New York.

US v. Franco Lupoi, et al., 14-cr-42, United States District Court for the Eastern District of New York.

US v. Joseph Massino, et al., 02-cr-307, United States District Court for the Eastern District of New York.

US (appellee) v. James Nicolapolous, et al. (appellants), 30 F. 3d 381, United States Court of Appeals, Second Circuit.

US v. Alex Rudaj, et al., 03-cr-1110, United States District Court for the Southern District of New York.

US v. Arnold Squitieri et al., 05-cr-228, United States District Court for the Southern District of New York.

US v. Gjavit Thaqi, et al., 11-cr-486, United States District Court for the Eastern District of New York.

US v. Spyredon Velentzas, et al., 91-cr-384, United States District Court for the Eastern District of New York.

Government Publications

The Activities and Associations of Persons Identified as Present at the Residence of Joseph Barbara Sr. at Apalachin, New York, on November 14, 1957, and the Reasons for Their Presence. Report by Arthur L. Reuter, Acting Commissioner of Investigation of the State of New York, to Averell Harriman, Governor of the State of New York, April 23, 1958.

New York State Joint Legislative Committee on Crime, Its Cause, Control and Effect on Society. Report for 1970, September 1970.

Police Department of the City of New York, *Annual Report for Year Ending December 31, 1912.*

Newspapers and News Organizations Consulted

Associated Press

Brooklyn Daily Eagle

The Evening World (NY)

The Illustrated American

National Police Gazette

Newsday (Long Island)

New York Daily News

New-York Daily Tribune

New York Herald

New York Magazine

New York Newsday

New York Post

New York Times
New York Tribune
Reuters
The Sun (NY)
Times Ledger (Queens)
Women's Wear Daily

Websites

https://archive.org
www.biography.com
www. bop.gov
www.bridgecafenyc.com
www.findagrave.com
www.fultonhistory.com
www.ganglandnews.com
www.green-wood.com
www.infamousnewyork.com
www.junipercivic.com
www.loc.gov
www.nymag.com
www.nypost.com
www.thecircle.org
www.thesmokinggun.com
www.usinflationcalculator.com
www.wikipedia.com

Articles

Baker, Russ. "The Cop Out," *New York Magazine*, December 12, 1994.
Fishman, Steven. "Louie Lump Lump's Bad Night at Rao's," *New York Magazine*, January 4, 2004.
Klein, Melissa. "The Mob Murder at Rao's that Was Sparked by a Song," *The New York Post*, December 29, 2013.

INDEX